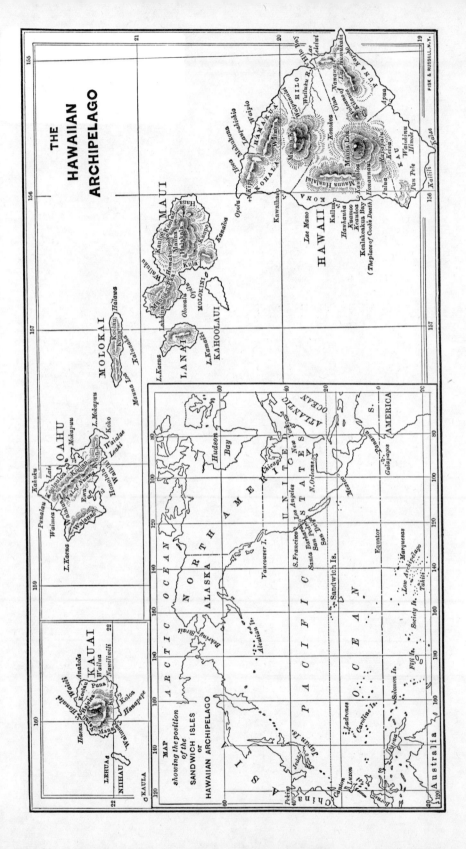

THE
HAWAIIAN
ARCHIPELAGO

MAP
showing the position
of the
SANDWICH ISLES
or
HAWAIIAN ARCHIPELAGO

FISK & RUSSELL, N.Y.

NORTHERN CALIFORNIA,

OREGON,

AND THE

SANDWICH ISLANDS.

By CHARLES NORDHOFF,

AUTHOR OF

"CALIFORNIA: FOR HEALTH, PLEASURE, AND RESIDENCE," &c., &c.

TEN SPEED PRESS
1974

This Centennial Edition
is dedicated by the publisher
to
Wallace E. Rankin

This is an unabridged edition of the original text. To retain the historical perspective of Nordhoff's study, no attempt has been made to expurgate his quaintly-expressed social attitudes.

Address all wholesale and
retail inquiries to:
Ten Speed Press
Box 4310
Berkeley, California 94704

TO MY FRIENDS,

MR. AND MRS. HENRY A. DIKE,

OF BROOKLYN, N. Y.

PREFACE.

THE favor with which my previous volume on California was received by the public induced me to prepare the present volume, which concerns itself, as the title sufficiently shows, with the northern parts of California, Oregon (including a journey through Washington Territory to Victoria, in Vancouver's Island), and the Sandwich Islands.

I have endeavored, as before, to give plain and circumstantial details, such as would interest and be of use to travelers for pleasure or information, and enable the reader to judge of the climate, scenery, and natural resources of the regions I visited; to give, in short, such information as I myself would like to have had in my possession before I made the journey.

Since this book went to press, Lunalilo, the King of the Sandwich Islands, has died of rapid consumption; and his successor is the Hon. David Kalakaua, a native chief, who has been prominent in the political affairs of the Islands, and was the rival of the late king after the death of Kamehameha V. Colonel Kalakaua is a man of education, of better physical stamina than the late king, of good habits, vigorous will, and a strong determination to maintain the independence of the Islands, in which he is supported by the people, who are of like mind with him on this point. His portrait is given on the next leaf.

KING KALAKAUA.

CONTENTS.

NORTHERN CALIFORNIA:

ITS AGRICULTURAL VALLEYS, DAIRIES, FORESTS, FRUIT-FARMS, ETC.

12 CONTENTS.

APPENDIX.

ILLUSTRATIONS.

DIAMOND HEAD AND WAIKIKI.

NORTHERN CALIFORNIA, OREGON,

AND

THE SANDWICH ISLANDS.

CHAPTER I.

HONOLULU AND THE ISLAND OF OAHU.

THE Hawaiian group consists, as you will see on the map, of eleven islands, of which Hawaii is the largest and Molokini the smallest. The islands together contain about 6000 square miles; and Hawaii alone has an area of nearly 4000 square miles, Maui 620, Oahu (which contains Honolulu, the capital) 530, and Kauai 500. Lanai, Kahoolawe, Molokai, Niihau, Kaula, Lehua, and Molokini are small islands. All are of volcanic origin, mountainous, and Hawaii contains the largest active crater in the world—Kilauea—one of the craters of Mauna Loa; while Maui contains the largest known extinct crater, Haleakala, the House of the Sun—a pit thirty miles in circumference and two thousand feet deep. Mauna Loa and Mauna Kea are nearly 14,000 feet high, as high as Mount Grey in Colorado; and you can not ride anywhere in the islands without seeing extinct craters, of which the hill called Diamond Head, near Honolulu, is an example.

2

HONOLULU—GENERAL VIEW.

The voyage from San Francisco to Honolulu is now very comfortably made in one of the Pacific Mail Company's steamers, which plies regularly between the two ports, and makes a round trip once in every month. The voyage down to the Islands lasts from eight to nine days, and even to persons subject to sea-sickness is likely to be an enjoyable sea-journey, because after the second day the weather is charmingly warm, the breezes usually mild, and the skies sunny and clear. In forty-eight hours after you leave the Golden Gate, shawls, overcoats, and wraps are discarded. You put on thinner clothing. After breakfast you will like to spread rugs on deck and lie in the sun, fanned by deliciously soft winds; and before you see Honolulu you will, even in winter, like to have an awning spread over you to keep off the sun. When they seek a tropical climate, our brethren on the Pacific coast have to endure no such rough voyage as that across the Atlantic. On the way you see flying-fish, and if you are lucky an occasional whale or a school of porpoises, but no ships. It is one of the loneliest of ocean tracks, for sailing-vessels usually steer farther north to catch stronger gales. But you sail over the lovely blue of the Pacific Ocean, which has not only softer gales but even a different shade of color than the fierce Atlantic.

We made the land at daylight on the tenth day of the voyage, and by breakfast-time were steaming through the Molokai Channel, with the high, rugged, and bare volcanic cliffs of Oahu close aboard, the surf beating vehemently against the shore. An hour later we rounded Diamond Head, and sailing past Waikiki, which is the Long Branch of Honolulu charmingly placed amidst groves of cocoa-nut-trees, turned sharp about, and steamed through a narrow channel into the landlocked little harbor of Honolulu, smooth as a mill-pond.

It is not until you are almost within the harbor that you get a fair view of the city, which lies embowered in palms and fine tamarind-trees, with the tall fronds of the banana peering above the low-roofed houses; and thus the tropics come after all somewhat suddenly upon you; for the land which you have skirted all the morning is by no means tropical in appearance, and the cocoa-nut groves of Waikiki will disappoint you on their first and too distant view, which gives them the insignificant appearance of tall reeds. But your first view of Honolulu, that from the ship's deck, is one of the pleasantest you can get: it is a view of gray house-tops, hidden in luxuriant green, with a background of volcanic mountains three or four thousand feet high, and an immediate foreground of smooth harbor, gay with man-of-war boats, native canoes and flags, and the wharf, with ladies in carriages, and native fruit-venders in what will seem to you brightly colored night-gowns, eager to sell you a feast of bananas and oranges.

There are several other fine views of Honolulu, especially that from the lovely Nuanu Valley, looking seaward over the town, and one from the roof of the prison, which edifice, clean, roomy, and in the day-time empty because the convicts are sent out to labor on public works and roads, has one of the finest situations in the town's limits, directly facing the Nuanu Valley.

From the steamer you proceed to a surprisingly excellent hotel, which was built at a cost of about $120,000, and is owned by the government. You will find it a large building, affording all the conveniences of a first-class hotel in any part of the world. It is built of a concrete stone made on the spot, of which also the new Parliament House is composed; and as it has roomy, well-shaded court-yards and deep, cool piazzas, and breezy halls and good rooms, and baths and gas, and a billiard-room, you might imagine yourself in San Francisco, were it not that you drive in under the shade of cocoa-nut, tama-

HAWAIIAN HOTEL, HONOLULU.

rind, guava, and algeroba trees, and find all the doors and windows open in midwinter; and ladies and children in white sitting on the piazzas.

It is told in Honolulu that the building of this hotel cost two of the late king's cabinet, Mr. Harris and Dr. Smith, their places. The Hawaiian people are economical, and not very enterprising; they dislike debt, and a considerable part of the Hawaiian national debt was contracted to build this hotel. You will feel sorry for Messrs. Harris and Smith, who were for many years two of the ablest members of the Hawaiian cabinet, but you will feel grateful for their enterprise also, when you hear that before this hotel was completed—that is to say, until 1871—a stranger landing in Honolulu had either to throw himself on the hospitality of the citizens, take his lodgings in the Sailors' Home, or go back to his ship. It is not often that cabinet ministers fall in so good a cause, or incur the public displeasure for an act which adds so much to the comfort of mankind.

The mercury ranges between 68° and 81° in the winter months and between 75° and 86° during the summer, in Honolulu. The mornings are often a little overcast until about half-past nine, when it clears away bright. The hottest part of the day is before noon. The trade-wind usually blows, and when it does it is always cool; with a south wind, it is sometimes sultry, though the heat is never nearly so oppressive as in July and August in New York. In fact, a New Yorker whom I met in the Islands in August congratulated himself as much on having escaped the New York summer as others did on having avoided the winter.

The nights are cool enough for sound rest, but not cold.

It is not by any means a torrid climate, and it has, perhaps, the fewest daily extremes of any pleasant climate in the world. For instance, the mercury ranged in January between 69° at 7 A.M., 75½° at 2 P.M., and 71½° at 10 P.M. The highest temperature in that month was 78°, and the lowest 68°. December and January are usually the coolest months in the year at Honolulu, but the variation is extremely slight for the whole year, the maximum of the warmest day in July (still at Honolulu) being only 86°, and this at noon, and the lowest mark being 62°, in the early morning in December. A friend of mine resident during twenty years in the Islands has never had a blanket in his house.

It is said that the climate is an excellent one for consumptives, and physicians here point to numerous instances of the kindly and healing effect of the mild air. At the same time, I suspect it must in the long-run be a little debilitating to Americans. It is a charming climate for children; and as sea-bathing is possible and pleasant at all times, those who derive benefit from this may here enjoy it to the fullest extent during all the winter months as well as in the summer.

Of course you wear thin, but not the thinnest, clothing. White is appropriate to the climate; but summer flannels are comfortable in winter. The air is never as sultry as in New York in July or August, and the heat is by no means oppressive, there being almost always a fresh breeze. Honolulu has the reputation of being the hottest place on the islands, and a walk through its streets at midday quickly tires one; but in a mountainous country like this you may choose your temperature, of course. The summits of the highest peaks on Hawaii are covered with almost perpetual snow; and there are sugar planters who might sit around a fire every night in the year.

Unlike California, the Islands have no special rainy season, though rain is more abundant in winter than during the summer months. But the trade-wind, which is also the rain-wind, greatly controls the rain-fall; and it is useful for visitors to bear in mind that on the weather side of every one of the Islands—that side exposed to the wind—rains are frequent, while on the lee side the rain-fall is much less, and in some places there is scarcely any. Thus an invalid may get at will either a dry or moist climate, and this often by moving but a few miles. Not only is it true that at Hilo it sometimes rains for a month at a time, while at Lahania they have a shower only about once in eighteen months; but you may *see* it rain every day from the hotel piazza in Honolulu, though you get not a drop in the city itself; for in the Nuanu and Manoa valleys there are showers every day in the year—the droppings of fragments of clouds which have been blown over the mountain summits; and if you cross the Pali to go the windward side of the island, though you set out from Honolulu amidst brilliant sunshine which will endure there all day unchanged, you will not ride three miles without needing a mackintosh. But the residents, knowing that during the greater part of the year the showers are light and of brief duration, take no precautions against them; and indeed an island shower seems to be harmless to any one but an invalid, for it is not a climate in which one easily "takes cold."

The very slight changes in temperature between day and night make the climate agreeable, and I think useful, to persons in tender health. But I do not believe it can be safely recommended for all cases of consumption. If the patient has the disease fully developed, and if it has been caused by lack of nutrition, I should think the island air likely to be insufficiently bracing. For persons who have "weak lungs" merely, but no actual disease, it is probably a good and perfectly safe climate; and if sea-bathing is part of your physician's prescription, it can, as I said before, be enjoyed in perfection here by the tenderest body all the year round.

Honolulu, being the capital of the kingdom, contains the government offices; and you will perhaps be surprised, as I was, to find an excellent public hospital,

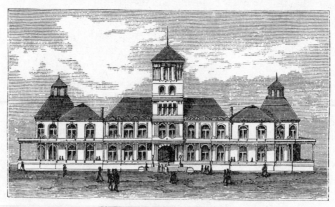

GOVERNMENT BUILDINGS, HONOLULU.

a reform school, and other proper and well-managed charities. When you have visited these and some of the numerous schools and the native churches, and have driven or ridden to Waikiki for a sea-bath, and have seen the Nuanu Valley and the precipice called the Pali, if you are American, and familiar with New England, it will be revealed to you that the reason why all the country looks so familiar to you is that it is really a very accurate reproduction of New England country scenery. The white frame houses with green blinds, the picket-fences whitewashed until they shine, the stone walls, the small barns, the scanty pastures, the little white frame churches scattered about, the narrow "front yards," the frequent school-houses, usually with but little shade: all are

New England, genuine and unadulterated; and you have only to eliminate the palms, the bananas, and other tropical vegetation, to have before you a fine bit of Vermont or the stonier parts of Massachusetts. The whole scene has no more breadth nor freedom about it than a petty New England village, but it is just as neat, trim, orderly, and silent also. There is even the same propensity to put all the household affairs under one roof which was born of a severe climate in Massachusetts, but has been brought over to these milder suns by the incorrigible Puritans who founded this bit of civilization.

ROYAL SCHOOL, HONOLULU.

In fact, the missionaries have left an indelible mark upon these islands. You do not need to look deep to know that they were men of force, men of the same kind as they who have left an equally deep impress upon so large a part of our Western States; men and women who had formed their own lives according to certain fixed and immutable rules, who knew no better country than New England, nor any better ways than New England ways, and to whom it never occurred to think that what was good and sufficient in Massachusetts was not equally good and fit in any part of the world. Patiently, and somewhat rigorously, no doubt, they sought from the beginning to make New England men and women of these Hawaiians; and what is wonderful is that, to a large extent, they have succeeded.

As you ride about the suburbs of Honolulu, and later as you travel about the islands, more and more you will be impressed with a feeling of respect and admiration for the missionaries. Whatever of material prosperity has grown up here is built on their work, and could not have existed but for their preceding labors; and you see in the spirit of the people, in their often quaint habits, in their universal education, in all that makes these islands peculiar and what they are, the marks of the Puritans who came here but fifty years ago to civilize a savage nation, and have done their work so thoroughly that, even though the

Hawaiian people became extinct, it would require a century to obliterate the way-marks of that handful of determined New England men and women.

Their patient and effective labors seem to me, now that I have seen the results, to have been singularly undervalued at home. No intelligent American can visit the islands and remain there even a month, without feeling proud that the civilization which has here been created in so marvelously short a time was the work of his country men and women; and if you make the acquaintance of the older missionary families, you will not leave them without deep personal esteem for their characters, as well as admiration of their work. They did not only form a written language for the Hawaiian race, and painfully write for them school-books, a dictionary, and a translation of the Scriptures and of a hymn-book; they did not merely gather the people in churches and

COURT-HOUSE, HONOLULU.

their children into schools; but they guided the race, slowly and with immense difficulty, toward Christian civilization; and though the Hawaiian is no more a perfect Christian than the New Yorker or Massachusetts man, and though there are still traces of old customs and superstitions, these missionaries have eradicated the grosser crimes of murder and theft so completely, that even in Honolulu people leave their houses open all day and unlocked all night, without thought of theft; and there is not a country in the world where the stranger may travel in such absolute safety as in these islands.

The Hawaiian, or Sandwich Islands, were discovered — or rediscovered, as some say — by Captain Cook, in January, 1778, a year and a half after our

Declaration of Independence.   The inhabitants were then what we call savages —that is to say, they wore no more clothing than the climate made necessary, and knew nothing of the Christian religion.   In the period between 1861 and 1865 this group had in the Union armies a brigadier-general, a major, several other officers, and more than one hundred private soldiers and seamen, and its people contributed to the treasury of the Sanitary Commission a sum larger than that given by most of our own States.

MRS. LUCY G. THURSTON.

In 1820 the first missionaries landed on the shores of these islands, and Mrs. Lucy G. Thurston, one of those who came in that year, still lives, a bright, active old lady, with a shrewd wit of her own.   Thirty-three years afterward, in 1853, the American Board of Missions determined that " the Sandwich Islands, having been Christianized, shall no longer receive aid from the Board ;" and in this year, 1873, the natives of these islands are, there is reason to be-

KAWAIAHO CHURCH—FIRST NATIVE CHURCH IN HONOLULU.

lieve, the most generally educated people in the world. There is scarcely a Hawaiian—man, woman, or child—of suitable age but can both read and write. All the towns and many country localities possess substantial stone or, more often, framed churches, of the oddest New England pattern; and a compulsory education law draws every child into the schools, while a special tax of two dollars on every voter, and an additional general tax, provide schools and teachers for all the children and youth.

Nine hundred and three thousand dollars were given by Christian people in the United States during thirty-five years to accomplish this result; and to-day the islands themselves support a missionary society, which sends the Gospel in the hands of native missionaries into other islands at its own cost, and not only supports more than a dozen "foreign" missionaries, but translates parts of the Bible into other Polynesian tongues.

Nor was exile from their homes and kindred the only privation the missionaries suffered. They came among a people so vile that they had not even a conception of right and wrong; so prone to murder and pillage that the first Kamehameha, the conqueror, gave as excuse for his conquest that it was necessary to make the paths safe; so debauched in their common conversation that the earlier missionaries were obliged for years rigidly to forbid their own children not only from acquaintance with the natives among whom they lived, but even from learning the native language, because to hear only the passing speech of their neighbors was to suffer the grossest contamination.

Of those who began this good work but few now remain. Most of them have gone to their reward, having no doubt suffered, as well as accomplished, much. Of the first band who came out from the United States, the only one living in 1873 is Mrs. Lucy G. Thurston, a bright, active, and lively old lady of seventy-five years, who drives herself to church on Sundays in a one-horse chaise, and has her own opinions of passing events. How she has lived in the tropics for fifty years without losing even an atom of the New England look puzzles you; but it shows you also the strength which these people brought with them, the tenacity with which they clung to their habits of dress

DR. JUDD.

and living and thought, the remorseless determination which they imported, with their other effects, around Cape Horn.

Then there was Dr. Judd, who has died since these lines were written, who

DR. COAN.

came out as physician to the mission, and proved himself in the islands, as the world knows, a very able man, with statesmanship for some great emergencies which made him for years one of the chief advisers of the Hawaiian kings. It was to me a most touching sight to see, on a Sunday after church, Mrs. Thurston, his senior by many years but still alert and vigorous, taking hold of his hand and tenderly helping him out of the church and to his carriage.

And in Hilo, when you go to visit the volcano, you will find Dr. Coan, one of the brightest and loveliest spirits of them all, the story of whose life in the remote island whose apostle he was, is as wonderful and as touching as that of any of the earlier apostles, and shows what great works unyielding faith and love can do in redeeming a savage people. When Dr. and Mrs. Coan came to the island of Hawaii, its shores and woods were populous; and through their labors and those of the Reverend Mr. Lyman and one or two others, thousands of men and women were instructed in the truths of Christianity, inducted into civilized habits of life, and finally brought into the church.

As you sail along the green coast of Hawaii from its northern point to Hilo, you will be surprised at the number of quaint little white churches which mark the distances almost with the regularity of mile-stones; if, later, you ride through this district or the one south of Hilo, you will see that for every church there is also a school-house; you will see native children reading and writing as well as our own at home; you may hear them singing tunes familiar in our own Sunday-schools; you will see the native man and woman sitting down to read their newspaper at the close of day; and if you could talk with them, you would find they knew almost as much about our late war as you do, for they took an intense interest in the war of the rebellion. And you must remember that when, less than forty years ago, Dr. and Mrs. Coan came to Hilo, the people were naked savages, with but one church and one school-house in the district, and almost without printed books or knowledge of reading. They flocked to hear the Gospel. Thousands removed from a distance to Hilo, where, in their rapid way, they built up a large town, and kept up surely the strangest " protracted meeting " ever held; and going back to their homes after many months, they took with them knowledge and zeal to build up Christian churches and schools of their own.

Over these Dr. Coan has presided these many years; not only preaching regularly on Sundays and during the week in the large native church at Hilo, and in two or three neighboring churches, but visiting the more distant churches at intervals to examine and instruct the members, and keep them all on the right track. He has seen a region very populous when he first came to it decrease until it has now many more deserted and ruined house-places than inhabited dwellings; but, also, he has seen a great population turned from darkness to light, a considerable part of it following his own blameless and loving life as an example, and very many living to old age steadfast and zealous Christians.

On your first Sunday at Honolulu you will probably attend one or other of the native churches. They are commodious buildings, well furnished; and a good organ, well played, will surprise you. Sunday is a very quiet day in the Islands: they are a church-going people, and the empty seats in the Honolulu native churches give you notice of the great decrease in population since these were built.

If you go to hear preaching in your own language, it will probably be to the Seamen's Chapel where the Rev. Mr. Damon preaches—one of the oldest and one of the best-known residents of Honolulu. This little chapel was brought around Cape Horn in pieces, in a whale-ship many years ago, and was, I believe, the first American church set up in these islands.   It is a curious old relic,

BETHEL CHURCH.

and has seen many changes.   Mr. Damon has lived here since 1846 a most zeal-ous and useful life as seamen's chaplain.   He is, in his own field, a true and untiring missionary, and to his care the port owes a clean and roomy Seamen's Home, a valuable little paper, *The Friend*, which was for many years the chief reading of the whalemen who formerly crowded the ports of Hawaii; and help in distress, and fatherly advice, and un-ceasing kindness at all times to a mul-titude of seamen during nearly thirty years.   The sailors, who quickly recog-nize a genuine man, have dubbed him "Father Damon;" and he deserves, what he has long had, their confidence and affection.

DR. DAMON.

The charitable and penal institutions of Honolulu are quickly seen, and de-serve a visit.   They show the care with which the Government has looked after the welfare of the people.   The Queen's Hospital is an admirably kept house.   At the Reform School you will see a number of boys trained and edu-cated in right ways.   The prison not only deserves a visit for itself, but from its roof you obtain, as I said before, one of the best views of Honolulu and the adjacent country and ocean.

Then there are native schools, elementary and academic, where you will see

QUEEN'S HOSPITAL, HONOLULU.

the young Hawaiian at his studies, and learn to appreciate the industry and thoroughness with which education is carried on all over these islands. You will see also curious evidence of the mixture of races here; for on the benches sit, and in the classes recite, Hawaiian, Chinese, Portuguese, half white and half Chinese children; and the little pig-tailed Celestial reads out of his primer quite as well as any.

NATIVE SCHOOL-HOUSE IN HONOLULU.

In the girls' schools you will see an occasional pretty face, but fewer than I expected to see; and to my eyes the Hawaiian girl is rarely very attractive.

Among the middle-aged women, however, you often meet with fine heads and large, expressive features. The women have not unfrequently a majesty of carriage and a tragic intensity of features and expression which are quite remarkable. Their loose dress gives grace as well as dignity to their movements, and whoever invented it for them deserves more credit than he has received. It is a little startling at first to see women walking about in what, to our perverted tastes, look like calico or black stuff night-gowns; but the dress grows on you as you become accustomed to it; it lends itself readily to bright ornamentation; it is eminently fit for the climate; and a stately Hawaiian dame, marching through the street in black *holaku*—as the dress is called—with a long necklace, or *le*, of bright scarlet or brilliant yellow flowers, bare and untrammeled feet, and flowing hair, surmounted often by a low-crowned felt hat, compares very favorably with a high-heeled, wasp-waisted, absurdly-bonneted, fashionable white lady.

COOOA-NUT GROVE, AND RESIDENCE OF THE LATE KING KAMEHAMEHA V., AT WAIKIKI, OAHU.

As you travel through the country, you see not unfrequently one of the tall, majestic, large women, who were formerly, it is said by old residents, more numerous than now. I have been assured by several persons that the race has dwindled in the last half century; and all old residents speak with admiration of the great stature and fine forms of the chiefs and their wives in the early days. It does not appear that these chiefs were a distinct race, but they were despotic rulers of the common people; and their greater stature is attributed by those who should know to their being nourished on better food, and to easier circumstances and more favorable surroundings.

When you have seen Honolulu and the Nuanu Valley, and bathed and drunk cocoa-nut milk at Waikiki, you will be ready for a charming excursion—the ride around the Island of Oahu. For this you should take several days. It is most pleasantly made by a party of three or four persons, and ladies, if they can sit in the saddle at all, can very well do it. You should provide yourself with a pack-mule, which will carry not only spare clothing but some provisions; and your guide ought to take care of your horses and be able, if necessary, to cook you a lunch. The ride is easily done in four days, and you will sleep every night at a plantation or farm. The roads are excellent for riding, and carriages have made the journey. It is best to set out by way of Pearl River and return by the Pali, as thus you have the trade-wind in your face all the way. If you are accustomed to ride, and can do thirty miles a day, you should sleep the first night at or near Waialua, the next at or near what is called the Mormon Settlement, and on the third day ride into Honolulu. If ladies are of your party, and the stages must be shorter, you can ride the first day to Ewa, which is but ten miles; the next, to Waialua, eighteen miles further; the third, to the neighborhood of Kahuku, twelve miles; thence to Kahana, fifteen miles; thence to Kaalaea, twelve miles; and the next day carries you, by an easy ride of thirteen miles, into Honolulu. Any one who can sit on a horse at all will enjoy this excursion, and receive benefit from it; the different stages of it are so short that each day's work is only a pleasure. On the way you will see, near Ewa, the Pearl Lochs, which it has recently been proposed to cede as a naval station to the United States; and near Waialua an interesting boarding-school for Hawaiian girls, in which they are taught not only in the usual school studies, but in sewing, and the various arts of the housewife. If you are curious to see the high valley in which the famous Waialua oranges are grown, you must take a day for that purpose. Between Kahuku and Kahana it is worth while to make a detour into the mountains to see the Kaliawa Falls, which are a very picturesque sight. The rock, at a height of several hundred feet, has been curiously worn by the water into the shape of a canoe. Here, also, the precipitous walls are covered with masses of fine ferns. At Kahana, and also at Koloa, you will see rice-fields, which are cultivated by Chinese. You pass also on your road several sugar-plantations; and if it is the season of sugar-boiling, you will be interested in this process. For miles you ride along the sea-shore, and your guide will lead you to proper places for a midday bath, preliminary to your lunch.

After leaving the Mormon Settlement, the scenery becomes very grand—it is, indeed, as fine as any on the Islands, and compares well with any scenery in the world. That it can be seen without severe toil gives it, for such people as myself, no slight advantage over some other scenery in these Islands and elsewhere, access to which can be gained only by toilsome and disagreeable journeys. There is a blending of sea and mountain which will dwell in your memory as not oppressively grand, and yet fine enough to make you thankful that Providence has made the world so lovely and fair.

As you approach the Pali, the mountain becomes a sheer precipice for some miles, broken only by the gorge of the Pali, up which, if you are prudent, you will walk, letting your horses follow with the guide—though Hawaiian horse-men ride both up and down, and have been known to gallop down the stone-paved and slippery steep. As you look up at these tall, gloomy precipices, you will see one of the peculiarities of a Sandwich Island landscape. The rocks are not bare, but covered from crown to base with moss and ferns; and these cling so closely to the surface that to your eye they seem to be but a short, close-textured green fuzz. In fact, these great rocks, thus adorned, reminded me constantly of the rock scenery in such operas as Fra Diavolo; the dark green being of a shade which I do not remember to have seen before in nature, though it is not uncommon in theatrical scenery.

The grass remains green, except in the dry districts, all the year round; and the common grass of the Islands is the *maniania,* a fine creeping grass which covers the ground with a dense velvety mat; and where it is kept short by sheep makes an admirable springy lawn. It has a fine deep color and bears drought remarkably well; and it is the favorite pasture grass of the Islands. I do not think it as fattening as the alfilleria of Southern California or our own timothy or blue grass; but it is a valuable grass to the stockmen, because it eats out every other and less valuable kind.

On your journey around Oahu you need a guide who can speak some English; you must take with you on the pack-mule provisions for the journey; and it is well to have a blanket for each of your party. You will sleep each night in a native house, unless, as is very likely to be the case, you have invitations to stop at plantation houses on your way. At the native houses they will kill a chicken for you, and cook taro; but they have no other supplies. You can usually get cocoa-nuts, whose milk is very wholesome and refreshing. The journey is like a somewhat prolonged picnic; the air is mild and pure; and you need no heavy clothing, for you are sure of bright sunny weather.

For your excursions near Honolulu, and for the adventure I have described, you can hire horses; though if you mean to stay a month or two it is better to buy. A safe and good horse, well saddled and bridled, brought to you every morning at the hotel, costs you a dollar a day. In that case you have no care or responsibility for the animal. But unless there are men-of-war in port you can buy a sufficiently good riding-horse for from twelve to twenty-five dollars, and get something of your investment back when you leave; and you can buy saddles and all riding-gear cheaply in Honolulu. The maintenance of a horse in town costs not over fifty cents per day.

Your guide for a journey ought to cost you a dollar a day, which includes his horse; when you stop for the day he unsaddles your horses and ties them out in a grass-field where they get sufficient nourishment. For your accommodation at a native house, you ought to pay fifty cents for each person of your party, including the guide. The proprietor of the Honolulu hotel is very obliging and readily helps you to make all arrangements for horses and guides; and if you have brought any letters of introduction, or make acquaintances in the place, you will find every body ready to assist you. Riding is the pleasantest way of getting about; but on Oahu the roads are sufficiently good to drive considerable distances, and carriages are easily obtainable.

One of the pleasant surprises which meet a northern traveler in these islands is the number of strange dishes which appear on the table and in the bill of fare. Strawberries, oranges—the sweetest and juiciest I have eaten anywhere, except perhaps in Rio de Janeiro—bananas and cocoa-nuts, you have at will; but besides these there are during the winter months the guava, very nice when it is sliced like a tomato and eaten with sugar and milk; taro, which is the potato of the country and, in the shape of poi, the main subsistence of the native Hawaiian; bread-fruit; flying-fish, the most tender and succulent of the fish kind ; and, in their season, the mango, the custard-apple, the alligator-pear, the water-melon, the rose-apple, the ohia, and other fruits.

Taro, when baked, is an excellent and wholesome vegetable, and from its

HAWAIIAN POI DEALER.

leaves is cooked a fine substitute for spinach, called *luau*. Poi also appears on your hotel table, being the national dish, of which many foreigners have become very fond. It is very fattening and easily digested, and is sometimes prescribed by physicians to consumptives. As you drive about the suburbs of Honolulu you will see numerous taro patches, and may frequently see the natives engaged in the preparation of poi, which consists in baking the root or tuber in underground ovens, and then mashing it very fine, so that if dry it would be a flour. It is then mixed with water, and for native use left to undergo a slight fermentation. Fresh or unfermented poi has a pleasant taste; when fermented it tastes to me like book-binder's paste, and a liking for it must be acquired rather than natural, I should say, with foreigners.

So universal is its use among the natives that the manufacture of poi is carried on now by steam-power and with Yankee machinery, for the sugar planters; and the late king, who was avaricious and a trader, incurred the dislike of his native subjects by establishing a poi-factory of his own near Honolulu. Poi is sold in the streets in calabashes, but it is also shipped in considerable quantities to other islands, and especially to guano islands which lie southward and westward of this group. On these lonely islets, many of which have not even drinking-water for the laborers who live on them, poi and fish are the chief if not the only articles of food. The fish, of course, are caught on the spot, but poi, water, salt, and a few beef cattle for the use of the white superintendents are carried from here.

Taro is a kind of *arum*. It grows, unlike any other vegetable I know of unless it be rice, entirely under water. A taro patch is surrounded by embankments; its bottom is of puddled clay; and in this the cutting, which is simply the top of the plant with a little of the tuber, is set. The plants are set out in little clumps in long rows, and a man at work in a taro patch stands up to his knees in water. Forty square feet of taro, it is estimated, will support a person for a year, and a square mile of taro will feed over 15,000 Hawaiians.

THE PALACE, HONOLULU.

By-the-way, you will hear the natives say *kalo* when they speak of taro; and by this and other words in common use you will presently learn of a curious obliquity in their hearing. A Hawaiian does not notice any difference in the sounds of *r* and *l*, of *k* and *t*, or of *b*, *p*, and *f*. Thus the Pali, or precipice near Honolulu, is spoken of as the Pari; the island of Kauai becomes to a resident of it Tauwai, though a native of Oahu calls it Kauai; taro is almost universally called *kalo ;* and the common salutation, *Aloha*, which means "Love to you," and is the national substitute for "How do you do?" is half the time *Aroha ;* Lanai is indifferently called Ranai; and Mauna Loa is in the mouths of most Hawaiians Mauna Roa. Indeed, in the older charts the capital of the kingdom is called Honoruru.

Society in Honolulu possesses some peculiar features, owing in part to the singularly isolated situation of this little capital, and partly to the composition of the social body. Honolulu is a capital city unconnected with any other place in the world by telegraph, having a mail once a month from San Francisco and New Zealand, and dependent during the remainder of the month upon its own resources. To a New Yorker, who gets his news hot and hot all day and night, and can't go to sleep without first looking in at the Fifth Avenue Hotel to hear the latest item, this will seem deplorable enough; but you have no idea how charming, how pleasant, how satisfactory it is for a busy or over-worked man to be thus for a while absolutely isolated from affairs; to feel that for a month at least the world must get on without your interfering hand; and though you may dread beforehand this enforced separation from politics and business, you will find it very pleasant in the actual experience.

As you stand upon the wharf in company with the élite of the kingdom to watch the steamer depart, a great burden falls from your soul, because for a month to come you have not the least responsibility for what may happen in any part of the planet.   Looking up at the black smoke of the departing ship, you say to yourself, "Who cares?"   Let what will happen, you are not respon-

EMMA, QUEEN OF KAMEHAMEHA IV.

sible.   And so, with a light heart and an easy conscience, you get on your horse (price $15), and about the time the lady passengers on the steamer begin to turn green in face, you are sitting down on a spacious *lanai* or veranda, in one of the most delightful sea-side resorts in the world, with a few friends who have determined to celebrate by a dinner this monthly recurrence of their non-intercourse with the world.

The people are surprisingly hospitable and kind and know how to make strangers at home; they have leisure, and know how to use it pleasantly; the climate controls their customs in many respects, and nothing is pursued at fever heat as with us.   What strikes you, when you have found your way into Honolulu society and looked around, is a certain sensible moderation and simplicity which is in part, I suspect, a remainder of the old missionary influence; there is a certain amount of formality, which is necessary to keep society from deteriorating, but there is no striving after effect; there are, so far as a stranger discovers, no petty cliques or cabals or coteries, and there is a very high average of intelligence: they care about the best things.

They know how to dine; and having good cooks and sound digestions, they add to these one requisite to pleasant dining which some more pretentious societies are without: they have leisure.   Nothing is done in haste in Honolulu, where they have long ago convinced themselves that "to-morrow is another day."   Moreover, you find them well-read, without being blue; they have not muddled their history by contradictory telegraphic reports of matters of no consequence; in fact, so far as recent events are concerned, they stand on tolerably firm ground, having perused only the last monthly record of current events. Consequently, they have had time to read and enjoy the best books; to follow with an intelligent interest the most notable passing events; and as most of them come from families or have lived among people who have had upon their own shoulders some conscious share of government, political, moral, or religious, these talkers are not pedantic, but agreeable. As to the ladies, you find them charming; beautifully dressed, of course, but they have not given the whole day and their whole minds to the dress; they are cheerful, easily excited to gayety, long accustomed to take life easily, and eating as though they did not know what dyspepsia was.

Indeed, when you have passed a month in the Islands you will have a better opinion of idleness than you had before, though in some respects the odd effects of a tropical climate will hardly meet your approval. Euchre, for instance, takes the place here which whist holds elsewhere as the amusement of sensible people.

Finally, society in Honolulu is respectable. It is fashionable to be virtuous, and if you were "fast," I think you would conceal it. The Government has always encouraged respectability, and discountenanced vice. The men who have ruled the Islands—not the missionaries alone, but the political rulers since—have been plain, honest, and, in the main, wise men; and they

A HAWAIIAN CHIEF.

have kept politics respectable in the little monarchy. The disreputable adventurer element which degrades our politics, and invades society too, is not found here. You will say the rewards are not great enough to attract this vile class. Perhaps not; but at any rate it is not there; and I do not know, in short, where else in the world you would find so kindly, so gracefully hospitable, and, at the same time, so simple and enjoyable a society as that of Honolulu.

No one can visit the Islands without being impressed by the boundless hospitality of the sugar planters, who, with their superintendents and managers, form, away from the few towns, almost the only white inhabitants. Hospitality so free-handed is, I suspect, found in few other parts of the world. Though Honolulu has now a commodious hotel, the residents keep up their old habits of graceful welcome to strangers. The capital has an excellent band, which plays in public places several times a week; and it does not lack social entertainments, parties, and dinners, to break the monotony of life. Not only the residents of foreign birth, but a few Hawaiians also, people of education, culture, and means, entertain gracefully and frequently.

As for the common people, they are by nature or long custom, or both, as kindly and hospitable as men can be. If you ask for lodgings at night-fall at a native hut, you are received as though you were conferring a favor; frequently the whole house, which has but one room, is set apart for you, the people going elsewhere to sleep; a chicken is slain in your honor, and for your exclusive supper; and you are served by the master of the house himself. The native grass-house, where it has been well built, is a very comfortable structure. It has but a single room, calico curtains serving as partitions by night; at one end a standing bed-place, running across the house, provides sleeping accommodations for the whole family, however numerous. This bed consists of mats; and the covers are either of tapa cloth—which is as though you should sleep under newspapers—or of blankets. The more prosperous people have often, besides this, an enormous bedstead curtained off and reserved for strangers; and you may see the women take out of their chests, when you ask hospitality, blankets, sheets, and a great number of little pillows for the bed, as well as often a brilliant silk coverlet; for this bed appears to be like a Cape Cod parlor—for ornament rather than use. The use of the dozen little pillows puzzled me, until I found that they were intended to tuck or wedge me in, so that I should not needlessly and uncomfortably roll about the vast bed. They were laid at the sides, and I was instructed to "chock" myself with them. On leaving, do not inquire what is the cost of your accommodations. The Hawaiian has vague ideas about price. He might tell you five or ten dollars; but if you pay him seventy-five cents for yourself and your guide, he will be abundantly and thoroughly satisfied.

THE CRATER OF KILAUEA—ONE PHASE.

CHAPTER II.

HILO, WITH SOME VOLCANOES.

HILO, as you will perceive on the map, lies on the eastern or windward side of the Island of Hawaii. You get there in the little inter-island steamer *Kilauea*, named after the volcano, and which makes a weekly tour of all the Islands except far-off Kauai, which it visits but once a month. The charge for passage is fifteen dollars from Honolulu to Hilo, and twenty-five dollars for the round trip.

The cabin is small; and as you are likely to have fine weather, you will, even if you are a lady, pass the time more pleasantly on deck, where the steward, a Goa man and the most assiduous and tactful of his trade, will place a mattress and blankets for you. You must expect to suffer somewhat from sea-sickness if you are subject to that ill, for the passage is not unlikely to be rough. On the way you see Lahaina, and a considerable part of the islands of Maui and Hawaii; in fact, you are never out of sight of land.

If you start on Monday evening you will reach Hilo on Wednesday—and "about this time expect rain," as the almanac-makers say. They get about seventeen feet of rain at Hilo during the year; and as they have sometimes several days without any at all, you must look for not only frequent but heavy showers. A Hilo man told me of a curious experiment which was once made there. They knocked the heads out of an oil-cask—so he said—and it rained in at the bung-hole faster than it could run out at the ends. You may disbelieve this story if you please; I tell it as it was told me; but in any case you will do well to provide yourself for Hilo and the volcano journey with stout water-proof clothing.

Hilo, on those days when the sun shines, is one of the prettiest places on the Islands. If you are so fortunate as to enter the bay on a fine day you will see a very tropical landscape—a long, pleasant, curved sweep of beach, on which the surf is breaking, and beyond, white houses nestling among cocoa-nut groves, and bread-fruit, pandanus, and other Southern trees, many of them bearing brilliant flowers; with shops and stores along the beach. Men and boys sporting in the surf, and men and women dashing on horseback over the beach, make up the life of the scene.

Hilo has no hotel; it has not even a carriage; but it has a very agreeable and intelligent population of Americans, and you will find good accommodations at the large house of Mr. Severance, the sheriff of Hawaii. If his house should be full you need not be alarmed, for some one will take you in.

This is the usual and most convenient point of departure for the volcano. Here you hire horses and a guide for the journey. Having gone to Hilo on the steamer, you will do best to return to Honolulu by schooner, which leaves you at liberty to choose your point and time of departure. Hawaii lies to windward of Oahu; and a schooner, which might need four or five days to beat up to Hilo, will run down from any part of Hawaii in twenty-four hours. If you are an energetic traveler, determined to see every thing, and able to endure a good deal of rough riding, you may spend six weeks on Hawaii. In that time you may not only see the active volcano of Kilauea, but may ascend Mauna Loa and Mauna Kea, whose immense slopes and lofty and in the winter snow-clad summits show gloriously on a clear day from Hilo; and you may ride from Hilo along the north-eastern coast, through the Hamakua and Kohala districts, ending your journey at Kealakeakua Bay where Captain Cook was killed. There you can take schooner for Honolulu; or if your energies hold out ride through Kau and Puna back to Hilo.

The Hamakua and Hilo coasts you will see from the steamer, which sails close along this bold and picturesque shore on her way to Hilo. This part of the island is but an extension of the vast slope of Mauna Kea; and all the waters which drain from its cloud-laden summit pour into the sea through numerous deep channels, or gorges which they have worn for themselves, and occasionally dash into the ocean from high cliffs, forming water-falls visible from the ship's deck. Of the gorges or cañons, there are seventy-nine in a distance of about thirty miles; many of them are from five to eight hundred feet deep;

KEALAKEAKUA BAY, WHERE CAPTAIN COOK WAS KILLED.

and as you ride along the coast, you have no sooner emerged from one of these deep pits than you descend by a road seldom easy, and often very steep indeed, into another. The sides of these gorges are lined with masses of the most magnificent ferns, and at their bottoms you find sparkling streams; and as you look up the cañons you see picturesque water-falls. In short, to the lover of bold and strange scenery this ride offers many pleasures; and that its difficulties may not be exaggerated to any one's apprehension, I will mention that during the spring of 1873 an English lady, taking with her only a native woman as guide, made the tour of the whole seventy-nine gulches, and thought herself amply rewarded for her toils by what she saw. As for myself, I must confess that four of these gulches—the four nearest Hilo—satisfied me; these I saw in visiting some sugar-plantations.

If you do not intend such a thorough exploration of Hawaii, but mean only to see the volcano of Kilauea, your pleasantest plan is to ride from Hilo by the direct road to the crater, and return by way of Puna. You will have ridden a trifle over one hundred miles through a very remarkable and in some parts a beautiful country; you will have slept one night in a native house, and will have seen much of Hawaiian life, and enjoyed a tiring but at the same time a very novel journey, and some sights which can not be matched outside of Iceland. To do this, and spend two or three days in pleasant sight-seeing near Hilo, will bring you back to Honolulu in from twelve to fourteen days after you left it.

Your traveling expenses will be sufficiently moderate. At Hilo you pay for board and lodgings eight dollars per week. The charge for horses is ten dollars each for the volcano journey, with a dollar a day for your guide. This guide relieves you of all care of the animals, and is useful in various ways. At the Volcano House the charge for horse and man is five dollars per day, and you pay half-price for your guide. There is a charge of one dollar for a special guide into the crater, which is made in your bill, and you will do well to promise this guide, when you go in, a small gratuity—half a dollar, or, if your party is large, a dollar—if he gives you satisfaction. He will get you specimens, carry a shawl for a lady, and make himself in other ways helpful.

When you get on your horse at Hilo for the volcano, leave behind you all hope of good roads. You are to ride for thirty miles over a lava bed, along a narrow trail as well made as it could be without enormous expense, but so rough, so full of mud-holes filled with broken lava in the first part of the jour-

THE VOLCANO HOUSE.

ney, and so entirely composed of naked, jagged, and ragged lava in the remainder, that one wonders how the horses stand it. A canter, except for two or three miles near the Volcano House, is almost out of the question; and though the Hawaiians trot and gallop the whole distance, a stranger will scarcely follow their example.

You should insist, by-the-way, upon having all your horses reshod the day before they leave Hilo; and it is prudent, even then, to take along an extra pair of shoes and a dozen or two horse-nails. The lava is extremely trying to the horse's shoes; and if your horse casts a shoe he will go lame in fifteen minutes, for the jagged lava cuts almost like glass.

Moreover, do not wait for a fine day; it will probably rain at any rate before you reach the Volcano House, and your wisest way is to set out resolutely, rain or shine, on the appointed morning, for the sun may come out two or three hours after you have started in a heavy rain. Each traveler should take his water-proof clothing upon his own saddle—it may be needed at any time—and the pack-mule should carry not only the spare clothing, well covered with India-rubber blankets, but also an abundant lunch to be eaten at the Half-way House.

India-rubber or leather leggings, and a long, sleeveless Mackintosh seemed to me the most comfortable and sufficient guards against weather. Ladies should ride astride; they will be most comfortable thus. There are no steep ascents or abrupt descents on the way. Kilauea is nearly four thousand feet higher than the sea from which you set out; but the rise is so gradual and constant that if the road were good one might gallop a horse the whole distance.

You should set out not later than half-past seven, and make up your mind not to be hurried on the way. There are people who make the distance in six hours, and boast about it; but I accomplished it with a party of ladies and children in ten hours with very little discomfort, and did not envy the six-hour people. There is nothing frightful, or dangerous, or disagreeable about the journey, even to ladies not accustomed to riding; and there is very much that is new, strange, and wonderful to Americans or Europeans. Especially you will be delighted with the great variety and beauty of the ferns, which range from minute and delicate species to the dark and grand fronds of the tree-fern, which rises in the more elevated region to a height of twenty feet, and whose stalk has sometimes a diameter of three or four feet. From a variety of this tree-fern the natives take a substance called pulu, a fine, soft, brown fuzz, used for stuffing pillows and mattresses.

Your guide will probably understand very little English: let him be instructed in your wishes before you set out. The native Hawaiian is the most kind and obliging creature in the world, and you will find your guide ready to do you every needful service. You can get nothing to eat on the road, except perhaps a little sugar-cane; therefore you must provide a sufficient lunch. At the Half-way House, but probably nowhere else, you will get water to drink.

When you reach the Volcano House, I advise you to take a sulphur vapor-bath, refreshing after a tedious ride; and after supper you will sit about a big open fire and recount the few incidents and adventures of the day.

The next day you give to the crater. Unless the night is very foggy you will have gone to sleep with the lurid light of Kilauea in your eyes. Madame Pele, the presiding goddess of the volcano, exhibits fine fire-works at night sometimes, and we saw the lava spurting up in the air above the edge of the smaller and active crater, one night, in a quite lively manner. On a moderately clear night the light from the burning lakes makes a very grand sight; and the bedrooms at the little Volcano House are so placed that you have Madame Pele's fire-works before you all night.

The house stands but a few feet from the edge of the great crater, and you have no tedious preliminary walk, but begin your descent into the pit at once. For this you need stout shoes, light clothing, and, if you have ladies in your party, a heavy shawl for each.   The guide takes with him a canteen of water, and also carries the shawls.   You should start about nine o'clock, and give the whole day to the crater, returning to dinner at five.

The great crater of Kilauea is nine miles in circumference, and perhaps a thousand feet deep.   It is, in fact, a deep pit, bounded on all sides by precipitous rocks.   The entrance is effected by a series of steps, and below these by a scramble over lava and rock débris.   It is not difficult, but the ascent is tiresome; and it is a prudent precaution, if you have ladies with you, to take a native man for each lady, to assist her over the rougher places, and up the steep ascent.   The greater part of the crater was, when I saw it, a mass of dead,

HAWAIIAN TEMPLE, FROM A RUSSIAN ENGRAVING, ABOUT 1790.

though not cold lava; and over this you walk to the farthest extremity of the pit, where you must ascend a tolerably steep hill of lava, which is the bank of the fiery lake.   The distance from the Volcano House to the edge of this lake is, by the road you take, three miles.

The goddess Pele, who, according to the Hawaiian mythology, presides over Kilauea, is, as some say all her sex are, variable, changeable, mutable.   What I shall tell you about the appearance of the crater and lake is true of that time; it may not have been correct a week later; it was certainly not true of a month before.   We climbed into the deep pit, and then stood upon a vast floor of lava, rough, jammed together, broken, jagged, steaming out a hot sulphurous breath at almost every seam, revealing rolls of later lava injections at every deep crack, with caverns and high ridges where the great mass, after cooling, was forced together, and with a steep mountain-side of lava at our left, along the foot of which we clambered.

This floor of lava, which seems likely to be a more or less permanent feature, was, three or four years ago, upon a level with the top of the high ridge, or ledge, whose base you skirt. The main part of the crater was then a floor of lava vaster even than it now is. Suddenly one day, and with a crash which persuaded one or two persons at the Volcano House that the whole planet was flying to pieces, the greater part of this lava floor sank down, or fell down, a depth of about five hundred feet, to the level whereon we now walked. The wonder-

LAVA FIELD, HAWAII—FLOW OF 1868.

ful tale was plain to us as we examined the details on the spot. It was as though a top-heavy and dried-out pie-crust had fallen in in the middle, leaving a part of the circumference bent down, but clinging at the outside to the dish.

After this great crash the lava seems from time to time to have boiled up from beneath through cracks, and now lies in great rolls upon the surface, or in the deeper cracks. It is related that later the lake or caldron at the farther end of the crater boiled over, and sent down streams of lava which meandered over the black plain; that, continuing to boil over at intervals, this lake increased the height of its own banks, for the lava cools very rapidly; and thus was built up a high hill, which we ascended after crossing the lava plains, in order to look down, in fear and wonder, upon the awful sight below.

What we saw there on the 3d of March, 1873, was two huge pits, caldrons, or lakes, filled with a red, molten, fiery, sulphurous, raging, roaring, restless mass of matter, to watch whose unceasing tumult was one of the most fascinating experiences of my life.

The two lakes were then separated by a narrow and low-lying ledge or peninsula of lava, which I was told they frequently overflow, and sometimes entirely melt down. Standing upon the northern bank we could see both lakes, and we estimated their shortest diameter to be about 500 feet, and the longest about one-eighth of a mile. Within this pit the surface of the molten lava was about eighty feet below us. It has been known to sink down 400 feet; last December it was overflowing the high banks and sending streams of lava into the great plain by which we approached it; and since I saw it, it has risen to within a few feet of the top of the bank, and has forced a way out at one side, where, in September, 1873, it was flowing out slowly on to the great lava plain which forms the bottom of the main crater.

What, therefore, Madame Pele will show you hereafter is uncertain. What we saw was this: two large lakes or caldrons, each nearly circular, with the lower shelf or bank, red-hot, from which the molten lava was repelled toward the centre without cessation. The surface of these lakes was of a lustrous and beautiful gray, and this, which was a cooling and tolerably solid scum, was broken by jagged circles of fire, which appeared of a vivid rose-color in contrast with the gray. These circles, starting at the red-hot bank or shore, moved more or less rapidly toward the centre, where, at intervals of perhaps a minute, the whole mass of lava suddenly but slowly bulged up, burst the thin crust, and flung aloft a huge, fiery wave, which sometimes shot as high as thirty feet in the air. Then ensued a turmoil, accompanied with hissing, and occasionally with a dull roar as the gases sought to escape, and spray was flung in every direction; and presently the agitation subsided, to begin again in the same place, or perhaps in another.

Meantime the fiery rings moved forward perpetually toward the centre, a new one re-appearing at the shore before the old was ingulfed; and not unfrequently the mass of lava was so fiercely driven by some force from the bank near which we stood, that it was ten or fifteen feet higher near the centre than at the circumference. Thus somewhat of the depth was revealed to us, and there seemed something peculiarly awful to me in the fierce glowing red heat of the shores themselves, which never cooled with exposure to the air and light.

Thus acted the first of the two lakes. But when, favored by a strong breeze, we ventured farther, to the side of the furthermost one, a still more terrible spectacle greeted us. The mass in this lake was in yet more violent agitation; but it spent its fury upon the precipitous southern bank, against which it dashed with a vehemence equal to a heavy surf breaking against cliffs. It had undermined this lava cliff, and for a space of perhaps one hundred and fifty feet the lava beat and surged into glaring, red-hot, cavernous depths, and was repelled with a dull, heavy roar, not exactly like the boom of breakers, because the lava is so much heavier than water, but with a voice of its own, less resonant, and, as we who listened thought, full of even more deadly fury.

It seems a little absurd to couple the word "terrible" with any action of mere inanimate matter, from which, after all, we stood in no very evident peril. Yet "terrible" is the only word for it. Grand it was not, because in all its action and voice it seemed infernal. Though its movement is slow and deliberate, it would scarcely occur to you to call either the constant impulse from one side toward the other, or the vehement and vast bulging of the lava wave as it explodes its thin crust or dashes a fiery mass against the cliff, majestic, for devilish seems a better word.

Meantime, though we were favored with a cool and strong breeze, bearing the sulphurous stench of the burning lake away from us, the heat of the lava on which we stood, at least eighty feet above the pit, was so great as to be almost unendurable. We stood first upon one foot, and then on the other, because the soles of our feet seemed to be scorching through thick shoes. A lady sitting down upon a bundle of shawls had to rise because the wraps began to scorch; our faces seemed on fire from the reflection of the heat below; the guide's tin water-canteen, lying near my feet, became presently so hot that it burned my fingers when I took it up; and at intervals there came up from behind us a draught of air so hot, and so laden with sulphur that, even with the strong wind carrying it rapidly away, it was scarcely endurable. It was while we were coughing and spluttering at one of these hot blasts, which came from the numerous fissures in the lava which we had passed over, that a lady of our party remarked that she had read an excellent description of this place in the New Testament; and so far as I observed, no one disagreed with her.

After the lakes came the cones. When the surface of this lava is so rapidly cooling that the action below is too weak to break it, the gases forcing their way out break small vents, through which lava is then ejected. This, cooling rapidly as it comes to the outer air, forms by its accretions a conical pipe of greater or less circumference, and sometimes growing twenty or thirty feet high, open at the top, and often with openings also blown out at the sides. There are several of these cones on the summit bank of the lake, all ruined, as it seemed to me, by some too violent explosion, which had blown off most of the top, and in one case the whole of it, leaving then only a wide hole.

Into these holes we looked, and saw a very wonderful and terrible sight. Below us was a stream of lava, rolling and surging and beating against huge, precipitous, red-hot cliffs; and higher up, suspended from other, also red or white hot overhanging cliffs, depended huge stalactites, like masses of fiercely glowing fern leaves waving about in the subterranean wind; and here we saw how thin was in some such places the crust over which we walked, and how near the melting-point must be its under surface. For, as far as we could judge, these little craters or cones rested upon a crust not thicker than twelve or fourteen inches, and one fierce blast from below seemed sufficient to melt away the whole place. Fortunately one can not stay very long near these openings, for they exhale a very poisonous breath; and so we were drawn back to the more fascinating but less perilous spectacle of the lakes; and then back over the rough lava, our minds filled with memories of a spectacle which is certainly one of the most remarkable our planet affords.

When you have seen the fiery lakes you will recognize a crater at sight, and every part of Hawaii and of the other islands will have a new interest for you;

VIEW OF THE CRATER OF SOUTH LAKE IN A STATE OF ERUPTION, FROM THE CREST OF THE NORTH LAKE.

for all are full of craters, and from Kilauea to the sea you may trace several lines of craters, all extinct, but all at some time belching forth those interminable lava streams over which you ride by the way of the Puna coast for nearly seventy miles back to Hilo.

I advise you to take this way back. Almost the whole of it is a land of desolation. A narrow trail across unceasing beds of lava, a trail which in spots was actually hammered down to make it smooth enough for horses' feet, and outside of whose limits in most places your horse will refuse to go, because he knows it is too rough for beast or man: this is your road. Most of the lava is probably very ancient, though some is quite recent; and ferns and guava bushes and other scanty herbage grow through it.

In some of the cavernous holes, which denote probably ancient cones or huge lava bubbles, you will see a cocoa-nut-tree or a pandanus trying to subsist; and by-and-by, after a descent to the sea-shore, you are rewarded with the pleasant sight of groves of cocoa-nuts and umbrageous arbors of pandanus, and occasionally with a patch of green.

Almost the whole of the Puna coast is waterless. From the Volcano House you take with you not only food for the journey back to Hilo, but water in bottles; and your thirsty animals get none until you reach the end of your first

HILO.

day's journey, at Kaimu. Here, also, you can send a more than half-naked native into the trees for cocoa-nuts, and drink your fill of their refreshing milk, while your jaded horses swallow bucketfuls of rain-water.

It will surprise you to find people living among the lava, making potato-patches in it, planting coffee and some fruit-trees in it, fencing in their small holdings, even, with lava blocks. Very little soil is needed to give vegetation a chance in a rainy reason, and the decomposed lava makes a rich earth. But except the cocoa-nut which grows on the beach, and seems to draw its sustenance from the waves, and the sweet-potato, which does very well among the lava, nothing seems really to thrive.

It will add much to the pleasure of your journey to Kilauea if you carry with you, to read upon the spot and along the road, Brigham's valuable Memoir

4

on the Hawaiian Volcanoes. With this in hand, you will comprehend the nature, and know also the very recent date of some important changes, caused
by earthquakes and lava flows, on the Puna coast. Near and at Kaimu, for
instance, there has been an apparent subsidence of the land, which is supposed
in reality, however, I believe, to have been caused rather by the breaking off of
a vast lava ledge or overhang, on which, covered as it was with earth and
trees, a considerable population had long lived. In front of the native house
in which you will sleep, at Kaimu, part of a large grove of cocoa-nut-trees was
thus submerged, and you may see the dead stumps still sticking up out of the
surf.

Kaimu is twenty-five miles from the Volcano House. The native house at
which you will pass the night is clean, and you may there enjoy the novelty of
sleeping on Hawaiian mats, and under the native cover of tapa. You must
bring with you tea or coffee, sugar, and bread, and such other food as is necessary to your comfort. Sweet-potatoes and bananas, and chickens caught after
you arrive, with abundant cocoa-nuts, are the supplies of the place. The water
is not good, and you will probably drink only cocoa-nut milk, until, fifteen miles
farther on, at Captain Eldart's, you find a pleasant and comfortable resting-
place for the second night, with a famous natural warm bath, very slightly min-
eral. Thence a ride of twenty-three miles brings you back to Hilo, all of it
over lava, most of it through a sterile country, but with one small burst of a
real paradise of tropical luxuriance, a mile of tall forest and jungle, which looks
more like Brazil than Hawaii.

One advantage of returning by way of the Puna coast, rather than by the
direct route from Kilauea, is that you have clear, bright weather all the way.
The configuration of the coast makes Puna sunny while Hilo is rainy.

If you desire a longer ride than that by the Puna coast, you can cross the
island, from the Volcano House, by way of Waiahino and Kapapala to Kau-
waloa on the western coast, whence a schooner will bear you back to Honolulu.
A brief study of the map of Hawaii in this volume will show the different
routes suggested in this chapter.

Moreover, when you are at Kilauea, you have done something toward the ascent of Mauna Loa; and guides, provisions, and animals for that enterprise can
be obtained at the Volcano House, as well as such ample details of the route
that I will not here attempt any directions. It is not an easy ride; and you
must carry with you warm clothing. A gentleman who slept at the summit in
September, 1873, told me the ice made over two inches thick during the night.

If Mauna Loa is active, a traveler on the Islands ought by all means to see
it; for Dr. Coan assures me that it is then one of the most terrific and grand
sights imaginable. I did not visit it, as it was not active while I was on the
Islands, though its fires were alive. The crater is a pit about three miles in
circumference, with precipitous banks about two thousand feet deep. At the

SURF BATHING.

bottom is the burning lake, which has a curious habit of throwing up a jet, more or less constant, of fiery lava, to the height, this last summer, of four or five hundred feet from the surface of the lake. It is a fine sight, but, of course, somewhat distant. I am told that this jet has at times reached nearly to the summit level of the crater; and it must then have been a glorious spectacle.

Near Hilo are some pretty water-falls and several sugar plantations, to which you can profitably give a couple of days, and on another you should visit Cocoa-nut Island, and—as interesting a spot as almost any on the Islands—a little lagoon on the main-land near by, in which you may see the coral growing, and pick it up in lovely specimens with the stones upon which it has built in these shallow and protected waters. Moreover, the surf-beaten rocks near by yield cowries and other shells in some abundance; and I do not know anywhere of a pleasanter picnic day than that you can spend there.

Finally, Hilo is one of the very few places on these islands where you can see a truly royal sport—the surf-board. It requires a rough day and a heavy surf, but with a good day it is one of the finest sights in the world.

The surf-board is a tough plank about two feet wide and from six to twenty feet long, usually made of the bread-fruit-tree. Armed with these, a party of tall, muscular natives swim out to the first line of breakers, and, watching their chance to duck under this, make their way finally, by the help of the undertow, into the smooth water far off beyond all the surf. Here they bob up and down on the swell like so many ducks, watching their opportunity. What they seek is a very high swell, before which they place themselves, lying or kneeling on the surf-board. The great wave dashes onward, but as its bottom strikes the ground, the top, unretarded in its speed and force, breaks into a huge comber, and directly before this the surf-board swimmer is propelled with a speed which we timed and found to exceed forty miles per hour. In fact, he goes like lightning, always just ahead of the breaker, and apparently downhill, propelled by the vehement impulse of the roaring wave behind him, yet seeming to have a speed and motion of his own.

It is a very surprising sight to see three or four men thus dashed for nearly a mile toward the shore at the speed of an express train, every moment about to be overwhelmed by a roaring breaker, whose white crest was reared high above and just behind them, but always escaping this ingulfment, and propelled before it. They look, kneeling or lying on their long surf-boards, more like some curious and swift-swimming fish—like dolphins racing, as it seemed to me—than like men. Once in a while, by some mischance the cause of which I could not understand, the swimmer *was* overwhelmed; the great comber overtook him; he was flung over and over like a piece of wreck, but instantly dived, and re-appeared beyond and outside of the wave, ready to take advantage of the next. A successful shot launched them quite high and dry on the beach far beyond where we stood to watch. Occasionally a man would stand erect upon his surf-board, balancing himself in the boiling surf without apparent difficulty.

The surf-board play is one of the ancient sports of Hawaii. I am told that few of the younger generation are capable of it, and that it is thought to require great nerve and coolness even among these admirable swimmers, and to be not without danger.

In your journeys to the different islands you need to take with you, as part of your baggage, saddle and bridle, and all the furniture of a horse. You can hire or buy a horse anywhere very cheaply; but saddles are often unattainable, and always difficult to either borrow or hire. " You might as well travel here without your boots as without your saddle," said a friend to me; and I found it literally true, not only for strangers, but for residents as well. Thus you may notice that the little steamer's hold, as she leaves Honolulu, contains but few trunks; but is crowded with a considerable collection of saddles and saddle-bags, the latter the most convenient receptacles for your change of clothing.

Riding on Hawaii is often tiresome, even to one accustomed to the saddle, by reason of the slow pace at which you are compelled to move. Wherever you stop, for lunch or for the night, if there are native people near, you will be greatly refreshed by the application of what they call "lomi-lomi." Almost everywhere you will find some one skillful in this peculiar and, to tired muscles, delightful and refreshing treatment.

To be lomi-lomied, you lie down upon a mat, loosening your clothing, or undressing for the night if you prefer. The less clothing you have on the more perfectly the operation can be performed. To you thereupon comes a stout native, with soft, fleshy hands but a strong grip, and, beginning with your head and working down slowly over the whole body, seizes and squeezes with a quite peculiar art every tired muscle, working and kneading with indefatigable patience, until in half an hour, whereas you were sore and weary and worn-out, you find yourself fresh, all soreness and weariness absolutely and entirely removed, and mind and body soothed to a healthful and refreshing sleep.

The lomi-lomi is used not only by the natives, but among almost all the foreign residents; and not merely to procure relief from weariness consequent on overexertion, but to cure headache, to relieve the aching of neuralgic or rheumatic pains, and, by the luxurious, as one of the pleasures of life. I have known it to relieve violent headache in a very short time. The old chiefs used to keep skillful lomi-lomi men and women in their retinues; and the late king, who was for some years too stout to take exercise, and was yet a gross feeder, had himself lomi-lomied after every meal, as a means of helping his digestion.

It is a device for relieving pain or weariness which seems to have no injurious reaction and no drawback but one—it is said to fatten the subjects of it.

LAHAINA, ISLAND OF MAUI.

CHAPTER III.

MAUI, AND THE SUGAR CULTURE.

MAUI lies between Oahu and Hawaii, and is somewhat larger than the first-named island. It contains the most considerable sugar-plantations, and yields more of this product than any one of the other islands. It is notable also for possessing the mountain of Haleakala, an extinct volcano ten thousand feet high, which has the largest crater in the world—a monstrous pit, thirty miles in circumference, and two thousand feet deep.

There is some reason to believe that Maui was originally two islands, the northern and southern parts being joined together by an immense sandy plain, so low that in misty weather it is hardly to be distinguished from the ocean; and some years ago a ship actually ran aground upon it, sailing for what the captain imagined to be an open passage.

Maui has also the famous Wailuku Valley, a picturesque gorge several miles deep, and giving you a very fair example of the broken, verdure-clad, and now lonely valleys of these islands; which are in reality steep, narrow cañons, worn out of the mountains by the erosion of water. The old Hawaiians seem to have cared little how difficult a piece of country was; they not only made their taro patches in the streams which roar at the bottoms of such gorges, but they fought battles among the precipices which you find at the upper ends of these valleys, where the defeated usually met their deaths by plunging down into the stream far below.

After seeing a live or burning crater like Kilauea, Haleakala, I thought, would be but a dull sight; but it is, on the contrary, extremely well worth a visit. The islands have no sharp or angular volcanic peaks. Mauna Loa and Mauna Kea, on Hawaii, though 14,000 feet high, are mere bulbs—vast hills, not mountains; and the ascent to the summit of Haleakala, though you surmount 10,000 feet, is neither dangerous nor difficult. It is tedious, however, for it involves a ride of about twelve miles, mostly over lava, uphill. It is best to ride up during the day, and sleep at or near the summit, where there are one or two so-called caves in the lava, broken lava-bubbles in fact, sufficiently roomy to

CASCADE AND RIVER OF LAVA—FLOW OF 1869.

accommodate several persons. You must take with you a guide, provisions, and blankets, for the nights are cold; and you find near the summit water, wood enough for a small fire, and forage for your horses. Each person should have water-proof clothing, for it is very likely to rain, at least on the Makawao side.

The great crater is best seen at sunrise, and, if you are so fortunate as to have a tolerably clear sky, you may see, lying far away below you, almost all of the islands. Hawaii lies far enough away to reveal its entire outline, with Mauna Loa and Mauna Kea rising near either end, and the depression near which lies Kilauea in the middle. The cloud effects at sunrise and sunset are marvelous, and alone repay the ascent.

But the crater itself, clear of fog and clouds in the early morning, and lighted up by the rising sun, is a most surprising sight. It is ten miles in diameter, and the bottom lies 2000 feet below where you stand. The vast irregular floor contains more than a dozen subsidiary craters or great cones, some of them 750 feet high, and nearly as large as Diamond Head. At the Kaupo and Koolau gaps, indicated on the map, the lava is supposed to have burst through and made its way down the mountain sides. The cones are distinctly marked as you look down upon them; and it is remarkable that from the summit the eye takes in the whole crater, and notes all its contents, diminished of course by their great distance. Not a tree, shrub, or even tuft of grass obstructs the view.

To describe such a scene is impossible. A study of the map, with the figures showing elevations, will give you a better idea of it than a long verbal description. It is an extraordinarily desolate scene. A few wild goats scramble over the rocks, or rush down the nearly perpendicular cliff; occasionally a solitary bird raises its harsh note; the wind howls fiercely; and as you lie under the lee of a mass of lava, taking in the scene and picking out the details as the rising sun brings them out one by one, presently the mist begins to pour into the crater, and often by ten o'clock fills it up completely.

The natives have no tradition of Haleakala in activity. There are signs of several lava flows, and of one in particular, clearly much more recent than the others. It must have presented a magnificent and terrible sight when it was in full activity. I did not ride into the crater, but it is possible to do so, and the natives have a trail, not much used, by which they pass. If you descend, be careful not to leave or lose this trail, for in many parts your horse will not be able to get back to it if you suffer him to stray off even a few yards, the lava is so sharp and jagged. As you descend the mountain on the Makawao side you will notice two finely shaped craters on the side of the mountain, which also in their time spewed out lava. Nearer the coast your eye, become familiar with the peculiar shape of these cones or craters, will notice yet others; and, indeed, to appreciate the peculiarities of Sandwich Island scenery, in which extinct craters and cones of all sizes have so great a part, it is necessary to have visited Kilauea and Haleakala. The latter name, by-the-way, means "House of the Sun;" and as you watch the rising sun entering and apparently taking possession of the vast gloomy depths, you will think the name admirably chosen.

If you carry a gun you are likely to have a shot at wild turkeys on your way up or down. It is remarkable that many of our domestic animals easily become wild on the islands. There are wild goats, wild cats, wild chickens and turkeys; the cattle run wild; and on Hawaii one man at least has been killed and torn to pieces by wild dogs, which run in packs in some parts of the island.

Sugar-plantations are found on all four of the larger islands; and on all of them there are successful examples of this enterprise; but Maui contains, I believe, the greatest number, and is thought to be the best fitted for the business. It is on this island, therefore, that the curious traveler can see this industry

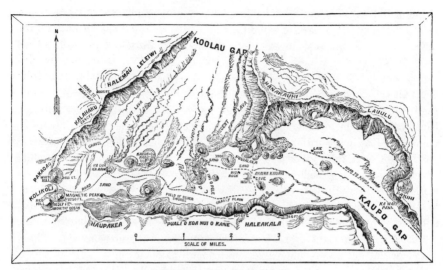

MAP OF THE HALEAKALA CRATER.

under its most favorable aspects.   There is no doubt that for the production
of sugar these islands offer some extraordinary advantages.

I have seen a field of thirty acres which two years ago produced nearly six
tons of sugar to the acre.   Four tons per acre is not a surprising crop; and,
from all I can hear, I judge that two and a half tons per acre may be considered a fair yield.   The soil, too, with proper treatment, appears to be inex-
haustible.   The common custom is to take off two crops, and then let the field
lie fallow for two years; but where they irrigate even this is not always done.
There is no danger of frost, as in Louisiana, and cane is planted in some part
of the islands in almost every month of the year.   In Lahaina it matures in
from fourteen to sixteen months; in some districts it requires eighteen months;
and at greater altitudes even two years.

But under all the varying circumstances, whether it is irrigated or not, whether it grows on bottoms or on hill slopes, in dry or in damp regions, everywhere
the cane seems to thrive, and undoubtedly it is the one product of the islands
which succeeds.   A worm, which pierces the cane near the ground and eats
out the pith, has of late, I am told, done some damage, and in some parts the
rat has proved troublesome.   But these evils do not anywhere endanger or
ruin the crop, as the blight has ruined the coffee culture and discouraged other
agricultural ventures.   The sugar product of the islands has constantly increased.   In 1860 they exported 1,444,271 pounds of sugar; in 1864, 10,414,441
pounds; in 1868, 18,312,926 pounds; and in 1871, 21,760,773 pounds of sugar.

What is remarkable is that, with this rapid increase in the production of
sugar, you hear that the business is unprosperous; and if to this you reply that

planters, like farmers, are hard to satisfy, they show you that the greater number of the plantations have at some time been sold by the sheriff, some of them more than once, and that, in fact, only six or seven are to-day in the hands of their founders.

I do not doubt that there has been bad management on many plantations, and that this accounts in part for these failures, by which many hundred thousand dollars have been lost. For the advantages of the sugar planter on these islands are very decided. He has not only, as I showed you above, a favorable climate and an extraordinarily fertile soil, but he has a laboring population, perhaps the best, the most easily managed, the kindliest, and—so far as habits affect the steadiness and usefulness of the laborer—the least vicious in the world. He does not have to pay exorbitant wages; he is not embarrassed to feed or house them, for food is so abundant and cheap that economy in its distribution is of no moment; and the Hawaiian is very cheaply housed.

But bad management by no means accounts for all the non-success. There are some natural disadvantages serious enough to be taken into the account. In the first place, you must understand that the rain-fall varies extraordinarily. The trade-wind brings rain; the islands are bits of mountain ranges; the side of the mountain which lies toward the rain-wind gets rain; the lee side gets scarcely any. At Hilo it rains almost constantly; at Lahaina they get hardly a shower a year. At Captain Makee's, one of the most successful plantations on·Maui, water is stored in cisterns; at Mr. Spencer's, not a dozen miles distant, also one of the successful plantations, which lies on the other side of Mount Haleakala, they never have to irrigate. Near Hilo the long rains make cultivation costly and difficult; but the water is so abundant that they run their fire-wood from the mountains and their cane from the fields into the sugar-houses in flumes, at a very great saving of labor. Near Lahaina every acre must be irrigated, and this work proceeds day and night in order that no water may run to waste.

Then there is the matter of shipping sugar. There are no good ports except Honolulu. Kaalui on Maui, Hanalei and Nawiliwili on Kauai, and one or two plantations on Oahu, have tolerable landings. But almost everywhere the sugar is sent over vile roads to a more or less difficult landing, whence it is taken in launches to the schooners which carry it to Honolulu, where it is stored, coopered, and finally reshipped to its market. Many landings are made through the surf, and I remember one which, last spring, was unapproachable by vessel or boat for nearly four weeks.

Each sugar planter has, therefore, problems of his own to solve. He can not pattern on his neighbors. He can not base his estimate on theirs. He can not be certain even, until he has tried, which of the ten or a dozen varieties of cane will do best on his soil. He must look out for wood, which is by no means abundant, and is often costly to bring down from the mountain; he must look out for his landing; must see that taro grows near at hand; must secure pasture for his draught cattle: in short, he must consider carefully and independently many different questions before he can be even reasonably sure of success. And if, with all this uncertainty, he embarks with insufficient capital, and must pay one per cent. a month interest, and turn his crop over to an agent in Honolulu, who is his creditor, and who charges him five per cent. for handling it, it will not be wonderful to any business man if he fails to grow rich, or if even he by-and-by becomes bankrupt. Many have failed. Of thirty-four plantations, the number worked in all the islands at this time, only six or seven are in the hands of their founders. Some, which cost one hundred thousand dollars, were sold by the sheriff for fifteen or eighteen thousand; some, which cost a quarter of a million, were sold for less than a hundred thousand.

If you speak with the planters, they will tell you that their great difficulty is to get a favorable market; that the duty on their sugar imported into San Francisco eats up their profits; and that the only cure—the cure-all, I should say, for all the ills they suffer—is a treaty with the United States, which shall admit their product duty free. Of course any one can see that if the sugar duty were remitted to them, the planters would make more money, or would lose less. An ingenuous planter summed up for me one day the whole of that side of the case, by saying, " If we had plenty of labor and a free market for our sugar, we should be thoroughly satisfied."

But I am persuaded that, as there are planters now who are prosperous and contented, and who make handsome returns even with the sugar duty against them, so, if that were removed, there would be planters who would continue their regular and slow march toward bankruptcy; and for whom the remitted duty would be but a temporary respite, while it would deprive them of a cheap and easy way to account for their failure. Wherever on the islands I found a planter living on his own plantation, managing it himself, and *out of debt*, I found him making money, even with low prices for his sugar, and even if the plantation itself was not favorably placed; not only this, but I found plantations yielding steady and sufficient profits, under judicious management, which in previous hands became bankrupt. But on the other hand, where I found a plantation heavily encumbered with debt and managed by a superintendent, the owner living elsewhere, I heard usually, though not always, complaints of hard times. If a sugar planter has his land and machinery heavily mortgaged at ten or twelve per cent. interest; if he must, moreover, borrow money on his crop in the field to enable him to turn that into sugar; if then he sends the product to an agent in Honolulu, who charges him five per cent. for shipping it to San Francisco; and if in San Francisco another agent charges him five per cent. more, *on the gross returns including freight and duty*, for selling it; if besides all this the planter buys his supplies on credit, and is charged one per cent. a month on these, compounded every three months until it is paid, and pays almost as much freight on his sugar from the plantation to Honolulu as from there to its final market—it is highly probable that he will, in the course of time, fail.

There are not many legitimate enterprises in the world which would bear such charges and leave a profit to the manager. But it is on this system that the planting of sugar has been, to a large extent, carried on for years in the Islands. Under it a good deal of money has been made, but not by the planters. Nor is this essentially unjust. In the majority of cases, planters began rashly with small means, and had to borrow largely to complete their enterprises and get to work. The capitalist of course took a part of the profits as interest. But the capitalist was in many cases also the agent and store-keeper in Honolulu; and he shaved off percentages—all in the way of business—until the planter was really no more than the foreman of his agent and creditor. When, under such circumstances, a planter complained that he did not make the fortune he anticipated, and reasoned that therefore sugar planting in the Islands is unprofitable, he seemed to me to speak beside the question—for his agent and creditor, his employer in fact, made no complaint: *he* always made money; and as he had invested the money to carry on the enterprise, this was but the natural result.

The planters make a grave mistake in not acting together and advising together on their most important interests. There are so few of them that it should be easy to unite; and yet for lack of concerted action they suffer important abuses to go on. For instance, it is a serious loss to the planter that when he ships or engages a hand he must pay a large "advance," amounting usually to at least half a year's pay. This custom is hurtful to the laborer, who wastes it, and it inflicts a serious loss upon the planter. Suppose he employs a hundred men, and pays fifty dollars advance, he invests at once five thousand dollars for which he gets no interest, though if, as is probable, he borrowed it, he must pay one per cent. a month. This abuse could be abolished in a day by the simple announcement that no planter would hereafter pay more than ten dollars advance. But it has gone on for years, and the sum paid gets higher every year merely by the planters outbidding each other.

Again, it is possible to ship sugar from some of the Islands direct to San Francisco, and for but little more than is now paid for shipping it to Honolulu. Half a dozen planters on Hawaii or Maui, clubbing together, could easily get a ship or half a dozen ships to come for their sugar, and thus save five per cent. on their gross returns, now paid to agents. But this is not done, partly because so many planters are in need of money, which they borrow in Honolulu, with the understanding that they will submit their produce to the management of agents there.

Again, the planters err, I think, in not giving personal study to the question of a market for their sugar. They leave this to the agents to manage. No doubt these gentlemen are competent; but it is easy to see that their interests may be somewhat different from those of the planter. For instance, some years ago an arrangement was offered by the San Francisco sugar refineries by which these agreed to take two-thirds of the product of the plantations in crude sugar, to furnish bags to contain this product, and to pay cash for it in Honolulu. Under this system the planter was saved the heavy expense of sugar kegs, and the cost of two agencies of five per cent. each, besides getting cash in Honolulu, whereas now his sugar is usually sold at three months in San Francisco, and he probably loses six months' interest, reckoning from the time his sugar leaves the plantation. This arrangement, several planters told me, was profitable to them; but it was discontinued—it was not to the advantage of the agents; its discontinuance was no doubt a blunder for the planters. Moreover, the Australian market has been too long neglected; but the advantage of possessing two markets instead of one is too obvious to require statement.

It is a reasonable conclusion, from all the facts in the case, that sugar planting can be carried on at a fair and satisfactory profit in the Hawaiian Islands, wherever skill and careful personal attention are given, and due economy enforced by a planter who has at the same time sufficient capital to carry on the business. The example of Captain Makee and Mr. A. H. Spencer on Maui, of Mr. Isenberg on Kauai and others sufficiently prove this.

If I seem to have given more space to this sugar question than it appears to deserve at the hands of a passing traveler, it is because sugar enters largely into the politics of the Islands. It is the sugar interest which urges the offer of Pearl River to the United States in exchange for a treaty of reciprocity; and it is when sugar is low-priced at San Francisco that the small company of annexationists raises its voice, and sometimes threatens to raise its flag.

There is room on the different islands for about seventy-five or eighty more plantations on the scale now common; and there are, I think, still excellent opportunities for making plantations. The sugar lands unoccupied are not high-priced; and men skilled in this industry, and with sufficient capital, can do well there, and live in a delightful climate and among pleasant society, in a country where, as I have before said, life and property are more absolutely secure than anywhere else in the world. But I strongly advise every one to avoid debt. It has been the curse of the planters, even of those who have kept out of debt, for it has prevented such unity of action among them as must have before this enabled them to effect important improvements. For instance, were they out of debt there is no reason that I can see why they should not succeed in making their market in Honolulu, and drawing purchasers thither instead of sending their sugar to far-off markets at their own risk and expense. If ships can afford to sail in ballast to more distant islands for guano, calling at Honolulu on the way, it is reasonable to suppose they could afford to come thither for the more valuable sugar cargoes.

WAILUKU, ISLAND OF MAUI.

The planters err, I think, in not planting the mountain sides, wherever these are accessible and have soil, with trees. The forests of the country are rapidly disappearing, especially from the higher plains and the grass-bearing slopes. Not only is the wood cut for burning, but the cattle browse down the young growth; and a pestilent grub has of late attacked the older trees and destroyed them in great numbers. Already complaints are heard of the greater dryness and infertility of certain localities, which I do not doubt comes from suffering the ground to become bare. At several points I was told that the streams were permanently lower than in former years—of course because evaporation goes on more rapidly near their head waters now that the ground is bare. But little care or forethought is exercised in such matters, however. A few extensive plantations of trees have been made, notably by Captain Makee on Maui, who has set out a large number of Australian gum trees. The universal habit of letting cattle run abroad, and the dearness of lumber for fencing, discourages tree planting, which yet will be found some day one of the most profitable investments in the islands, I believe; and I was sorry to see in many places cocoa-nut groves dying out of old age and neglect, and no young trees planted to replace them.

It remains to describe to you the "contract labor" system by which the sugar-plantations are carried on. This has been frequently and, as it seems to me, unjustly abused as a system of slavery. The laborers hire themselves out for a stated period, usually, in the case of natives, for a year, and in the case of Chinese for five years. The contract runs in English and in Hawaiian or Chinese, and is sufficiently simple. Thus:

"**This Agreement,** made and entered into this —— day of ——, A.D. 18—, by and between the owners of the —— plantation, in the island of ——, party of the first part, and —— ——, party of the second part, witnesseth:

"I. The said party of the second part promises to perform such labor upon the —— plantation, in the district of ——, island of ——, as the said party of the first part shall direct, and that he will faithfully and punctually perform the same as becomes a good workman, and that he will obey all lawful commands of the said party of the first part, their agents or overseers, during the term of —— months, each month to consist of twenty-six working days.

"II. The party of the first part will well and truly pay, or cause to be paid, unto the said party of the second part, at the end of each month during which this contract shall remain in force, compensation or wages at the rate of —— dollars for each month, if said party of the second part shall well and truly perform his labor as aforesaid."

The law requires that this contract shall be signed before a notary public. The wages are usually eight dollars per month and food, or eleven dollars per month without food; from which you will see that three dollars per month will buy sufficient poi, beef, and fish to support a native laborer in these islands. The engagement is entirely voluntary; the men understand what they contract to do, and in all the plantations where they are well treated they re-enlist with great regularity. The vicious custom of "advances" mentioned above has become a part of the system; it arose, I suppose, from the fact that the natives who shipped as whalemen received advance pay; and thus the plantation laborers demanded it too. The laborers are commonly housed in detached cottages, and live with their families, the women forming an important, irregular laboring force at seasons when the work is hurried. But they are not "contract" laborers, but paid by the day. It has been found the best plan on most of the plantations to feed the people, and food is so cheap that it is supplied without stint.

This system has been vigorously, but, I believe, wrongly, attacked. The recent census is an uncommonly barren document; but there is strong reason to believe that while there is a general decrease in the population, on the plantations there is but little if any decrease. In fact, the Hawaiian living in his valley on his kuliana or small holding, leads an extremely irregular life. He usually sups at midnight, sleeps a good deal during the day, and has much idle time on his hands. On the plantations he works regularly and not too hard, eats at stated intervals, and sleeps all night. This regularity conduces to health. Moreover, he receives prompt and sufficient medical attendance, he lives a more social and interesting life, and he is as well fed, and mostly better lodged. There are very few instances of abuse or cruelty; indeed, a plantation manager said to me, " If I were to wrong or abuse one of my men, he would persuade a dozen or twenty others not to re-enlist when their terms are out, and would fatally embarrass me;" for it is not easy to get laborers.

There is good reason to believe, therefore, that the plantation laborers are healthier, more prosperous, and just as happy as those who live independently; and it is a fact that on most of the islands the greater part of the younger people are found on the plantations. Churches are established on or very near all the sugar estates, and the children are rigorously kept at school there as elsewhere. The people take their newspaper, discuss their affairs, and have usually a leader or two among the foremen. On one plantation one of the foremen in the field was pointed out to me: he was a member of the Legislature.

There is a good deal of complaint of a scarcity of labor. If more plantations were opened it would be necessary to import laborers; but for the present, it seems to me, the supply is not deficient. Doubtless, however, many planters would extend their operations if they could get workmen readily. Chinese have been brought over, though not in great numbers; and of late the absurd and cruel persecution of these people in California has driven several hundred to take refuge in the Islands, where they are kindly treated and can live comfortably.

The machinery used in the sugar-houses is usually of the best; the larger plantations all use vacuum-pans; and the planters are usually intelligent gentlemen, familiar with the best methods of producing sugar, and with the latest improvements. Yet it is a question whether the expensive machinery is not in the long run a disadvantage, as it disables them from profitably making those low grades of sugar which can be cheaply turned out with the help of an " open train," and which appear to have, in these days, the most ready sale and the best market.

KEAPAWEO MOUNTAIN, KAUAI.

CHAPTER IV.

KAUAI, WITH A GLANCE AT CATTLE AND SHEEP.

KAUAI lies farthest to leeward of the main islands of the Hawaiian group; the steamer visits it usually but once a month; and the best way to see it without unnecessary waste of time is to take passage in a schooner, so timing your visit as to leave you a week or ten days on the island before the steamer arrives to carry you back.

We took passage on a little sugar schooner, the *Fairy Queen*, of about seventy-five tons, commanded by a smart native captain, and sailing one afternoon about two o'clock, and sleeping comfortably on deck wrapped in rugs, were landed at Waimea the following morning at day-break.

When you travel on one of these little native schooners you must provide food for yourself, for poi and a little beef or fish make up the sea ration as well as the land food of the Hawaiian. In all other respects you may expect to be treated with the most distinguished consideration and the most ready and thoughtful kindness by captain and crew; and the picturesque mountain scenery of Oahu, which you have in sight so long as daylight lasts, and the lovely star-lit night, with its soft gales and warm air, combine to make the voyage a delightful adventure.

As usual in these Islands, a church was the first and most conspicuous land-mark which greeted our eyes in the morning. Abundant groves of cocoa-nuts, for which the place is famous, assured us of a refreshing morning draught. The little vessel was anchored off the shore, and our party, jumping into a whale-boat, were quickly and skillfully steered through the slight surf which pours upon the beach. The boat was pulled upon the black sand; and the lady who was of my party found herself carried to the land in the stout arms of the captain; while the rest of us watched our chance, and, as the waves receded, leaped ashore, and managed to escape with dry feet. The sun had not yet risen; the early morning was a little overcast. A few natives, living on the beach, gathered around and watched curiously the landing of our saddles and saddle-bags from the boat; presently that pushed off, and our little company sat down upon an old spar, and watched the schooner as she hoisted sails

CHAIN OF EXTINCT VOLCANOES NEAR KOLOA, ISLAND OF KAUAI.

and bore away for her proper port, while we waited for the appearance of a native person of some authority to whom a letter had been directed, request-ing him to provide us with horses and a guide to the house of a friend with whom we intended to breakfast. Presently three or four men came gallop-ing along the beach, one of whom, a burly Hawaiian, a silver shield on whose jacket announced him a local officer of police, reported that he was at our serv-ice with as many horses as we needed.

It is one of the embarrassing incidents of travel on these Islands that there are no hotels or inns outside of Honolulu and Hilo. Whether he will or no the traveler must accept the hospitality of the residents, and this is so general and so boundless that it would impose a burdensome obligation, were it not offered in such a kindly and graceful way as to beguile you into the belief that you are conferring as well as receiving a favor. Nor is the foreigner alone generous; for the native too, if you come with a letter from his friend at a distance, places himself and all he has at your service. When we had reached our friend's house, I asked my conductor, the policeman, what I should pay him for the use of three horses and his own services. He replied that he was but too happy to have been of use to me, as I was the friend of his friend. I managed to force upon him a proper reward for his attention, but I am persuaded that he would have been content without.

Kauai is probably the oldest of the Hawaiian group; according to the geologists it was the first thrown up; the bottom of the ocean began to crack, up there to the north-west, and the rent extended gradually in the south-easterly direction necessary to produce the other islands. It would seem that Kauai must be a good deal older than Hawaii; for, whereas the latter is covered with undecayed lava and has two active volcanoes, the former has a rich and deep covering of soil, and, except in a few places, there are no very plain or conspicuous cones or craters. Of course the whole island bears the clearest traces of its volcanic origin; and near Koloa there are three small craters in a very good state of preservation.

Having thus more soil than the other islands, Kauai has also more grass; being older, not only are its valleys somewhat richer, but its mountains are also more picturesque than those of Maui and Hawaii, as also they are much lower. The roads are excellent for horsemen, and for the most part practicable for carriages, of which, however, there are none to be hired.

The best way to see the island is to land, as we did, at Waimea; ride to a singular spot called the " barking sands "—a huge sand-hill, sliding down which you hear a dull rumble like distant thunder, probably the result of electricity. On the way you meet with a mirage, remarkable for this that it is a constant phenomenon—that is to say, it is to be seen daily at certain hours, and is the apparition of a great lake, having sometimes high waves which seem to submerge the cattle which stand about, apparently, in the water.

From the sands you return to Waimea, and can ride thence next day to Koloa in the forenoon, and to Na-Wiliwili in the afternoon. The following day's ride will bring you to Hanalei, a highly picturesque valley which lies on the rainy side of the island, Waimea being on the dry side. At Hanalei you should take the steamer and sail in her around the Palis of Kauai, a stretch of precipitous cliff twenty-five miles long, the whole of which is inaccessible from the sea, except by the native people in canoes; and many parts of which are very lovely and grand. Thus voyaging, you will circumnavigate the island, returning to Na-Wiliwili, and thence in a night to Honolulu.

It is easy and pleasant to see Kauai, taking a store of provisions with you and lodging in native houses. But if you have made some acquaintances in Honolulu you will be provided with letters of introduction to some of the hospitable foreign families on this island; and thus the pleasure of your visit will be greatly increased. I do not, I trust, violate the laws of hospitality if I say something here of one of these families—the owners of the little island of Niihau, who have also a charming residence in the mountains of Kauai. They came to Honolulu ten or twelve years ago from New Zealand in a ship of their own, containing not only their household goods, but also some valuable sheep. Thus fitted out they were sailing over the world, looking for such a little empire to

WAIALUA FALLS, ISLAND OF KAUAI.

own as they found in Niihau; and here they settled, selling their ship; and here they remain, prospering, and living a quiet, peaceful, Arcadian life, with cattle and sheep on many hills, and with a pleasant, hospitable house, where children and grandchildren are clustered together, and where the stranger receives the heartiest of welcomes. It was a curious adventure to undertake, this sailing over the great Pacific to seek out a proper home; and I did not tire of listening to the account of their voyage and their settlement in this new and out-of-the-way land, from the cheery and delightful grandmother of the family, a Scotch lady, full of the sturdy character of her country people, and altogether one of the pleasantest acquaintances I made on the Islands.

Kauai has many German residents, mostly, like these Scotch people I have spoken of, persons of education and culture, who have brought their libraries with them, and on whose tables and shelves you may see the best of the recent literature, as well as the best of the old. A New Yorker who imagines, cockney-like, that civilization does not reach beyond the sound of Trinity chimes is startled out of this foolish fancy when he finds among the planters and missionaries here, as in other parts of these Islands, men and women of genuine culture maintaining all the essential forms as well as the realities of civilization; yet living so free and untrammeled a life that he who comes from the high-pressure social atmosphere of New York can not help but envy these happy mortals, who seem to have the good without the worry of civilization, and who have caught the secret of how to live simply and yet gently.

Kauai has four or five sugar-plantations, some of which are now successful, though they were not always so. Success has been attained by a resolute expenditure of money in irrigation ditches, which have made the land yield constant and remunerative crops. But I could see here, as elsewhere, that close and careful management—the eye of the master and the hand of the master—insured the success.

But a large part of the island is given up to cattle. In the mountains they have gone wild, and parties are made to hunt and shoot these. But on the plains, of course, they are owned and herded. The raising of cattle is an important and considerable business on all the Islands; and at present, I believe, the cattle owners are making a good deal of money. In 1871, 19,384 hides were exported, as well as 185,240 pounds of tallow, 58,900 goat skins, and 471,706 pounds of wool.

The market for beef is limited, and the stockman boils down his beeves. In many cases the best machinery is used for this purpose; the boiling is done in closed vessels, and the business is carried on with precision. It seemed to me, who remembered the high price of beef in our Eastern States, like a sad waste to see a hundred head of fat steers driven into a corral, and one after the other knocked on the head, slaughtered, skinned, cut up, and put into the boilers to be turned into tallow. But it is the only use to make of the beasts. The refuse, however, is here always wasted, which appeared to me unnecessary, for it might well be applied to the enrichment of the pastures.

On many of the ranchos you see open try pots used; it is a more wasteful process, I imagine, but it is simpler and requires a smaller expenditure of capital for machinery. The cattle are managed here, as in California, on horseback and with the help of the lasso; and he who on our Pacific coast is called a *vaquero*, or cow-herd, is here known as a "Spaniol." Such a native man is pointed out to you as an excellent Spaniol. This comes from the fact that in the early days of cattle-raising here the natives knew nothing of their management, and Spaniards had to be imported from California to teach them the business. The native people now make excellent vaqueros; they are daring horsemen, and as they work cheaply and are easily fed and lodged, the management of cattle costs less here, I imagine, than even in California. But it is necessary to take care that the pastures shall not be overstocked; and the vast number of horses kept by the natives is on all the Islands a serious injury to the pasturage of both sheep and cattle.

The Hawaiian, who seventy-five years ago did not know that there existed such a creature as a horse, and even fifty years ago beheld it as a rarity, now can not live without this beast. There are probably more horses than people on the Islands; and the native family is poor, indeed, which has not two or three hardy, rough, grass-fed ponies, easy to ride, sometimes tricky but more often quite trustworthy, and capable of living where a European donkey would die in disgust. At a horse auction you see a singular collection of good and bad horses; and it is one of the jokes of the Islands to go to a horse auction and buy a horse for a quarter of a dollar. The Government has vainly tried to put a check to the reckless increase of horseflesh by laying a tax on these animals, and by impounding them if the tax is not paid. I was told of a planter who bought on one occasion fifty horses out of a pound, at twenty-five cents a head, and had them all shot and put into a manure pile. But if the horse is worth his tax it is pretty certain to be paid; and it is not easy to keep them off the pastures.

Cattle ranchos usually extend over from fifteen to thirty thousand acres of land; though many are smaller, and some, on Hawaii, larger. The grass is of different varieties, but the most useful, as well as now the most abundant, is the *manienie*, of which I have before made mention. Horses and sheep, as well as cattle, become very fond of this grass, and eat it down very close. The handling of the cattle is intrusted to native people, who live on the rancho or estate; and the planter or stock farmer has an advantage, in these Islands, in finding a laboring population living within the bounds of his own place. The large estates were formerly the property of the chiefs. They are the old "lands." But when the kuliana law was made, the common people were allowed to take out for themselves such small holdings as they held in actual cultivation. These kulianas they still hold; and thus it often happens that within the bounds of a large estate fifty or sixty families will live on their little freeholds; and these form a natural and cheap laboring force for the plantation or rancho.

On the Island of Niihau, I was told, there are still about three hundred native people. The sheep are allowed to run at large on the island, there being no wild animals to disturb them; at lambing and shearing times the proprietors hire their native tenants to do the necessary work; and these people at other times fish, raise water-melons and other fruits, and make mats which are famous for their fine texture and softness, and sell at handsome prices even in Honolulu.

Where, as is the case almost universally, the relations between the stockman and the native people are kindly, there is a reciprocity of good offices, and a ready service from the people, in return for management and protection by the great proprietor, which is mutually agreeable, and in which the proprietor stands in some such relation to the people as the chief in old times, though of course with not a tithe of the power the ancient rulers had.

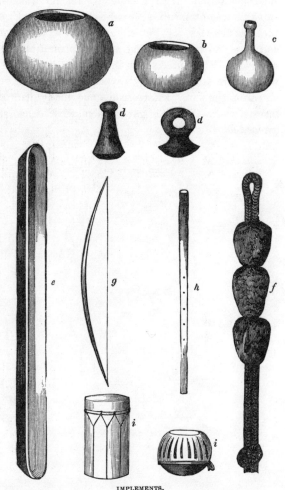

At Kauai you will also see rice growing. This is one of the products which is rapidly increasing in the Islands. Of rice and paddy, or unhulled rice, the exports were in 1871, 417,011 pounds of the first, and 867,452 of the last. In 1872 there were exported 455,121 pounds of rice and 894,382 pounds of paddy.

The taro patches make excellent rice fields; and it is an industry in which the Chinese, who understand it, invest their savings. They employ native labor; and it is not uncommon to find that a few Chinese have hired all the taro patches in a valley from their native owners, and then employ these natives to work for them; an arrangement which is mutually beneficial, and agreeable besides to the Hawaiian,

IMPLEMENTS.

a, Calabash for *poi.*—*b*, Calabash for fish.—*c*, Water bottle.—*d d*, *Poi* mallets.—*e*, *Poi* trough.—*f*, Native bracelet.—*g*, Fiddle.—*h*, Flute.— *i i*, Drums.

who has not much of what we call "enterprise," and does not care to accumulate money. The windward side of the Islands of Oahu and Kauai produces a great deal of rice, and this is one of the products which promises to increase largely. The rice is said to be of excellent quality.

Kauai contained once the most important coffee-plantations; and the large sugar-plantation of Princeville at Hanalei was originally planted in coffee. But this tree or shrub is so subject to the attacks of a leaf-blight that the culture has decreased. Yet coffee grows wild in many of the valleys and hills, and here and there you find a small plantation of a few hundred trees which does well. The coffee shrub thrives best in these Islands among the lava rock, where there seems scarcely any soil; and it must be sheltered from winds and also from the sun. I have seen some young plantations placed in the midst of forests where the trees gave a somewhat dense shade, and these seemed to grow well.

GRASS HOUSE.

CHAPTER V.

THE HAWAIIAN AT HOME: MANNERS AND CUSTOMS.

AS we rode one day near the sea-shore I heard voices among the rocks, and sending the guide ahead with the horses, I walked over to the shore with the lady and children who were my companions. There we saw a sight characteristic of these islands. Three women decently clothed in a garment which covered them from head to foot, and a man with only a breech-clout on, were dashing into the surf, picking up sea-moss, and a little univalve shell, a limpet, which they flung into small baskets which hung from their shoulders. They were, in fact, getting their suppers, and they were quite as much surprised at our appearance as we at theirs. They came out politely, and showed the children what was in their baskets; the man, understanding that our horses had gone ahead, kindly volunteered to pilot us over the rocks to a village near by. I do not imagine that he was embarrassed at his lack of clothing, and after the first shock of surprise I am quite sure we were more inclined to admire his straight muscular figure and his shining dark skin than to complain of his nakedness. Presently, however, he slipped away into the bush, and re-appeared in a hat, and a shirt which was so short that even my little girl burst into laughter at this ridiculous and futile effort toward decency; and thus arrayed, and with the kindly and gracious smile which illuminates a Hawaiian's face when he puts himself to some trouble on your account, this funny guide led us to our horses.

In the evening I related this incident to our host, an old resident, and said, "I suppose this man could read?" "Read!" he replied; "he can read and write as well as you. I know him very well; he is a prosperous man, and is to be the next justice of the peace in that district. He doubtless went home and spent the remainder of the afternoon in reading his newspaper."

Native life in the Islands is full of such contrasts, and I found, on examining the labor contracts on several sugar-plantations, that almost without exception the working people signed their own names.

According to a census taken in December, 1872, the Hawaiian Islands contained 56,897 souls, of whom 51,531 were natives and half-castes, and 5366 were foreigners. In six years the native population had decreased 7234, and the foreigners had increased 1172. Since 1866, therefore, the Islands have lost 6062 souls.

Of the foreigners the Chinese are the most numerous, outnumbering all the other foreign nationalities together except the Americans. Chinese have been brought over here as coolie laborers on the plantations. They readily intermarry with the native women, and these unions are usually fruitful of healthy and bright children. It is said that the Chinese insist upon taking better care of their children than the native women, uninstructed, usually give them, and that therefore the Chinese half-caste families are more thrifty than those of the pure blood Hawaiians. Moreover, the Chinaman takes care of his wife. He endeavors to form her habits upon the pattern of his own; and requires of her the performance of fixed duties, which add to her happiness and health. In fact, the number of half-castes of all races has increased thirty per cent. in the last six years.

The native population is admirably cared for by the authorities. The Islands are divided for various governmental purposes into districts; and in every district where the people are much scattered the government places a physician— a man of skill and character—to whom it gives a small salary for attending upon the common people, and he is, I believe, expected to make a tour of his district at stated intervals. Of course he is allowed to practice besides for pay. The sugar planters also usually provide medical attendance for their laborers.

The Government maintains a careful guard over the schools. A compulsory education law obliges parents, under fixed penalties, to send their children to school; and besides the common or primary schools, there are a number of academies, most of which receive some help from the Government, while all are under Government supervision. The census gives the number of children between six and fifteen years of age at 8931; and there are 324 teachers, or one teacher for every twenty-seven children in the whole group. Attendance at school is, I suspect, more general here than in any other country in the world. The last report of W. P. Kamakau, the President of the Board of Education, made in March, 1872, returns 8287 children actually attending upon 245 schools of various grades, 202 being common schools. Under this system there is scarcely a Hawaiian of proper age who can not both read and write.

Churches they maintain by voluntary effort, and their contributions are very liberal. They take a pride in such organizations. Dr. Coan's native church at Hilo contributes $1200 per year to foreign missions.

There are no beggars, and no public paupers except the insane, who are cared for in an asylum near Honolulu, and the lepers, who are confined upon a part of Molokai. The convicts and the boys in the reform school contribute to their own support by their labor. The Queen's Hospital is only for curable cases, and the people take care of their own infirm, aged and otherwise incapable dependents.

It seems to me that very unusual judgment has been shown in the manner in which benevolent and penal institutions have been created and managed among these people; for the tendency almost everywhere in countries which call themselves more highly civilized is to make the poor dependent upon charity, and thus a fatal blow is struck at their character and respectability. Here, partly of course because the means of living are very abundant and easily got, but also, I think, because the government has been wisely managed, the people have not been taught to look toward public charity for relief; and though we Americans, who live in a big country, are apt to think slightingly of what some one called a toy kingdom, any one who has undertaken to manage or organize even a small community at home will recognize the fact that it is a task beset by difficulties.

But in these Islands a state, a society, has been created within a quarter of a century, and it has been very ably done. I am glad that it has been done mainly by Americans. Chief-justice Lee, now dead, but whose memory is deservedly cherished here; Dr. Judd, who died in August, 1873; Mr. C. C. Harris, lately Minister of Foreign Relations, and for many years occupying different prominent positions in the Government; Dr. J. Mott Smith, lately the Minister of Finance; Chief-justice Allen, and Mr. Armstrong, long at the head of the Educational Department, the father of General Armstrong, President of the Hampton University in Virginia, deserve, perhaps, the chief credit for this work. They were the organizers who supplemented the labors of the missionaries; and, fortunately for the native people, they were all men of honor, of self-restraint, of goodness of heart, who knew how to rule wisely and not too much, and who protected the people without destroying their independence. What they have done would have given them fame had it not been done two thousand miles from the nearest continent, and at least five thousand from any place where reputations are made.

Of a total native population of 51,531, 6580 are returned by the census as free-holders—more than one in every eight.   Only 4772 are returned as plantation laborers, and of these probably a third are Chinese; 2115 returned themselves as mechanics, which is a very large proportion of the total able-bodied popula-tion.   I believe that both freeholders and mechanics find employment on the plantations as occasional laborers.

A people so circumstanced, well taught in schools, freeholders to a large ex-tent, living in a mild and salubrious climate, and with cheap and proper food, ought not, one would say, to decrease.   There are, of course, several reasons for their very rapid decrease, and all of them come from contact with the whites.   These brought among them diseases which have corrupted their blood, and made them infertile and of poor stamina.   But to this, which is the chief cause, must be added, I suspect, another less generally acknowledged.

The deleterious habit of wearing clothes has, I do not doubt, done much to kill off the Hawaiian people.   If you think for a moment, you will see that to adopt civilized habits was for them to make a prodigious change in their ways of life.   Formerly the maro and the slight covering of the tapa alone shielded them from the sun and rain.   Their bodies became hardy by exposure.   Their employments—fishing, taro-planting, tapa-making, bird-catching, canoe-making —were all laborious, and pursued out-of-doors.   Their grass houses, with open-ings for doors and windows, were, at any rate, tolerably well ventilated.   Take the man accustomed thus to live, and put shoes on his feet, a hat on his head, a shirt on his back, and trowsers about his legs, and lodge him in a house with close-shutting doors and windows, and you expose his constitution to a very se-rious strain, especially in a country where there is a good deal of rain.   Being, after all, but half civilized, he will probably sleep in a wet shirt, or cumber his feet with wet shoes; he will most likely neglect to open his windows at night, and poison himself and his family with bad air, to the influence of which, be-sides, his unaccustomed lungs will be peculiarly liable; he will live a less active life under his changed conditions; and altogether the poor fellow must have an uncommonly fine constitution to resist it all and escape with his life.   At the best, his system will be relaxed, his power of resistance will be lessened, his chances of recovery will be diminished in the same degree as his chances of falling ill are increased.   If now you throw in some special disease, corrupting the blood, and transmitted with fatal certainty to the progeny, the wonder is that a people so situated have not died out in a single generation.

In fact they have died out pretty fast, though there is reason to believe that the mortality rate has largely decreased in the last three years; and careful observers believe even that in the last year there has been an actual increase, rather than a decrease in the native and half-caste population.   In 1832 the Islands had a population of 130,315 souls; in 1836 there were but 108,579; in 1840, only 84,165, of whom 1962 were foreigners; in 1850, 69,800, of whom

3216 were foreigners; and in 1860, 62,959, of whom 4194 were foreigners. The native population has decreased over sixty per cent. in forty years.

In the same period the foreigners have increased very slowly, until there are now in all 5366 foreigners and persons born here, but of foreign parentage, on the Islands. You will see that while the Hawaiians have so rapidly decreased that all over the Islands you notice, in waste fields and desolate house places, the marks of this loss, foreigners have not been attracted to fill up their places. And this in spite of the facts that the climate is mild and healthful, the price of living cheap, the Government liberal, the taxes low, and life and property as secure as in any part of the world. One would think that a country which offers all these advantages must be a paradise for poor men; and I do not wonder that in the United States there is frequent talk of "annexing the Islands." But, in fact, they offer no advantages, aside from those I have named, to white settlers, and they have such serious natural disabilities as will always —or, at least, for the next two or three millions of years—repel our American people, and all other white settlers.

In the first place, there is very little of what we call agricultural land on the Islands. They are only mountains rising from the sea, with extremely little alluvial bottom, and that usually cut up by torrents, and water-washed into gulches, until it is difficult in many parts to find a fair field of even fifty acres. From these narrow bottoms, where they exist, you look into deep gorges or valleys, out of which issue the streams which force their way through the lower fields into the sea. These valleys are never extensive, and are always very much broken and contracted. They are useless for common agricultural purposes. In several the culture of coffee has been begun; but they are so inaccessible, the roads into them are so difficult, and the area of arable soil they contain is, after all, so insignificant, that, even for so valuable a product as coffee, transportation is found to be costly.

But it is along and in the streams which rush through the bottoms of these narrow gorges that the Hawaiian is most at home. Go into any of these valleys, and you will see a surprising sight: along the whole narrow bottom, and climbing often in terraces the steep hill-sides, you will see the little taro patches, skillfully laid so as to catch the water, either directly from the main stream, or from canals taking water out above.

Such a taro patch oftenest contains a sixteenth, less frequently an eighth of an acre. It consists of soil painfully brought down from above, and secured by means of substantial stone walls, plastered with mud and covered with grass, strong enough to resist the force of the torrent. Each little patch or flat is so laid that a part of the stream shall flow over it without carrying away the soil; indeed, it is expected to leave some sediment. And as you look up such a valley you see terrace after terrace of taro rising before you, the patches often fifty or sixty feet above the brawling stream, but each receiving its proper proportion of water.

Near by or among these small holdings stand the grass houses of the pro-prietors, and you may see them and their wives, their clothing tucked up, stand-ing over their knees in water, planting or cultivating the crop. Here the Ha-waiian is at home. His horse finds its scanty living on the grass which fringes the taro patches; indeed, you may see horses here standing belly deep in fresh water, and feeding on the grasses which grow on the bottom; and again you find horses raised in the drier parts of the islands that do not know what water is, never having drunk any thing wetter than the dew on the grass. Among the taro patches the house place is as narrow as a fishing schooner's deck—"two steps and overboard." If you want to walk, it must be on the dikes within which the taro land is confined; and if you ride, it must be in the mid-dle of the rapid mountain torrent, or along a narrow bridle-path high up on the precipitous side of the mountain.

Down near the shore are fish ponds, with wicker gates which admit the small fry from the sea, but keep in the large fish. Many of these ponds are hundreds of acres in area, and from them the Hawaiian draws one of his favorite dishes. Then there may be cocoa-nuts; there are sure to be bananas and guavas. Beef costs but a trifle, and hogs fatten on taro. The pandanus furnishes him mate-rial for his mats, and of mats he makes his bed, as well as the floor of his house.

In short, such a gorge or valley as I have tried to describe to you furnishes in its various parts, including the sea-shore, all that is needed to make the Ha-waiian prosperous; and I have not seen one which had not its neatly kept school-house and church, and half a dozen framed houses scattered among the humbler grass huts, to mark the greater wealth of some—for the Hawaiian holds that the wooden house is a mark of thrift and respectability.

But the same valley which now supports twenty or thirty native families in comfort and happiness, and which, no doubt, once yielded food and all the ap-pliances of life in abundance to one or two hundred, would not tempt any white man of any nation in the world to live in it, and a thousand such gorges would not add materially to the prosperity of any white nation. That is to say, the country is admirably adapted to its native people. It favors, as it doubtless compelled and formed, all their habits and customs. But it would repel any one else, and an American farmer would not give a hundred dollars for the whole Wailuku Valley—if he had to live in it and work it—though it would be worth many thousands to the natives if it were once more populous as of old.

As you examine the works of the old Hawaiians, their fish ponds, their irri-gation canals, their long miles of walls inclosing ponds and taro fields, you will not only see the proofs that the Islands were formerly far more populous than now, but you will get a respect for the feudal system of which these works are the remains.

The Hawaiian people, when they first became known to the world, were sev-eral stages removed from mere savagery. They had elaborated a tolerably perfect system of government and of land tenure, which has since been swept away, as was inevitable, but which served its day very well indeed. Under this system the chiefs owned every thing. The common people were their retainers —followers in war and servants in peace. The chief, according to an old Hawaiian proverb, owned "all the land, all the sea, and all the iron cast up by the sea."

HAWAIIAN WARRIORS.

The land was carefully parceled out among the chiefs, upon the plan of securing to each one from his own land all that he and his retainers needed for their lives. What they chiefly required was taro ground, the sea for fish, the mulberry for tapa, and timber land for canoes; but they required also *ti* leaves in which to wrap their parcels, and flowers of which to make their *les*, or flower necklaces. And I have seen modern surveys of old "lands" in which the lines were run very irregularly, and in some cases even outlying patches were added, because a straight line from mountain to sea was found to exclude some one product, even so trifling as the yellow flowers of which *les* are often made.

On such a "land," and from it, the chief and his people lived. He appears to have been the brains and they the hands to work it. They owed him two days' labor in every seven, in which they cultivated his taro, cleaned his fish pond, caught fish for him, opened paths, made or transported canoes, and did generally what he required. The remainder of the time was their own, to cultivate such patches of taro as he allowed them to occupy, or to do what they pleased. For any important public work he could call out all his people, and oblige them to labor as long as he chose, and thus were built the surprisingly solid and extensive walls which inclose the old fish ponds, and many irrigating canals which show not only long continued industry, but quite astonishing skill for so rude a people.

The chief was supreme ruler over his people; they lived by his tolerance, for they owned absolutely nothing, neither land, nor house, nor food, nor wife, nor child. A high chief was approached only with abject gestures, and no one dared resist his acts or dispute his will. The sense of obedience must have been very strong, for it has survived every change; and only the other day a friend of mine saw a Hawaiian lady, a chiefess, but the wife of an American, and herself tenderly nurtured and a woman of education and refinement, boxing the ears of a tall native, whom she had caught furiously abusing his wife, and the man bore his punishment as meekly as a child. "Why?" "He knows I am his chief, and he would not dare raise even an angry look toward me; he would not think of it, even," was her reply, when she was asked how she had courage to interfere in what was a very violent quarrel. Yet the present law recognizes no allegiance due to a chief.

When the young king Lunalilo returned to the palace after the coronation, the pipe-bearer, an old native retainer, approached him on his knees, and was shocked at being ordered to get up and act like a man. The older natives to this day approach a chief or chiefess only with humble and deprecatory bows; and wherever a chief or chiefess travels, the native people along the road make offerings of the fruits of the ground, and even of articles of clothing and adornment. One of the curious sights of Honolulu to us travelers, last spring, was to see long processions of native people, men, women, and children, marching to the palace to lay their offerings before the king, who is a high chief. Each brought something—a man would walk gravely along with a pig under his arm; after him followed perhaps a little child with half a dozen bananas, a woman with a chicken tied by a string, a girl with a handkerchief full of eggs, a boy with a cocoa-nut, an old woman with a calabash of poi, and so on. In the palace yard all this was laid in a heap before the young king, who thereupon said thank you, and, with a few kind words, dismissed the people to their homes.

As an illustration of the power of the old chiefs, as well as of the density of the population in former times, it is related that when the wall inclosing a cer-

LUNALILO.

tain fish pond on the windward side of Oahu was to be built, the chief then ruling over that land gave notice that on a certain day every man, woman, and child within his domain must appear at a designated point, bearing a stone. The wall, which stands yet, is half a mile long, well built, and probably six feet high; and it was begun and completed in that one day.

6

I was shown, on Kauai, a young man of insignificant appearance, and of no particular merit or force of character. To him an old woman recently dying had by a will, written out for her by a friend of my own, left all her property—a taro patch, a house, and some other land. My friend asked why. He is my chief, was the reply; and sure enough, on inquiry my friend discovered, what he had not before known, that the man was a descendant of one of the chief families, of whom this old woman had in her early days been a subject.

As the chief was the ruler, the people looked to him for food in a time of scarcity. He directed their labors; he protected them against wrong from others; and as it was his pride that his retainers should be more numerous and more prosperous than those of the neighboring chief, if the head possessed brains, no doubt the people were made content. Food was abundant; commerce was unknown; the chief could not eat or waste more than his people could easily produce for him; and until disturbing causes came in with Captain Cook, no doubt feudalism wrought satisfactory results here. One wonders how it was invented among such a people, or who it was that first had genius enough to insist on obedience, to make rules, to prescribe the tabu, and, in short, to evolve order out of chaos.

The tabu was a most ingenious and useful device; and when you hear of the uses to which it was put, and of its effectiveness, you feel surprised that it was not found elsewhere as an appurtenance of the feudal machinery. Thus the chief allowed his people to fish in the part of the ocean which he owned—which fronted his "land," that is to say. He tabued one or two kinds of fish, however; these they were forbidden to catch; but as a fisherman can not, even in these islands, exercise a choice as to the fish which shall enter his net or bite at his hook, it followed that the tabued fish were caught—but then they were at once rendered up to the chief. One variety of taro, which makes poi of a pink color, was tabued and reserved for the chiefs. Some birds were tabued on account of their feathers; one especially, a black bird which has a small yellow feather under each wing. The great feather cloak of Kamehameha I., which is still kept as a sign of royalty, is made of these feathers, and contains probably several thousand of them, thus gathered, two from each bird.

Further, a tabu prohibited women from eating with men, even with their husbands; and when, on the death of the first Kamehameha, his Queen Kahumanu, an energetic and fearless virago, dared for the first time to eat with her son, a cry of horror went up as though "great Pan was dead;" and this bold act really broke the power of the heathen priests.

A tabu forbade women to eat cocoa-nuts and some other articles of food; and the prohibition appears to have been used also to compel sanitary and other useful restraints, for I have been told that a tabu preserved girls from marriage until they had attained a certain age, eighteen, I believe; and to this and some other similar regulations, rigorously enforced in the old times, I have heard old residents attribute the fertility of the race before foreigners came in.

He who violated a tabu was at once killed. Capital punishment seems to have been an effective restraint upon crime among these savages, contrary to the theories of some modern philosophers; probably it was effective for two reasons, because it was prompt and because it was certain. One wonders how long the tabu would have been respected, had a violator of it been lodged in jail for eighteen months, allowed to appeal his case through three courts, and at last been brained amidst the appeals for mercy of the most respectable people of his tribe, and had his funeral ceremonies performed by the high-priest, and closed with a eulogy upon his character, and insinuations

KAMEHAMEHA I.

against the sound judgment and uprightness of the chief who ordered the execution.

The first Kamehameha, who seems to have been a savage of considerable merit, and a firm believer in capital punishment, subdued the Islands to his own rule, but he did not aim to break the power of the chiefs over their people. He established a few general laws, and insisted on peace, order, and obedience to

QUEEN OF KAMEHAMEHA I.

himself. By right of his conquest all lands were supposed to be owned by him; he gave to one chief and took away from another; he rewarded his favorites, but he did not alter the condition of the people.

But as traders came in, as commerce began, as

money came into use, the feudal system began to be oppressive.   Sandal-wood was long one of the most precious products of these islands—their Chinese name, indeed, is "Sandal-wood Islands."   The chiefs, greedy for money, or for what the ships brought, forced their unhappy retainers into the mountains to gather this wood.   Exposed to cold, badly fed, and obliged to bear painful burdens, they died in great numbers, so that it was a blessing to the Islanders when the wood became scarce.   Again, supplies of food were sold by the chiefs to the ships, and this necessitated unusual labor from the people.   One famous chief for years used his retainers to tow ships into the narrow harbor of Honolulu, sending them out on the reef, where, up to their middle in water, they shouldered the tow-line.

Thus when, in 1848, the king, at the instance of that excellent man and upright judge, Chief-justice Lee, gave the kuliana rights, he relieved the people of a sore oppression, and at a single blow destroyed feudalism.   The kuliana is the individual holding.   Under the kuliana law each native householder became entitled to the possession in fee of such land as he had occupied, or chose to occupy and cultivate.   He had only to make application to a government officer, have the tract surveyed, and pay a small sum to get the title.   It is creditable to the chiefs that, under the influence of the missionaries, they consented to this important change, fully knowing that it meant independence to the common people and an end of all feudal rights; but it must be added that a large part of their lands remained in their hands, making them, of course, still wealthy proprietors.

Thus the present system of land tenure on the Islands is much the same as our own; but the holdings of the common people are generally small, and the chiefs, or their successors in many cases foreigners, still maintain their right to the sea fisheries as against all who live outside the old boundaries of their own "lands."

The families of most of the great chiefs have become extinct.   Their wealth became a curse to them when foreigners came in with foreign vices and foreign luxuries.   They are said to have been remarkable as men and women of extraordinary stature and of uncommon perfection of form.   I have been told of many chiefesses nearly or quite six feet in height, and many chiefs from six feet two inches to six feet six, and in one case six feet seven inches high.   There is no reason to doubt the universal testimony that they were, as a class, taller and finer-looking than the common people; but the older missionaries and residents believe that this arose not from their being of a different race, but because they were absolutely relieved from hard work, were more abundantly and carefully fed, and used the lomi-lomi constantly.   It is supposable, too, that in the wars which prevailed among the tribes the weaklings, if any such were among the chiefs, were pretty sure to be killed off; and thus a natural selection went on which weeded out the small and inefficient chiefs.

Their government appears to have been a "despotism tempered by assassination," for great as was the respect exacted by a chief, and implicit as was the obedience he commanded, if he pushed his tyranny too far, his people rose and slew him. Thus on Kauai, in the lower part of the Hanapepe Valley, a huge cliff is shown, concerning which the tradition runs that it was once the residence of the chief who ruled this valley. This person, with a Titanic and Rabellaisian humor, was accustomed to descend into the valley in the evening, seize a baby and carry it to his stronghold to serve him as a pillow. Having slept upon it he slew it next morning; and thus with a refinement of luxury he required a fresh baby every evening. When patience had ceased to be a virtue, according to our more modern formula, the people went up one night and knocked his brains out; and there was a change of dynasties.

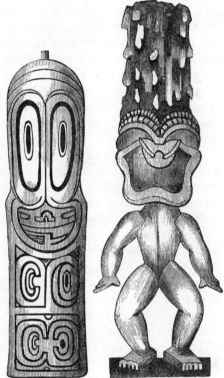

ANCIENT GODS OF HAWAII.

The Hawaiian of the present day reads his Bible and newspaper, writes letters, wears clothes, owns property, serves in the Legislature or Parliament, votes, teaches school, acts as justice of the peace and even as judge, is tax collector and assessor, constable and preacher. In spite of all this, or rather with it, he retains the oddest traces of the habits and customs of another age. For instance, he will labor for wages; but he will persistently and for years give away to his relations all his pay except what he needs for his actual subsistence, and if he is prosperous he is pretty sure to have quite a swarm of people to support. A lady told me that having repeatedly clothed her nurse in good apparel, and finding this liberal soul, every time, in a day or two reduced to her original somewhat shabby clothing, she at last reproached her for her folly. "What can I do?" the woman replied; "they come and ask me for the holaku, or the handkerchief, or whatever I have. Suppose you say they are yours—then I will not give them away." Accordingly, the next new suit was formally declared to belong to the mistress: it was not given away. An old woman, kept chiefly for her skill in lomi-lomi by an American family, asked her master one day for ten dollars. He gave her two five-dollar gold pieces, and, to his amazement, saw her hand them over immediately, one to a little girl and one to a boy, who had evidently come to get the money—not for her use at all. A cook in my own family asked for the wages due him, which he had been saving for some time; he received forty-four dollars, and gave the whole amount at once to his father-in-law, who had come from another island on purpose to get this money. Nor was it grudged to him, so far as any of us could see. "By-and-by, if we are poor and in need, they will do as much for us," is the excuse.

As you ride along in the country, you will see your guide slyly putting a stone or a bunch of grass on a ledge near some precipice. If you look, you will see other objects of the same kind lying there. Ask him about it and he will tell you, with a laugh, that his forefathers in other times did so, and he does the same. It is, in fact, a peace offering to the local divinity of the place. Is he, then, an idolater? Not at all; not necessarily, at least. He is under the compulsion of an old custom; and he will even tell you that it is all nonsense. The same force leads him to treat with respect and veneration a chief or chiefess even if abjectly poor, though before the law the highest chief is no better than the common people.

They are hearty and even gross feeders; and probably the only christianized people who live almost entirely on cold victuals. A Hawaiian does not need a fire to prepare a meal; and at a *luau*, or feast, all the food is served cold, except the pig, which ought to be hot.

Hospitable and liberal as he is in his daily life, when the Hawaiian invites his friends to a *luau* he expects them to pay. He provides for them roast pig, poi, baked ti-root, which bears a startling resemblance in looks and taste to New England molasses-cake; raw fish and shrimps, limu, which is a sea-moss of villainous odor; kuulaau, a mixture of taro and cocoa-nut, very nice; paalolo, a mixture of sweet-potato and cocoa-nut; raw and cooked cuttle-fish, roast dog, sea-eggs, if they can be got; and, if the feast is something above the ordinary, raw pickled salmon with tomatoes and red-pepper.

The object of such a luau is usually to enable the giver to pay for his new house, or to raise money for some private object of his own. Notice of the coming feast is given months beforehand, as also of the amount each visitor is expected to give. It will be a twenty-five cent, or a fifty cent, or a dollar luau. The pigs—the centre-piece of the feast—have been fattening for a year before. The affair is much discussed. It is indispensable that all who attend shall come in brand-new clothing, and a native person will rather deny himself the feast than appear in garments which have been worn before. A few of the relatives of the feast-giver act as stewards, and they must be dressed strictly alike. At one luau which I had the happiness to attend the six men who acted as stewards were arrayed in green cotton shirts and crimson cotton trowsers, and had green wreaths on their heads. I need not say that they presented a truly magnificent appearance.

To such a luau people ride thirty or forty miles; arriving often the evening beforehand, in order to be early at the feast next day. When they sit down each person receives his abundant share of pig, neatly wrapped in ti-leaves; to the remainder of the food he helps himself as he likes. They eat, and eat, and eat; they beat their stomachs with satisfaction; they talk and eat; they ride about awhile, and eat again; they laugh, sing, and eat. At last a man finds he can hold no more. He is "pau"—done. He declares himself "mauna"— a mountain; and points to his abdomen in proof of his statement. Then, unless he expects a recurrence of hunger, he carefully wraps up the fragments and bones which remain of his portion of pig, and these he must take with him. It would be the height of impoliteness to leave them; and each visitor scrupulously takes away every remaining bit of his share. If now you look you will see a calabash somewhere in the middle of the floor, into which each, as he completes his meal, put his quarter or half dollar.

In the evening there are dancing and singing, and then you may hear and see the extremely dramatic meles of the Hawaiians—a kind of rapid chant, the tones of which have a singular fascination for my ears. A man and woman, usually elderly or middle-aged people, sit down opposite each other, or side by side facing the company. One begins and the other joins in; the sound is as of a shrill kind of drone; it is accompanied by gesticulations; and each chant lasts about two or three minutes, and ends in a jerk. The swaying of the lithe figures, the vehement and passionate movements of the arms and head, the tragic intensity of the looks, and the very peculiar music, all unite to fasten one's attention, and to make this spectacle of mele singing, as I have said, singularly fascinating.

The language of the meles is a dialect now unused, and unintelligible even to most of the people. The whole chant concerns itself, however, with a detailed description of the person of the man or woman or child to which or in whose honor it is sung. Thus a mele will begin with the hair, which may be likened in beauty to the sea-moss found on a certain part of Kauai; or the teeth, which "resemble the beautiful white pebbles which men pick up on the beach of Kaalui Bay on Maui;" and so on. Indeed an ancient Hawaiian mele is probably, in its construction, much like the Song of Solomon; though I am told that the old meles concerned themselves with personal details by no means suitable for modern ears. A mele is always sung for or about some particular person. Thus I have heard meles for the present king; meles for a man or woman present; meles for a chief; and on one occasion I was told they sang a mele for me; and I judged, from the laughter some parts of it excited, that my feelings were saved by my ignorance of the language.

On all festive occasions, and on many others, the Hawaiian loves to dress his head with flowers and green wreaths. Les or garlands are made of several substances besides flowers; though the most favorite are composed of jasmine flowers, or the brilliant yellow flowers of one kind of ginger, which give out a somewhat overpowering odor. These are hung around the neck. For the head they like to use wreaths of the maile shrub, which has an agreeable odor, something like that of the cherry sticks which smokers like for pipe stems. This ornamentation does not look amiss on the young, for to youth much is forgiven; but it is a little startling, at a luau, to see old crones and grave grandfathers arrayed with equal gayety; and I confess that though while the flowers and leaves are fresh the decorated assembly is picturesque, especially as the women wear their hair flowing, and many have beautiful wavy tresses, yet toward evening, when the maile has wilted and the garlands are rumpled and decaying, this kind of ornamentation gives an air of dissipation to the company which it by no means deserves.

Finally, the daily life of the Hawaiian, if he lives near the sea-coast and is master of his own life, is divided between fishing, taro planting, poi making, and mat weaving. All these but the last are laborious occupations; but they do not make hard work of them. Two days' labor every week will provide abundant food for a man and his family. He has from five to ten dollars a year of taxes to pay, and this money he can easily earn. The sea always supplies him with fish, sea-moss, and other food. He is fond of fussing at different things; but he also lies down on the grass a good deal—why shouldn't he? —he reads his paper, he plays at cards, he rides about a good deal, he sleeps more or less, and about midnight he gets up and eats a hearty supper. Altogether he is a very happy creature, and by no means a bad one. You need not lock your door against him; and an election and a luau occasionally, give him all the excitement he craves, and that not of an unwholesome kind.

What there is happy about his life he owes to the fine climate and the missionaries. The latter have given him education enough to read his Bible and newspaper, and thus to take some interest in and have some knowledge of affairs in the world at large. They and their successors, the political rulers, have made life and property secure, and caused roads and bridges to be built and maintained; and the Hawaiian is fond of moving about. The little inter-island steamer and the schooners are always full of people on their travels; and as they do not have hotel bills to pay, but live on their friends on these visits, there is a great deal of such movement.

It would hardly do to compare the Hawaiian people with those of New England; but they will compare favorably in comfort, in intelligence, in wealth, in morals, and in happiness with the common people of most European nations; and when one sees here how happily people can live in a small way, and without ambitious striving for wealth or a career, he can not but wonder if, after all, in the year 2873, our pushing and hard-pushed civilization of the nineteenth century will get as great praise as it gets from ourselves, its victims.

HAWAIIANS EATING POI.

CHAPTER VI.

COMMERCIAL AND POLITICAL.

COMMERCIAL relations form and foster political alliances, especially between a weak state and a strong one. The annual report for 1872 of imports and exports, made up by the Collector-general of the Hawaiian Kingdom, shows how completely the Islands depend upon the United States.

Of 146 merchant vessels and steamers entered at Hawaiian ports during 1872, 90 were American, only 15 were English; 6 were German, 9 belonged to other nations, and 26 were Hawaiian. Of a total of 98,647 tons of shipping, 73,975 were American, 6714 Hawaiian, and but 7741 British. Of 47 whaling vessels calling at Island ports during the year, 42 were American, 2 Hawaiian, and 3 British.

Of a little less than 16,000,000 pounds of sugar exported during the same year, 14,500,000 were sent to the United States; of 39,000 pounds of coffee 34,000 were sent to us; of 1,349,503 pounds of rice and paddy exported, 1,317,203 pounds came to the United States. All the cotton, all the goat-skins, nearly all the hides, all the wool, the greater part of the peanuts and the pulu, in short, almost the whole exports of the Islands, are sent to the United States.

On the other hand, of $1,234,147, the value of duty-paying merchandise imported during 1872 into the Islands, $806,111 worth came from the United States, $155,939 from Great Britain, and $205,396 from Germany. Besides this, of the total value of bonded goods, $349,435, the large amount of $135,487 was brought from sea by whalemen, almost all of whom were Americans; and $99,567 worth was goods from the United States; or $235,000 of American products against $21,801 of British, and $23,904 of German importation, in bond.

It is plain that the Island trade is so largely in our hands that no other nation can be said to dispute it with us. If our flag flew over Honolulu we could hardly expect to have a more complete monopoly of Hawaiian commerce than we already enjoy. Moreover, almost all the sugar-plantations—the most productive and valuable property on the Islands—are owned by Americans; and the same is true of the greater number of stock farms.

Our political predominance on the Islands is as complete as the commercial. In the present cabinet all the ministers except one are Americans. This was true also of the cabinet of the late king. Of the Supreme Court, two of the judges are Americans, and one is German. Almost all the executive and administrative offices are in the hands of Americans or Hawaiians.

Nor can any foreign power rightly find fault with this state of things. What the Islands are they are because of American effort, American enterprise, American capital. American missionaries civilized them; Americans gave them laws wisely adapted to the customs and habits of their people; American enterprise and Boston capital established the sugar culture and other of the important industries; perhaps I ought to add that American sailors spread among the Islands the vices and diseases which, more than all else, have caused the rapid decrease of the population, and to combat and check which added toil and trouble to the labors of the American missionaries.

The government of the Hawaiian Islands consists of a king and a Parliament. The Parliament meets once in two years; and under the late king consisted of but a single House. The present king has promised to call together two Houses, of which but one will be elected. The other consists of "Nobles," who are nominated or created by the king for life, but have no title nor salary unless they are called to office. By the Constitution the reigning king appoints his successor, but his nomination must be confirmed by the Nobles. As, however, he may at pleasure increase the number of Nobles, the appointment virtually rests with him. If he dies without naming a successor, the Parliament has the right and duty to elect a new sovereign.

There is a slight property qualification for voters, and a heavier one for members of Parliament.

The revenue of the Government, which amounts to about half a million per annum, is derived from the various sources specified in the official returns of the Minister of Finance, which I copy below. It must be understood that this report covers two years:

The balance in the Treasury at the close of the last fiscal period (March 31, 1870) was........				$61,580 20
And there has been received from Foreign Imports............			$396,418 15	
"	"	"	Fines, Penalties, and Costs .	47,289 13	
"	"	"	Internal Commerce..........	98,982 51	
"	"	"	" Taxes.................	215,962 51	
"	"	"	Fees and Perquisities.........	22,194 45	
"	"	"	Government Realizations....	124,071 37	
"	"	"	Miscellaneous Sources........	60,038 23	
				964,956 35
				$1,026,536 55

The expenditures during two years are detailed thus in the same report:

For Civil List...............		$50,000 00	
" Permanent Settlements.........		18,000 00	
" Legislature and Privy Council.................		15,281 63	
" Department of Judiciary................		73,562 61	
"	"	Foreign Affairs and War..............	98,028 24
"	"	Interior.................	396,806 41
"	"	Finance.............	141,345 29
"	"	Attorney-general.............	88,412 17
" Bureau of Public Instruction		88,347 79	
			969,784 14
Balance on hand March 31, 1872.............			56,752 41
			$1,026,536 55

The internal taxes include the property tax, which is quite low, one and a half per cent. Every male adult pays a poll tax of one dollar, a school tax of two dollars, and a road tax of two dollars. The following is the detail of the internal taxes for the two years 1870–72:

Real Estate and Personal Property........................	$97,685 11
Horses	53,006 00
Dogs..	22,271 40
Mules..	6,140 00
Carriages	3,125 00
Poll..	27,841 00
Native Seamen...	5,894 00
	$215,962 51

Among the licenses the monopoly of opium selling brings the Government $22,248, a prodigious sum when it is considered that there are but 2500 Chinese in the Islands; these being the chief, though not the only consumers. There is, besides, a duty of ten per cent. on the opium when imported, and the merchant must make his profit. I had the curiosity to look a little into the opium consumption. It is said that its use is slowly spreading among the natives, particularly where these are employed with Chinese on the plantations. But the quantity used by the Chinese themselves is prodigious. I was shown one man, a cook, whose wages, fourteen dollars per month, were entirely spent on opium; and whose master supplied the poor creature with clothes, because he had nothing left out of his pay. In other cases the amount spent was nearly as great.

Eight thousand two hundred and sixty-five dollars were also realized for awa licenses. Awa is a root the use of which produces a frightful kind of intoxication, in which the victim falls into stupor, his features are contorted, and he has seizures resembling epilepsy. The body of the habitual awa drinker becomes covered with white scales; and it is said that awa drinking predisposes to leprosy. The manner of preparing awa is peculiarly disgusting. The root is chewed by women, and they spit out well-chewed mouthfuls into a calabash. Here it settles, and the liquor is then drunk. It is said that in old times the chiefs used to get together the prettiest young girls to chew awa for them.

The king receives a salary of $22,500 per annum; the cabinet ministers and the chief-justice receive $5000, and the two associate justices $4000 per annum. These are the largest salaries paid; and in general the public service of the Islands is very cheaply as well as ably and conscientiously conducted. There is an opportunity for retrenchment in abolishing some of the offices; but the saving which could thus be effected would after all not be great. The present Government means, I have been told, to undertake some reforms; these will probably consist in getting the king to turn the crown lands into public lands, to be sold or leased for the benefit of the treasury. They are now leased, and the income is a perquisite of the king, a poor piece of policy, for the chiefs from among whom a sovereign is selected are all wealthy; the present king, for instance, has an income of probably $25,000 per annum from private property of his own. It is also proposed to lessen the number of cabinet ministers; but this will scarcely be done. They are but four in number now, having charge of Foreign Affairs, Finance, and the Interior and Law Departments.

There is a debt of about $300,000 which is entirely held within the kingdom; and the public property is of value sufficient to pay three times this sum. It is probable, however, that, like many other governments, the Hawaiian ministry will have to deal with a deficit when the next Legislature meets; and this will probably bring reform and retrenchment before them. There is not much hope of increasing the revenue from new and still untouched sources, for there are but few such.

The taxable industries and wealth of the Islands can not be very greatly increased.

Finding yourself in a tropical country, with a charming and equable climate, and with abundant rains, you are apt to think that, given only a little soil, many things would grow and could be profitably raised. It is one of the surprises of a visitor to the Hawaiian group to discover that in reality very few products succeed here.

Coffee was largely planted, and promised to become a staple of the Islands; but a blight attacked the trees and proved so incurable that the best plantations were dug up and turned into sugar; and the export of coffee, which has been very variable, but which rose to 415,000 pounds in 1870, fell to 47,000 pounds in the next year, and to 39,276 pounds in 1872.

Sea-island cotton would yield excellent crops if it were not that a caterpillar devours the young plants, so that its culture has almost ceased. Only 10,000 pounds were exported in 1872. The orange thrives in so few localities on the Islands that it is not an article of commerce: only two boxes were exported last year, though San Francisco brings this fruit from Otaheite by a voyage of thirty days. A bur worse than any found in California discourages the sheep-raiser in some of the Islands. The cacao-tree has been tried, but a blight kills it. In the garden of Dr. Hillebrandt, near Honolulu, I saw specimens of the cinnamon and allspice trees; but again I was told that the blight attacked them, and did not allow them to prosper. Wheat and other cereals grow and mature, but they are subject to the attacks of weevil, so that they can not be stored or shipped; and if you feed your horse oats or barley in Honolulu, these have been imported from California. Silk-worms have been tried but failed. Rice does well, and its culture is increasing.

Moreover, there is but an inconsiderable local market. A farmer on Maui told me he had sent twenty bags of potatoes to Honolulu, and so overstocked the market that he got back only the price of his bags. Eggs and all other perishable products, for the same reason, vary much in price, and are at times high-priced and hardly attainable. It will not do for the farmer to raise much for sale. The population is not only divided among different and distant islands, but it consists for much the largest part of people who live sufficiently well on taro, sweet-potatoes, fish, pork, and beef—all articles which they raise for themselves, and which they get by labor and against disadvantages which few white farmers would encounter.

For instance, the Puna coast of Hawaii is a district where for thirty miles there is so little fresh water to be found that travelers must bring their own supplies in bottles; and Dr. Coan told me that in former days the people, knowing that he could not drink the brackish stuff which satisfied them, used to collect fresh water for his use when he made the missionary tour, from the drippings of dew in caves. Wells are here out of the question, for there is no soil except a little decomposed lava, and the lava lets through all the water which comes from rains. There are few or no streams to be led down from the mountains.   There are no fields, according to our meaning of the word.

Formerly the people in this district were numbered by thousands: even yet there is a considerable population, not unprosperous by any means.   Churches and schools are as frequent as in the best part of New England.   Yet when I asked a native to show me his sweet-potato patch, he took me to the most curious and barren-looking collection of lava you can imagine, surrounded, too, by a very formidable wall made of lava, and explained to me that by digging holes in the lava where it was a little decayed, carrying a handful of earth to each of these holes, and planting there in a wet season, he got a very satisfactory crop. Not only that, but being desirous of something more than a bare living, this man had planted a little coffee in the same way, and had just sold 1600 pounds, his last crop.   He owned a good wooden house; politely gave up his own mats for me to sleep on; possessed a Bible and a number of other works in Hawaiian; after supper called his family together, who squatted on the floor while he read from his Scriptures, and, after singing a hymn, knelt in family prayers; and finally spent half an hour before going to bed in looking over his newspaper.   This man, thoroughly respectable, of good repute, hospitable, comfortable in every way so far as I could see, lived, and lived well, on twenty or thirty acres of lava, of which not even a Vermonter would have given ten cents for a thousand acres; and which was worthless to any one except a native Hawaiian.

Take next the grazing lands.   In many parts they are so poorly supplied with water that they can not carry much stock.   They also are often astonishingly broken up, for they frequently lie high up on the sides of the mountains, and in many parts they are rocky and lava-covered beyond belief.   On Hawaii, the largest island, lava covers and makes desolate hundreds of thousands of acres, and on the other and smaller islands, except, perhaps, Kauai, there is corresponding desolation.   Thus the area of grazing lands is less than one would think.   But on the other hand, cattle are very cheaply raised.   They require but little attention; and the stock-owners, who are now boiling down their cattle and selling merely the hides and tallow, are said to be just at this time the most prosperous people on the Islands.   Sheep are kept too, but not in great flocks except upon the small island of Niihau, which was bought some years ago by two brothers, Sinclair by name, who have now a flock of fifteen or eighteen thousand sheep there, I am told; on Molokai and part of Hawaii; and upon the small island of Lanai, where Captain Gibson has six or eight thousand head.

One of the conspicuous trees of the Hawaiian forests is the Kukui or candlenut.   Its pale green foliage gives the mountain sides sometimes a disagreeable look; though where it grows among the Ko trees, whose leaves are of a dark green, the contrast is not unpleasant.   From its abundance I supposed the candle-nut might be made an article of export; but the country is so rough that the gathering of the nuts is very laborious; and several persons who have experimented in expressing the oil from the nut have discovered that it did not pay cost. Only two thousand pounds of Kukui nuts were exported in 1872.

Sandal-wood was once a chief article of export. It grows on the higher mountain slopes, and is still collected, for 20,232 pounds were exported in 1872, and a small quantity is worked up in the Islands. The cocoa-nut is not planted in sufficient quantities to make it an article of commerce. Only 950 nuts were exported last year. Of pulu 421,227 pounds were shipped; this is a soft fuzz taken from the crown of a species of fern; it is used to stuff bedding, and is as warm, though not as durable, as feathers. Also 32,161 pounds of "fungus," a kind of toad-stool which grows on decaying wood, and is used in China as an article of food.

NATIVE HAY PEDDLER.

There has been no lack of ingenuity, enterprise, or industry among the inhabitants. The Government has imported several kinds of trees and plants, as the cinnamon, pepper, and allspice, but they have not prospered. Private effort has not been wanting either. But nature does not respond. Sugar and rice are and must it seems continue to be the staples of the Islands; and the culture of these products will in time be considerably increased.

This, it appears to me, decides the future of the Islands and the character of their population. A sugar or rice plantation needs at most three or four American workmen aside from the manager. The laboring force will be Hawaiians or Chinese; for they alone work cheaply, and will content themselves in the situation of plantation laborers. It is likely, therefore, that the future population of the Islands will consist largely, as it does now, of Hawaiians and Chinese, and a mixture of these two races; and, no doubt, these will live very happily there.

For farming, in the American sense of the word, the Islands are, as these facts show, entirely unfit. I asked again and again of residents this question: "Would you advise your friend in Massachusetts or Illinois, a farmer with two or three thousand dollars in money, to settle out here?" and received invariably the answer, "No; it would be wrong to do so." Transportation of farm products from island to island is too costly; there is no local market except Honolulu, and that is very rapidly and easily overstocked; Oregon or California potatoes are sold in the Islands at a price which would leave the local farmer without a profit. In short, farming is not a pursuit in the Islands. A farmer would not starve, for beef is cheap, and he could always raise vegetables enough for himself; but he would not get ahead. Moreover, perishable fruits, like the banana, have but a limited chance for export. The Islands, unluckily, lie to windward of California; and a sailing vessel, beating up to San Francisco, is very apt to make so long a passage that if she carries bananas they spoil on the way. Hence but 4520 bunches were shipped from the Islands in 1872 —which was all the monthly steamer had room for.

These circumstances seem to settle the question of annexation, which is sometimes discussed. To annex the Islands would be to burden ourselves with an outlying territory too distant to be cheaply defended; and containing a population which will never be homogeneous with our own; a country which would neither attract nor reward our industrious farmers and mechanics; which offers not the slightest temptation to emigration, except a most delightful climate, and which has, and must by its circumstances and natural formation continue to have, chiefly a mixed population of Chinese and other coolies, whom it is assuredly not to our interest to take into our family. I suppose it is a proper rule that we should not encumber ourselves with territory which by reason of unchangeable natural causes will repel our farmers and artisans, and which, therefore, will not become in time Americanized. If this is true, we ought not to annex the Hawaiian Islands.

Moreover, there is no excuse for annexation, in the desire of the people. The present Government is mild, just, and liked by the people. They can easily make it cheaper whenever they want to. The native people are very strongly opposed to annexation; they have a strong feeling of nationality, and considerable jealousy of foreign influence. Annexation to our own or any other country would be without their consent.

As to the residents of foreign birth, a few of them favor annexation to the United States; but only a few. A large majority would oppose it as strenuously as the native people. Most of the planters see that it would break up their labor system, demoralize the workmen, and probably for years check the production of sugar.

One thing is certain, however. If the Islands ever offer themselves to any foreign power, it will be to the United States. Their people, foreign as well as native, look to us as their neighbors and friends; and the king last summer blurted out one day when too much wine had made him imprudent, this truth: that if annexation came, it must be to the United States.

As I write a negotiation has been opened with the United States Government, for the purpose of offering us Pearl River in exchange for a reciprocity treaty. Pearl River is an extensive, deep, and well-protected bay, about ten miles from Honolulu. It would answer admirably for a naval station; and if the United States were a second-rate power likely to be bullied by other nations, we might need a naval station in the Pacific Ocean. In our present condition, when no single power dares to make war with us, and when, unless we become shamelessly aggressive, no alliance of European powers against us for purposes of war is possible, the chief use of distant naval stations appears to me to be as convenient out-of-the-way places for wasting the public money.

HULA-HULA, OR DANCING-GIRLS.

Pearl River would be an admirable spot for a dozen pleasant sinecures, and the expenditure of three or four millions of money. It seems to me, therefore, that it would be a dear bargain. For the accommodation of merchant steamers and ships and their repair, Honolulu offers sufficient facilities. There are ingenious American mechanics there who have even taken a frigate upon a temporary dry-dock, and repaired her hull.

But justice, kindly feeling, and a due regard for our future interests in the Pacific Ocean ought to induce us to establish at once a reciprocity treaty with the Hawaiian Government. We should lose but little revenue; and should make good that loss by the greater market which would be opened for our

7

own products, in the Islands.   Such a treaty would bring more capital to the Islands, increase their prosperity, and, at the same time, bind them still more closely and permanently to us.   It would pave the way to annexation, if that should ever become advisable.

The politics of the Hawaiian Kingdom are not very exciting.   In those fortunate Isles the Legislature troubles itself chiefly about the horse and dog tax. The late king, who was of an irascible temper, did not always treat his faithful Commons with conspicuous civility.   He sometimes told them that they had talked long enough and had better adjourn; and they usually took his advice. The present king, who belonged to "his majesty's opposition" during the late reign, has yet to develop his qualities as a ruler.   He has shown sound judgment in the nomination of his cabinet; and he is believed to have the welfare of the people at heart.   He is unmarried; but is not likely to marry; and he will probably nominate a successor from one of the chief or ruling families still remaining.   The list from which he can choose is not very long; and it is most probable, as this is written, that he will nominate to succeed him Mrs. Bernice Pauahi Bishop, wife of the present Minister of Foreign Affairs.   Mrs. Bishop is a lady of education and culture, of fine presence, every way fit to rule over her people; and her selection would be satisfactory to the foreign residents as well as to the best of the Hawaiian people.

HAWAIIAN STYLE OF DRESS.

CHAPTER VII.

THE LEPER ASYLUM ON MOLOKAI.

SO much has been said and written of late about the disease called leprosy
and its ravages in the Sandwich Islands that I had the curiosity to visit
the asylum for lepers at Molokai, where now very nearly all the people suffering from this disease have been collected, under a law which directs this
seclusion.

The steamer *Kilauea* left Honolulu one evening at half-past five o'clock, and
dropped several of us about two o'clock at night into a whale-boat near a point
on the lee side of Molokai. Here we were landed, and presently mounted
horses and rode seven or eight miles to the house of a German, Mr. Meyer,
who is the superintendent of the leper settlement, and also, I believe, of a cattle
farm which belongs to the heirs of the late king.

Mr. Meyer has lived on Molokai since 1853. He is married to a Hawaiian, and has a large family of sons and daughters who have been carefully and excellently brought up, I was told. Mrs. Meyer, who presided at breakfast, is one of those tall and grandly proportioned women whom you meet among the native population not infrequently, who enable you to realize how it was that in the old times the women exercised great influence in Hawaiian politics. She seemed born to command, and yet her benevolent countenance and friendly smile of welcome showed that she would probably rule gently.

From Mr. Meyer's we rode some miles again, until at last we dismounted at the top or edge of the great precipice, at the foot of which, two thousand feet below, lies the plain of Kalawao, occupied by the lepers. At the top we four dismounted, for the trail to the bottom, though not generally worse than the trail into the Yosemite Valley, has some places which would be difficult and, perhaps, dangerous for horses.

From the edge of the Pali or precipice the plain below, which contains about 16,000 acres, looks like an absolute flat, bounded on three sides by the blue Pacific. Horses awaited us at the bottom, and we soon discovered that the plain possessed some considerable elevations and depressions. It is believed to have been once the bottom of a vast crater, of which the Pali we clambered down formed one of the sides, the others having sunk beneath the ocean, leaving a few traces on one side. It has yet one considerable cone, a hill two hundred feet high, a well-preserved subsidiary crater, on whose bottom grass is now growing, while a little pool of salt water, which rises and falls with the tide, shows a connection with the ocean. A ride along the shore showed me also several other and smaller cones.

The whole great plain is composed of lava stones, and to one unfamiliar with the habits of these islanders would seem to be an absolutely sterile desert. Yet here lived, not very many years ago, a considerable population, who have left the marks of an almost incredible industry in numerous fields inclosed between walls of lava rock well laid up; and in what is yet stranger, long rows of stones, like the windrows of hay in a grass field at home, evidently piled there in order to secure room in the long, narrow beds thus partly cleared of lava which lay between, to plant sweet-potatoes. As I rode over the trails worn in the lava by the horses of the old inhabitants, I thought this plain realized the Vermonter's saying about a piece of particularly stony ground, that there was not room in the field to pile up the rocks it contained.

Yet on this apparently desert space, within a quarter of a century more than a thousand people lived contentedly and prosperously, after their fashion; and this though fresh water is so scarce that many of them must have carried their drinking water at least two or even three miles. And here now live, among the lepers, or rather a little apart from them at one side of the plain, about a hundred people, the remnant of the former population, who were too much attached to their homes to leave them, and accepted sentence of perpetual seclusion here, in common with the lepers, rather than exile to a less sterile part of the island.

When we had descended the cliff, a short ride brought us to the house of a luna, or local overseer, a native who is not a leper; and of this house, being uncontaminated, we took possession.

By a law of the kingdom it is made the duty of the Minister of the Interior, and under him of the Board of Health, to arrest every one suspected of leprosy; and if a medical examination shows that he has the disease, to seclude the leper upon this part of Molokai.

Leprosy, when it is beyond its very earliest stage, is held to be incurable. He who is sent to Molokai is therefore adjudged civilly dead. His wife, upon application to the proper court, is granted a decree of absolute divorce, and may marry again; his estate is administered upon as though he were dead. He is incapable of suing or being sued; and his dealings with the world thereafter are through and with the Board of Health alone.

In order that no doubtful cases may be sent to Molokai there is a hospital at Kalihi, near Honolulu, where the preliminary examinations are made, and where Dr. Trousseau, the skillful physician of the Board of Health, son of the famous Paris physician of the same name, retains people about whom he is uncertain.

The leper settlement at Molokai was begun so long ago as 1865; but the law requiring the seclusion of lepers was not enforced under the late king, who is believed to have been himself a sufferer from this disease, and who, at any rate, by constantly granting exemptions, discouraged the officers of the law. Since the accession of the present king, however, it has been rigidly enforced, and it is this which has caused the sudden and great outcry about leprosy, which has reached even to the United States, and has caused many people, it seems, to fear to come to the Islands, as though a foreigner would be liable to catch the disease.

You must understand that the native people have no fear of the disease. Until the accession of the present king lepers were commonly kept in the houses of their families, ate, drank, smoked, and slept with their own people, and had their wounds dressed at home. If the disease were quickly or readily contagious, it must have spread very rapidly in such conditions; and that it did not spread greatly or rapidly is one of the best proofs that it is not easily transmitted. When I remember how commonly, among the native people, a whole family smokes out of the same pipe, and sleeps together under the same tapa, I am surprised that so few have the disease.

There are at this time eight hundred and four persons, lepers, in the settlement, besides about one hundred non-lepers, who prefer to remain there in their ancient homes. Since January, 1865, when the first leper was sent here, one thousand one hundred and eighty have been received, of whom seven hundred and fifty-eight were males and four hundred and twenty-two females. Of this number three hundred and seventy-three have died, namely, two hundred and forty-six males and one hundred and twenty-seven females. Forty-two died between April 1 and August 13 of the present year. The proportion of women to men is smaller than I thought; and there are about fifty leper children, between the ages of six and thirteen. Lepers are sterile, and no children have been born at the asylum.

So great has been the energy and the vigilance of the Board of Health and its physician, Dr. Trousseau, that there are not now probably fifty lepers at large on all the islands, and these are persons who have been hidden away in the mountains by their relatives. In fact if there was ever any risk to foreign visitors from leprosy, this is now reduced to the minimum; and as the disease is not caused by the climate, and can be got, as the widest experience and the best authorities agree, only by intimate contact, united with peculiar predisposition of the blood, there is not the least ground for any foreign visitor to dread it.

When a leper is sent to Molokai, the Government provides him a house, and he receives, if an adult, three pounds of paiai or unmixed poi, per day, and three pounds of salt salmon, or five pounds of fresh beef, per week. Beef is generally preferred.

They are allowed and encouraged to cultivate land, and their products are bought by the Health Board; but the disease quickly attacks the feet and hands, and disables the sufferers from labor.

There are two churches in the settlement, one Protestant, with a native pastor, and one Catholic, with a white priest, a young Frenchman, who has had the courage to devote himself to his co-religionists.

There is a store, kept by the Board of Health, the articles in which are sold for cost and expenses. The people receive a good deal of money from their relatives at home, which they spend in this store. The Government also supplies all the lepers with clothing; and there is a post-office. The little schooner which carried me back to Honolulu bore over two hundred letters, the weekly mail from the leper settlement.

For the bad cases there is a hospital, an extensive range of buildings, where one hundred patients lay when I visited it. These, being helpless, are attended by other lepers, and receive extra rations of tea, sugar, bread, rice, and other food.

Almost every one strong enough to ride has a horse; for the Hawaiians can not well live without horses. Some of the people live on the shore and make salt, which you see stored up in pandanus bags under the shelter of lava bubbles. When I was there a number were engaged in digging a ditch in which to lay an iron pipe, intended to convey fresh water to the denser part of the settlement.

Such is the life on the leper settlement of Molokai; a precipitous cliff at its back two thousand feet high; the ocean, looking here bluer and lovelier than ever I saw it look elsewhere on three sides of it; the soft trade-wind blowing across the lava-covered plain; eternal sunshine; a mild air; horses; and the weekly excitement of the arrival of the schooner from Honolulu with letters. There is sufficient employment for those who can and like to work—and the Hawaiian is not an idle creature; and altogether it is a very contented and happy community. The Islander has strong feelings and affections, but they do not last long, and the people here seemed to me to have made themselves quickly at home. I saw very few sad faces, and there were mirth and laughter, and ready service and pleasant looks all around us, as we rode or walked over the settlement.

And now, you will ask, what does a leper look like? Well, in the first place, he is not the leper of the Scriptures; nor, I am assured, is the disease at all like that which is said to occur in China. Indeed, the poor Chinese have been unjustly accused of bringing this disease to the Islands. With the first ship-load of Chinese brought to these Islands came two lepers "white as snow," having, that is to say, a disease very different from that which now is called leprosy here. They were not allowed to land, but were sent back in the ship which brought them out.

The Hawaiian leprosy, on the other hand, has been known here for a quarter of a century, and men died of it before the first Chinese were brought hither. The name Mai-Pakeh was given it by an accident, a foreigner saying to a native that he had a disease such as they had in China. There are but six Chinese in the Molokai leper settlement, and there are three white men there.

The leprosy of the Islands is a disease of the blood, and not a skin disease. It can be caught only, I am told, by contact of an abraded surface with the matter of the leprous sore; and doubtless the familiar habit of the people, of many smoking the same pipe, has done much to disseminate it.

Its first noticeable signs are a slight puffiness under the eyes, and a swelling of the lobes of the ears. To the practiced eyes of Dr. Trousseau these signs were apparent where I could not perceive them until he laid his finger on them. Next follow symptoms which vary greatly in different individuals; but a marked sign is the retraction of the fingers, so that the hand comes to resemble a bird's claw. In some cases the face swells in ridges, leaving deep furrows between; and these ridges are shiny and without feeling, so that a pin may be stuck into one without giving pain to the person. The features are thus horribly deformed in many instances; I saw two or three young boys of twelve who looked like old men of sixty. In some older men and women, the face was at first sight revolting and baboon-like; I say at first sight, for on a second look the mild sad eye redeemed the distorted features; it was as though the man were looking out of a horrible mask.

At a later stage of the disease these rugous swellings break open into festering sores; the nose and even the eyes are blotted out, and the body becomes putrid.

In other cases the extremities are most severely attacked. The fingers, after being drawn in like claws, begin to fester. They do not drop off, but seem rather to be absorbed, the nails following the stumps down; and I actually saw finger-nails on a hand that had no fingers. The nails were on the knuckles; the fingers had all rotted away.

The same process of decay goes on with the toes; in some cases the whole foot had dropped away; and in many the hands and feet were healed over, the fingers and toes having first dropped off. But the healing of the sore is but temporary, for the disease presently breaks out again.

Emaciation does not seem to follow. I saw very few wasted forms, and those only in the hospitals and among the worst cases. There appears to be an astonishing tenacity of life, and I was told they mostly choke to death, or fall into a fever caused by swallowing the poison of their sores when these attack the nose and throat.

Those diseased give out soon a very sickening odor, and I was much obliged to a thoughtful man in the settlement, who commanded the lepers who had gathered together to hear an address from the doctor to form to leeward of us. I expected to be sickened by the hospitals; but these are so well kept, and are so easily ventilated by the help of the constantly blowing trade-wind, that the odor was scarcely perceptible in them.

You will, perhaps, ask how the disease is contracted. I doubt if any one knows definitely. But from all I heard, I judge that there must be some degree of predisposition toward it in the person to be contaminated. I believe I have Dr. Trousseau's leave to say that the contact of a wounded or abraded surface with the matter of a leprous sore will convey the disease; this is, of course, inoculation; and he seemed to think no other method of contamination probable. I was careful to provide myself with a pair of gloves when I visited the settlement, to protect myself in case I should be invited to shake hands; but I noticed that the doctor fearlessly shook hands with some of the worst cases, even where the fingers were suppurating and wrapped in rags.

There are several women on the Islands, confirmed lepers, whose husbands are at home and sound; one, notably, where the husband is a white man. On the other hand, a woman was pointed out to me who had had three husbands, each of whom in a short time after marrying her became a leper. There are children lepers, whose parents are not lepers; and there are parents lepers, whose children are at home and healthy.

There are three white men on the island, lepers, two of them in a very bad state. So far as I could learn the particulars of their previous history, they had lived flagitiously loose lives; such as must have corrupted their blood long before they became lepers. In some other cases of native lepers I came upon similar histories; and while I do not believe that every case, or indeed perhaps a majority of cases, involves such a previous career of vice, I should say that this is certainly a strongly predisposing cause.

As to the danger of infection to a foreign visitor, there is absolutely none, unless he should undertake to live in native fashion among the natives, smoking out of their pipes, sleeping under their tapas, and eating their food with them; and even in such an extreme case his risk would be very slight now, so thoroughly has the disease been "stamped out" by the energetic action of Mr. Hall, the Minister of the Interior, Mr. Samuel G. Wilder, the head of the Board of Health, and Dr. Trousseau, its physician. In short, there is no more risk of a white resident or traveler catching leprosy in the Hawaiian Islands than in the city or State of New York.

I have heard one reason given why this disease has been more frequent in the last ten years. Ten or twelve years ago the Islands were visited by small-pox. This disease made terrible ravages, and the Government at once ordered

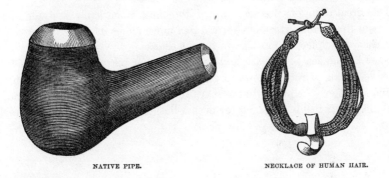

NATIVE PIPE.   NECKLACE OF HUMAN HAIR.

the people to be vaccinated. There seems to be no doubt that the vaccine matter used was often taken from persons not previously in sound health; this was perhaps unavoidable; but intelligent men, long resident in the Islands, believe that vaccination thus performed with impure matter had a bad effect upon the people, leaving traces of a resulting corruption of their blood.

The choice of the plain of Kalawao as the spot on which to seclude the lepers from all the Islands was very happy. It can not be said that to an agile native the place is inaccessible, for there are, no doubt, several points in the great precipice where men and women could make their way down or up; and there are instances of women swimming around the precipitous and surf-beaten shore, seven or eight miles, to reach husbands or friends in the settlement to whom they were devotedly attached. But it is easily guarded, and, for all practical purposes, the seclusion is perfect.

A singular tradition, related to me on the island, points to its use for such a purpose, and gives a sad significance to the leper settlement. It is said that in the time of the first Kamehameha, the conqueror and hero of his race, upon an occasion when he visited Molokai, an old sorceress or priestess sent him word that she had made a garment for him—a robe of honor—which she desired him to come and get. He returned for answer a command that she should bring it to him; and when the old hag appeared, the king desired her to tell him something of the future. She replied that he would conquer all the Islands, and rule over them but a brief time; that his own posterity would die out; and that finally all his race would be gathered together on Molokai; and that this small island would be large enough to hold them all.

It is probable, of course, that this tale is of recent origin, and that no priestess of Kamehameha the First possessed so fatal and accurate a gift of prophecy; but the tale, told me in the midst of the leper asylum, pointed to the gloomy end of the race with but too plain a finger. The Hawaiians, once so numerous as to occupy almost all the habitable parts of all the Islands, have so greatly decreased that they might almost find their support on the little island of Molokai alone. Happily the decrease has now ceased.

The great Pali of Molokai, one of the most remarkable and picturesque sights of the Islands, stretches for a dozen miles along its windward coast. It is a sheer precipice, in most parts from a thousand to two thousand feet high, washed by the sea at its base, and having, in most parts, not a trace of beach. This vast wall of rock is an impressive sight; here the shipwrecked mariner would be utterly helpless; but would drown, not merely in sight of land, but with his hands vainly grasping for even a bush, or root, or a projecting rock.

NORTHERN CALIFORNIA:

ITS AGRICULTURAL VALLEYS, DAIRIES, FORESTS, FRUIT-FARMS, ETC.

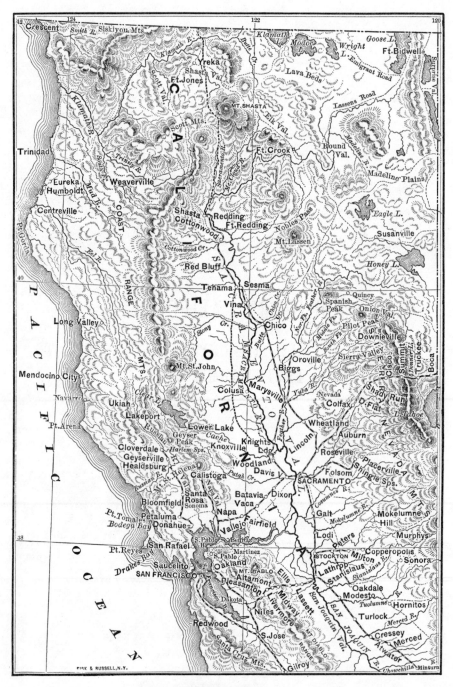

NORTHERN CALIFORNIA.

A CALIFORNIA VINEYARD.

CHAPTER I.

THE SACRAMENTO VALLEY: A GENERAL VIEW, WITH HINTS TO TOURISTS AND SPORTSMEN.

THE State of California extends over somewhat more than ten degrees of latitude. If it lay along the Atlantic as it lies along the Pacific coast, its boundaries would include the whole shore-line from Cape Cod to Hilton Head, and its limits would take in the greater portion of ten of the original States.

It contains two great mountain ranges—the Sierra Nevada and the Coast Range. These, running parallel through the State, approach each other so closely at the south as to leave only the narrow Tejon Pass between them; while at the north they also come together, Mount Shasta rearing its splendid snow-covered summit over the two mountain chains where they are joined.

Inclosed within these mountain ranges lies a long, broad, fertile valley, which was once, no doubt, a great inland sea. It still contains in the southern part three considerable lakes—the Tulare, Kern, and Buena Vista—and is now drained from the south by the San Joaquin River, flowing out of these lakes, and from the north by the Sacramento, which rises near the base of Mount Shasta. These two rivers, the one flowing north, the other south, join a few miles below Sacramento, and empty their waters into the bay of San Francisco.

That part of the great inland plain of California which is drained by the Sacramento is called after its river. It is more thickly inhabited than the southern or San Joaquin Valley, partly because the foot-hills on its eastern side were the scene of the earliest and longest continued, as well as the most successful, mining operations; partly because the Sacramento River is navigable for a longer distance than the San Joaquin, and thus gave facilities for transportation which the lower valley had not; and, finally, because the Sacramento Valley had a railroad completed through its whole extent some years earlier than the San Joaquin Valley.

The climate of the Sacramento Valley does not differ greatly from that of the San Joaquin, yet there are some important distinctions. Lying further north, it has more rain; in the upper part of the valley they sometimes see snow; there is not the same necessity for irrigation as in the lower valley; and though oranges flourish in Marysville, and though the almond does well as far north as Chico, yet the cherry and the plum take the place of the orange and lemon; and men build their houses somewhat more solidly than further south.

The romance of the early gold discovery lies mostly in the Sacramento Valley and the adjacent foot-hills. Between Sacramento and Marysville lay Sutter's old fort, and near Marysville is Sutter's farm, where you may still see his groves of fig-trees, under whose shade the country people now hold their picnics; his orchards, which still bear fruit; and his house, which is now a country tavern.

Of all his many leagues of land the old man has, I believe, but a few acres left; and of the thousands who now inhabit and own what once was his, not a dozen would recognize him, and many probably scarcely know his name. His riches melted away, as did those of the great Spanish proprietors; and he who only a quarter of a century ago owned a territory larger than some States, and counted his cattle by the thousands—if, indeed, he ever counted them—who lived in a fort like a European noble of the feudal times, had an army of Indians at his command, and occasionally made war on the predatory tribes who were his neighbors, now lives upon a small annuity granted him by the State of California. He saved little, I have heard, from the wreck of his fortunes; and of all who were with him in his earlier days, but one, so far as I know— General Bidwell, of Chico, an able and honorable gentleman, once Sutter's manager—had the ability to provide for the future by retaining possession of his own estate of twenty thousand acres, now by general consent the finest farm in California.

As you go north in California the amount of rain-fall increases. In San Diego County they are happy with ten inches per annum, and fortunate if they get five; in Santa Barbara, twelve and a half inches insure their crops;

the Sacramento Valley has an average rain-fall of about twenty inches, and eighteen inches insure them a full crop on soil properly prepared. In 1873 they had less, yet the crops did well wherever the farmers had summer-fallowed the land. This practice is now very general, and is necessary, in order that the grain may have the advantage of the early rains. When a farmer plows and prepares his land in the spring, lets it lie all summer, and sows his grain in November just as the earliest rain begins, he need not fear for his crop.

There is less difference in climate than one would suppose between the Sacramento and the San Joaquin valleys. Cattle and sheep live out-of-doors, and support themselves all the year round in the Shasta Valley on the north as constantly as in Los Angelos or any other of the southern counties. The seasons are a little later north than south, but the difference is slight; and as

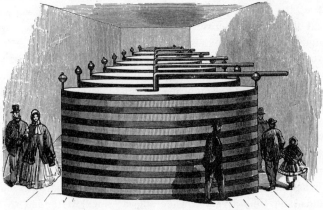

WINE VATS.

far north as Red Bluff, in the interior, they begin their harvest earlier than in Monterey County, far south but on the coast. Snow rarely lies on the ground in the northern counties more than a day. The best varieties of the foreign grapes are hardy everywhere. Light frosts come in December; and in the flower-gardens the geranium withers to the ground, but springs up from the roots again in March. The eucalyptus flourishes wherever it has been planted in Northern California; and as far north as Redding, at the head of the valley, the mercury very rarely falls below twenty-five degrees, and remains there but a few hours.

As you travel from Marysville, either northward or southward, you will see before and around you a great wide plain, bounded on the west by the blue out-lines of the Coast Range, and on the east by the foot-hills of the Sierra: a great level, over which as far as your eye can reach are scattered groves of grand and picturesque white oaks, which relieve the solitude of the plain, and make it resemble a well-planted park. Wherever the valley is settled, you will see neat board fences, roomy barns, and farm-houses nestling among trees, and flanked by young orchards. You will not find a great variety of crops, for wheat and barley are the staple products of this valley; and though the farms here are in general of 640 acres or less, there are not wanting some of those immense estates for which California is famous; and a single farmer in this valley is said to have raised on his own land last year one-twentieth of the entire wheat crop of the State.

Northwest of Marysville the plain is broken by a singularly lovely range of mountains, the Buttes. They rise abruptly from the plain, and their peaks reach from two to three thousand feet high. It is an extremely pretty miniature mountain range, having its peaks, passes, and cañons—all the features of the Sierra—and it is well worth a visit. Butte is a word applied to such isolated mountains, which do not form part of a chain, and which are not uncommon west of the Mississippi. Shasta is called a butte; Lassen's Peaks are buttes; and the traveler across the continent hears the word frequently applied to mountain. It is pronounced with the u long.

Along the banks of the Sacramento there are large quantities of land which is annually overflowed by the river, and much of which is still only used for pasturage during the dry season, when its grasses support large herds of cattle and sheep, which are driven to the uplands when the rains begin to fall. But much of this swamp and tule land has been drained and diked, and is now used for farm land. It produces heavy crops of wheat, and its reclamation has been, and continues to be, one of the successful speculations in land in this State. It will not be long before the shores of the Sacramento and its tributaries will be for many miles so diked that these rivers will never break their bounds, and thus a very considerable area will be added to the fertile farming lands of the State.

Already, however, the Yuba, the Feather, and the American rivers, tributaries of the Sacramento, have been leveed at different points for quite another reason. These rivers, once clear and rapidly flowing within deep banks, are now turbid, in many places shallow, and their bottoms have been raised from twenty to thirty feet by the accumulation of the washings from the gold mines in the foot-hills. It is almost incredible the change the miners have thus produced in the short space of a quarter of a century. The bed of the Yuba has been raised thirty feet in that time; and seeing what but a handful of men have effected in so short a period, the work of water in the denudation of mountains, and the scouring out or filling up of valleys during geological periods becomes easily comprehensible.

All our Northern fruits grow thriftily in the Sacramento Valley, and also the almond, of which thousands of trees have been planted, and a few considerable orchards are already in bearing. The cherry and the plum do remarkably

well, the latter fruit having as yet no curculio or blight; and the canning
and drying of peaches, plums, apricots, nectarines, and pears are already, as I
shall show in detail farther on, a considerable as well as very profitable business. Dried plums, in particular, sell at a price which
makes the orchards of this fruit very valuable. Excellent raisins have also been made, and they sell in the
open market of San Francisco for a price very little less
than that of the best Malaga raisins. The climate, with
its long dry summer, is very favorable to the drying and
curing of every fruit: no expensive houses, no ovens or
other machinery, are needed. The day is not distant
when the great Sacramento plain will be a vast orchard,
and the now unoccupied foot-hills will furnish a large

TRAINING A VINE.

part of the raisins consumed in the United States. For the present the population is scant, and cattle, horses, and especially sheep, roam over hundreds of
thousands of acres of soil which needs only industrious farmers to make it
bloom into a garden.

The farmer in this State is a person of uncommon resources and ingenuity.
I think he uses his brains more than our Eastern farmers. I do not mean to
say that he lives better, for he does not. His house is often shabby, even
though he be a man of wealth, and his table is not unfrequently without milk;
he buys his butter with his canned vegetables in San Francisco, and bread and
mutton are the chief part of his living, both being universally good here. But
in managing his land he displays great enterprise, and has learned how to fit
his efforts to the climate and soil.

The gathering of the wheat crop goes on in all the valley lands with headers, and you will find on all the farms in the Sacramento Valley the best labor-
saving machinery employed, and human labor, which is always the most costly,
put to its best and most profitable uses. They talk here of steam-plows and
steam-wagons for common roads, and I have no doubt the steam-plow will be
first practically and generally used, so far as the United States are concerned,
in these Californian valleys, where I have seen furrows two miles long, and ten
eight-horse teams following each other with gang-plows.

Withal, they are somewhat ruthless in their pursuit of a wheat crop. You
may see a farmer who plows hundreds of acres, but he will have his wheat
growing up to the edge of his veranda. If he keeps a vegetable garden, he
has performed a heroic act of self-denial; and as for flowers, they must grow
among the wheat or nowhere.

Moreover, while he has great ingenuity in his methods, the farmer of the
Sacramento plain has but little originality in his planting. He raises wheat
and barley. He might raise a dozen, a score, of other products, many more
profitable, and all obliging him to cultivate less ground, but it is only here and

8

there you meet with one who appreciates the remarkable capabilities of the soil and climate. Near Tehama some Chinese have in the last two years grown large crops of pea-nuts, and have, I was told, realized handsome profits from a nut which will be popular in America, I suppose, as long as there is a pit or a gallery in a theatre; but the pea-nut makes a valuable oil, and as it produces enormously here, it will some day be raised for this use, as much as for the benefit of the old women who keep fruit-stands on the street corners. It would not be surprising if the Chinese, who continue to come over to California in great numbers, should yet show the farmers here what can be done on small farms by patient and thorough culture. As yet they confine their culture of land mainly to vegetable gardens.

To the farmer the valley and foot-hill lands of the Sacramento will be the most attractive; and there are still here thousands of acres in the hands of the Government and the railroad company to be obtained so cheaply that, whether for crops or for grazing, it will be some time before the mountainous lands and the pretty valleys they contain, north of Redding, the present terminus of the railroad, will attract settlers. But for the traveler the region north of Redding to the State line offers uncommon attractions.

The Sacramento Valley closes in as you journey northward; and at Red Bluff, which is the head of navigation on the river, you have a magnificent view of Lassen's Peaks on the east—twin peaks, snow-clad, and rising high out of the plain—and also of the majestic snow-covered crag which is known as Shasta Butte, which towers high above the mountains to the north, and, though here 120 miles off, looks but a day's ride away.

Redding, thirty miles north from Shasta, lies at the head of the Sacramento Valley. From there a line of stage-coaches proceeds north into Oregon, through the mass of mountains which separates the Sacramento Valley in California from the Willamette Valley in Oregon. The stage-road passes through a very varied and picturesque country, one which few pleasure travelers see, and which yet is as well worth a visit as any part of the western coast. The Sacramento River, which rises in a large spring near the base of Mount Shasta, has worn its way through the high mountains, and rushes down for nearly a hundred miles of its course an impetuous, roaring mountain stream, abounding in trout at all seasons, and in June, July, and August filled with salmon which have come up here through the Golden Gates from the ocean to spawn. The stage-road follows almost to its source the devious course of the river, and you ride along sometimes nearly on a level with the stream, and again on a road-bed cut out of the steep mountain side a thousand or fifteen hundred feet above the river; through fine forests of sugar-pines and yellow pines many of which come almost up to the dimensions of the great sequoias.

The river and its upper tributaries abound in trout, and this region is famous among Californian sportsmen for deer and fish. Many farm-houses along the road accommodate travelers who desire to stay to enjoy the fine scenery, and to hunt and fish; and a notable stopping-place is Fry's Soda Spring, fourteen hours by stage from Redding, kept by Isaac Fry and his excellent wife— a clean, comfortable little mountain inn, where you get good and well-cooked food, and where you will find what your stage ride will make welcome to you —a comfortable bath. The river is too cold for bathing here in the mountains because of the snow-water of which it is composed. About ten miles south of Fry's lies Castle Rock, a remarkable and most picturesque mountain of white granite, bare for a thousand feet below its pinnacled summit, which you see as you drive past it on the stage.

Fry's lies in a deep cañon, with a singular, almost precipitous, mountain opposite the house, which terminates in a sharp ridge at the top, one of those "knife-edge" ridges of which Professor Whitney and Clarence King often speak in their descriptions of Sierra scenery. If you are a mountain climber, you have here an opportunity for an adventure, and an excellent guide in Mr.

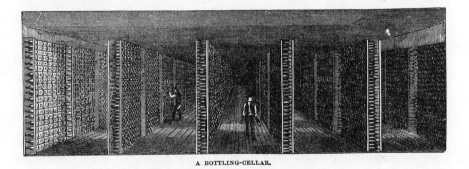

A BOTTLING-CELLAR.

Fry, who told me that this ridge is sharp enough to straddle, and that on the other side is an almost precipitous descent, with a fine lake in the distance. If you wish to hunt deer or bear, you will find in Fry an expert and experienced hunter. He has a tame doe, which, I was told, is better than a dog to mark game on a hunt, its sharp ears and nose detecting the presence of game at a great distance. If you are a fisherman, there are within three minutes' walk of the house pools abounding in trout, and you may fish up and down the river as far as you please, with good success everywhere. In June and July, when the salmon come up to spawn, they, too, lie in the deepest pools, and with salmon eggs for bait you may, if you are expert enough with your rod, take many a fat salmon.

It is astonishing to see how the salmon crowd the river at the spawning season. The Indians then gather from a considerable distance, to spear and trap these fish, which they dry for winter use; and you will see at this season many picturesque Indian camps along the river. They set a crotch of two sticks in a salmon pool, and lay a log from the shore to this crotch. Upon this log the Indian walks out, with a very long spear, two-pronged at the end and there armed with two bone spear-heads, which are fastened to the shaft of the spear by very strong cord, usually made of deer's sinews. The Indian stands very erect and in a really fine attitude, and peers into the black pool until his eye catches the silver sheen of a salmon. Then he darts, and instantly you see a commotion in the water as he hauls up toward the surface a struggling twenty-five or thirty pound fish. The bone spear heads, when they have penetrated the salmon, come off from the spear, and the fish is held by the cord. A squaw stands ready on the shore to haul him in, and he is beaten over the head with a club until he ceases to struggle, then cleaned, and roasted on hot stones. When the meat is done and dry it is picked off the bones, and the squaws rub it to a fine powder between their hands, and in this shape it is packed for future use.

From one of these pools a dozen Indian spearmen frequently draw out four hundred salmon in a day, and this fish forms an important part of their food. Of course they kill a great many thousand female salmon during the season; but so far, I believe, this murderous work has not been found to decrease the number of the fish which annually enter the river from the ocean, and go up to its head waters to spawn.

If you visit this region during the last of June or in July, you may watch the salmon spawning, a most curious and remarkable sight. The great fish then leave the deep pools in which they have been quietly lying for some weeks before, and fearlessly run up on the shallow ripples. Here, animated by a kind of fury, they beat the sand off the shoals with their tails, until often a female salmon thus labors till her tail fins are entirely worn off. She then deposits her eggs upon the coarse gravel, and the greedy trout, which are extravagantly fond of salmon eggs, rush up to eat them as the poor mother lays them. They are, I believe, watched and beaten off by the male salmon, which accompanies the female for this purpose. When the female salmon has deposited her eggs, and the male salmon has done his part of the work, the two often bring stones of considerable size in their mouths to cover up the eggs and protect them from the predatory attacks of the trout. .

And thereupon, according to the universal testimony of the fishermen of these waters, the salmon dies. I was assured that the dead bodies often cumber the shore after the spawning season is over; and the mountaineers all assert that the salmon, having once spawned up here, does not go down to the ocean again. They hold that the young salmon stay in the upper waters for a year, and go to sea about eighteen months after hatching; and it is not uncommon, I believe, for fishermen hereabouts to catch grilse weighing from two to four pounds. These bite sometimes at the fly. The salmon bite, too, when much smaller, for I caught one day a young salmon not more than six inches long. This little fellow was taken with a bait of salmon eggs, and his bright silvery sides made him quite different from the trout which I was catching out of the same pool. His, head, also had something of the fierce, predatory, hawk-like form which the older salmon's has.

Fry is an excellent fisherman himself, and knows all the best pools within reach of his house, and, if you are a mountaineer, will take you a dozen miles through the woods to other streams, where you may fish and hunt for days or weeks with great success, for these woods and waters are as yet visited by but few sportsmen.

And if you happen to come upon Indian fishermen on your way—they are all peaceful hereabouts—you may get the noble red man's opinion of the great Woman Question. As I stood at the road-side one day I saw an Indian emerging from the woods, carrying his rifle and his pipe. Him followed, at a respectful distance, his squaw, a little woman not bigger than a twelve-year-old boy; and *she* carried, first, a baby; second, three salmon, each of which weighed not less than twenty pounds; third, a wild goose, weighing six or eight pounds; finally, a huge bundle of some kind of greens. This cumbrous and heavy load the Indian had lashed together with strong thongs, and the squaw carried it on her back, suspended by a strap which passed across her forehead.

When an Indian kills a deer he loads it on the back of his squaw to carry home. Arrived there, he lights his pipe, and she skins and cleans the animal, cuts off a piece sufficient for dinner, lights a fire, and cooks the meat. This done, the noble red man, who has calmly or impatiently contemplated these labors of the wife of his bosom, lays down his pipe and eats his dinner. When he is done, the woman, who has waited at one side, sits down to hers and eats what he has left.

" Who would be free, themselves must strike the blow." Miss Anthony and Mrs. Cady Stanton have good missionary ground among these Indians. One wonders in what language an Indian brave courts the young squaw whom he wishes to marry ; what promises he makes her ; what hopes he holds out ; with what enticing views of wedded bliss he lures the Indian maiden to the altar or whatever may be the Digger substitute for that piece of church furniture. One wonders that the squaws have not long ago combined and struck for at least moderately decent treatment ; that marriages have not ceased among them ; that there has not arisen among the Diggers, the Pit River Indians, and all the Indian tribes, some woman capable of leading her sex in a rebellion.

But, to tell the truth, the Indian women are homely to the last degree. " Ugly," said an Oregonian to me, as we contemplated a company of squaws— " ugly is too mild a word to apply to such faces ;" and he was right. Broad-faced, flat-nosed, small-eyed, unkempt, frowzy, undersized, thickset, clumsy, they have not a trace of beauty about them, either young or old. They are just useful, nothing more ; and as you look at them and at the burdens they bear, you

wonder whether, when the Woman's Rights movement has succeeded, and when
women, dressed like frights in such Bloomer costume as may then be prescribed,
go out to their daily toil like men, and on an equality with men—when they
have cast off the beauty which is so scornfully spoken of in the conventions,
and have secured their rights—whether they will be any better off than these
squaws. When you have thoughtfully regarded the Indian woman perhaps

INDIAN RANCHERIA.

you will agree with Gail Hamilton that it is woman's first duty to be useless;
for it is plain that here, as in a higher civilization, when women consent to
work as men, they are sure to have the hardest work and the poorest pay.

As you ascend the Sacramento you near Mount Shasta, and when you reach
Strawberry Valley, a pretty little mountain vale, you are but a short ride from
its base. It is from this point that tourists ascend the mountain. You can

hire horses, guides, and a camp outfit here, and the adventure requires three days. You ride up to the snow-line the first day, ascend to the top the following morning, descend to your camp in the afternoon, and return to the valley on the third day. Mount Shasta has a glacier, almost, but not quite, the only one, I believe, within the limits of the United States. The mountain is an extinct volcano. Its summit is composed of lava, and if your eye is familiar with the peculiar shape of volcanic peaks, you can easily trace the now broken lines of this old crater as you view the mountain from the Shasta plain on the north.

There are many extremely pretty valleys scattered through these mountains, and these are used by small farmers, and by sheep and cattle owners who in the winter take their stock into the lower valleys, but ascend into the mountains in May, and remain until October. This is also a timber region, and as it is well watered by permanent streams you see frequent saw-mills, and altogether more improvement than one expects to find. But, proceeding further north you come upon a large plain, the Shasta Valley, in which lies the considerable town of Yreka, notable during the last winter and spring as the point from which news came to us about the Modoc war.

From Yreka you may easily visit the celebrated "lava beds," where the Indians made so stubborn and long-continued a defense against the United States troops; and at Yreka you may hear several opinions upon the merits of the Modocs and their war. You will hear, for instance, that the Indians were stirred up to hostilities by mischievous and designing whites, that white men were not wanting to supply them with arms and ammunition, and that, had it not been for the unscrupulous management of some greedy and wicked whites, we should not have been horrified by the shocking incidents of this costly Indian trouble, in which the United States Government for six months waged war against forty-six half-starved Modocs.

The Shasta Valley is an extensive plain, chiefly used at present as a range for cattle and sheep. But its soil is fertile, and the valley contains some good farms. Beyond Yreka gold mining is pursued, and, indeed, almost the whole of the mountain region north of Redding yields "the color;" and at many points along the Upper Sacramento and the mountain streams which fall into it, gold is mined profitably. One day, at the Soda Spring, several of us asked Mr. Fry whether he could find gold near the river. He took a pan, and digging at random in his orchard, washed out three or four specks of gold; and he related that when he was planting this orchard ten years ago he found gold in the holes he dug for his apple-trees. But he is an old miner, and experience has taught him that a good apple orchard is more profitable, in the long run, than a poor gold mine.

A large part of the Sacramento Valley is still used for grazing purposes, but the farmers press every year more and more upon the graziers; and the policy of the Government in holding its own lands within what are called "railroad limits"—that is to say, within twenty miles on each side of the railroad—for settlement under the pre-emption and homestead laws, as well as the policy of the railroad company in selling its lands, the alternate sections for twenty miles on each side of the road, on easy terms and with long credit to actual settlers, prevents land monopoly in this region. There is room, and cheap and fertile land, for an immense population of industrious farmers, who can live here in a mild climate, and till a fertile soil, and who need only intelligence and enterprise to raise profitably raisins, orchard fruits, castor-oil, peanuts, silk, and a dozen other products valuable in the world's commerce, and not produced elsewhere in this country so easily. It is still in this region a time of large farms poorly tilled; but I believe that small farms, from 160 to 320 acres, will prove far more profitable in the end.

The progress of California in material enterprises is something quite wonderful and startling. A year brings about changes for which one can hardly look in ten years. It is but eighteen months ago that the idea of a system of irrigation, to include the whole of the San Joaquin Valley, was broached, and then the most sanguine of the projectors thought that to give their enterprise a fair start would require years, and a great number of shrewd men believed the whole scheme visionary. But a few experiments showed to land-owners and capitalists the enormous advantages of irrigation, and now this scheme has sufficient capital behind it, and large land-holders are offering subsidies and mortgaging their lands to raise means to hasten the completion of the canal. Two years ago the reclamation of the tule lands, though begun, advanced slowly, and arguments were required to convince men that tule land was a safe investment. But this year eight hundred miles of levee will be completed, and thousands of acres will bear wheat next harvest which were overflowed eighteen months ago. Two years ago the question whether California could produce good raisins could not be answered; but last fall raisins which sold in the San Francisco market beside the best Malagas were cured by several persons, and it is now certain that this State can produce—and from its poorest side-hill lands—raisins enough to supply the whole Union. Not a year passes but some new and valuable product of the soil is naturalized in this State; and one who has seen the soil and who knows the climate of the two great valleys, who sees that within five, or, at most, ten years all their overflowed lands will be diked and reclaimed, and all their dry lands will be irrigated, and who has, besides, seen how wide is the range of products which the soil and climate yield, comes at last to have what seems to most Eastern people an exaggerated view of the future of California.

But, in truth, it is not easy to exaggerate, for the soil in the great valleys is deep and of extraordinary fertility; there are no forests to clear away, and farms lie ready-made to the settlers' hands; the range of products includes all those of the temperate zone and many of the torrid; the climate is invigorating, and predisposes to labor; and the seasons are extraordinarily favorable to the labors of the farmer and gardener. The people have not yet settled down to hard work. There are so many chances in life out there that men become overenterprising — a speculative spirit invades even the farm-house; and as a man can always live — food being so abundant and the climate so kindly—and as the population is as yet sparse, men are tempted to go from one avocation to another, to do many things superficially, and to look for sudden fortunes by the chances of a shrewd venture, rather than be content to live by patient and continued labor. This, however, is the condition of all new countries; it will pass away as population becomes more dense. And, meantime California has gifts of nature which form a solid substratum upon which will, in a few years, be built up a community productive far beyond the average of wealthy or productive communities. This is my conclusion after seeing all parts of this State more in detail than perhaps any one man has taken the trouble to examine it.

PIEDRAS BLANCAS.

CHAPTER II.

WINE AND RAISINS—PROFITS OF DRYING FRUITS.

I HAVE now seen the grape grow in almost every part of California where wine is made. The temptation to a new settler in this State is always strong to plant a vineyard; and I am moved, by much that I have seen, to repeat here publicly advice I have often given to persons newly coming into the State: Do not make wine. I remember a wine-cellar, cheaply built, but with substantial and costly casks, containing (because the vineyard was badly placed) a mean, thin, fiery wine; and on a pleasant sunny afternoon, around these casks, a group of tipsy men—hopeless, irredeemable beasts, with nothing much to do except to encourage each other to another glass, and to wonder at the Eastern man who would not drink. There were two or three Indians staggering about the door; there was swearing and filthy talk inside; there was a pretentious tasting of this, that, and the other cask by a parcel of sots, who in their hearts would have preferred "forty-rod" whisky. And a little way off there was a house with women and children in it, who had only to look out of the door to see this miserable sight of husband, father, friends, visitors, and hired men spending the afternoon in getting drunk.

I do not want any one to understand that every vineyard is a nest of drunkards, for this is not true. In the Napa and Sonoma valleys, in the foot-hills of the Sierra, at Anaheim and elsewhere in the southern country, you may find many men cultivating the grape and making wine in all soberness. But everywhere, and in my own experience

POINT ARENA LIGHT-HOUSE.

nearly as often, you will see the proprietor, or his sons or his hired men, bearing the marks of strong drink; and too often, if you come unexpectedly, you will see some poor wretch in the wine-house who about four o'clock is maudlin.

Seeing all this, I advise no new settler in the State to make wine. He runs too many risks with children and laborers, even if he himself escapes.

In giving this advice, I do not mean to be offensive to the great body of wine growers in California, which numbers in its list a great many able, careful, and sober men, who are doing, as they have done, much and worthily for the prosperity of the State and for the production of good wine, and whose skill and enterprise are honorable to them. But the best and most thoughtful of these men will bear me out when I say that wine growing and making is a business requiring eminent skill and great practical good sense, and that not every one who comes to California with means enough to plant a vineyard ought to enter this business or can in the long run do so safely or profitably.

Fortunately, no one need make wine, though every man may raise grapes; for it is now a fact, established by sufficient and practical trial, that raisins, equal in every respect to the best Malaga, can be made in California from the proper varieties of grapes, and can be sold for a price which will very handsomely pay the maker, and with a much smaller investment of capital and less skill than are required to establish a wine-cellar and make wine. The vineyard owners already complain that they can not always readily sell their crude wine at a paying price; but the market for carefully-made raisins is, as I am told by the principal fruit dealers in San Francisco, open and eager. To make wine requires uncommon skill and care, and to keep it so that age shall give it that merit which commands a really good price demands considerable capital in the necessary outlay for casks. While the skillful wine-maker undoubtedly gets a large profit on his vines, it begins to be seen here that there is an oversupply of poorly-made wine.

But any industrious person who has the right kind of grapes can make raisins; and raisin-making, which in 1871 had still a very uncertain future in this State, may now safely be called one of the established and most promising industries here.

In 1872 I ate excellent raisins in Los Angeles, and tolerable ones in Visalia; but they sell very commonly in the shops what they call "dried grapes," which are not raisins at all, but damp, sticky, disagreeable things, not good even in puddings. This year, however, I have seen in several places good native raisins; and the head of the largest fruit-importing house in San Francisco told me that one raisin-maker last fall sold the whole of his crop there at $2 per box of twenty-five pounds, Malagas of the same quality bringing at the same time but $2.37½. There is a market for all well-made raisins that can be produced in the State, he said, and they are preferred to the foreign product.

At Folsom, Mr. Bugby told me he had made last year 1700 boxes of raisins, and he was satisfied with the pecuniary return; and I judge from the testimony of different persons that at seven cents per pound raisins will pay the farmer very well. The Malaga and the White Muscat are the grapes which appear here to make the best raisins. Nobody has yet tried the Seedless Sultana, which, however, bears well here, and would make, I should think, an excellent cooking raisin.

For making raisins they wait until the grape is fully ripe, and then carefully cut off the bunches and lay them either on a hard clay floor, formed in the open air, or on brown paper laid between the vine rows. They do not trim out poor grapes from the bunches, because, as they assert, there are none; but I suspect this will have to be done for the very finest raisins, such as would tempt a reluctant buyer. The bunches require from eighteen to twenty-four days of exposure in the sun to be cured. During that time they are gently turned from time to time, and such as are earliest cured are at once removed to a raisin-house.

This is fitted with shelves, on which the raisins are laid about a foot thick, and here they are allowed to sweat a little. If they sweat too much the sugar candies on the outside, and this deteriorates the quality of the raisin. It is an object to keep the bloom on the berries. They are kept in the raisin-house, I was told, five or six weeks, when they are dry enough to box. It is as yet customary to put them in twenty-five pound boxes, but, no doubt, as more experience is gained, farmers will contrive other parcels. Chinese do all the work in raisin-making, and are paid one dollar a day, they supplying themselves with food. There is no rain during the raisin-making season, and, consequently, the whole outdoor work may be done securely as well as cheaply.

Enormous quantities of fruit are now put up in tin cans in this State; and you will be surprised, perhaps—as I was the other day—to hear of an orchard of peach and apricot trees, which bears this year (1873) its first full crop, and for one hundred acres of which the owners have received ten thousand dollars cash, gold, selling the fruit on the trees, without risk of ripening or trouble of picking.

Yet peaches and apricots are not the most profitable fruits in this State, for the cherry—the most delicious cherries in the world grow here—is worth even more; and I suspect that the few farmers who have orchards of plums, and carefully dry the fruit, make as much money as the cherry owners. There has sprung up a very lively demand for California dried plums. They bring from twenty to twenty-two cents per pound at wholesale in San Francisco, and even as high as thirty cents for the best quality; and I am told that last season a considerable quantity was shipped Eastward and sold at a handsome profit in New York.

The plum bears heavily and constantly north of Sacramento, and does not suffer from the curculio, and the dried fruit is delicious and wholesome.

Some day the farmers who are now experimenting with figs will, I do not doubt, produce also a marketable dried fig in large quantities. At San Francisco, in October, 1873, I found in the shops delicious dried figs, but not in great quantities, nor so thoroughly dried as to bear shipment to a distance. The tree flourishes in almost all parts of the State. Usually it bears two and often three crops a year, and it grows into a noble and stately tree.

I am told that when Smyrna figs sell for twenty to thirty cents per pound, California figs bring but from five to ten cents. The tree comes into full bearing, where its location is favorable, in its third or fourth year; and ought to yield then about sixty pounds of dried figs. I suspect the cost of labor will control the drying of figs, for they must be picked by hand. If they fall to the ground they are easily bruised, and the bruised part turns sour.

They are dried in the shade, and on straw, which lets the air get to every part. Irrigation is not good after the tree bears, as the figs do not dry so readily. Birds and ants are fond of the fruit; and in one place I was told the birds took almost the whole of the first crop. There are many varieties of the fig grown in this State, but the White Smyrna is, I believe, thought to be the best for market. There are no large plantations of this tree in the State, but it is found on almost every farm and country place, and is a very wholesome fruit when eaten green.

When the farmers of the Sacramento Valley become tired of sowing wheat, and when the land comes into the hands of small farmers, as it is now doing to some extent, it will be discovered that fruit-trees are surer and more profitable than grain. A considerable emigration is now coming into California; and I advise every one who goes there to farm to lose no time before planting an orchard. Trees grow very rapidly, and it will be many years before such fruits as the cherry, plum, apricot, or the raisin-grape are too abundant to yield to their owners exceptionally large profits.

SHIPPING LUMBER, MENDOCINO COUNTY.

CHAPTER III.

THE TULE LANDS AND LAND DRAINAGE.

WHILE you are talking about redeeming the New Jersey marshes these go-ahead Californians are actually diking and reclaiming similar and, in some cases, richer overflowed lands by the hundred thousand acres.

If you will take, on a map of California, Stockton, Sacramento, and San Francisco for guiding points, you will see that a large part of the land lying between these cities is marked "swamp and overflowed." Until within five or six years these lands attracted but little attention. It was known that they were extremely fertile, but it was thought that the cost and uncertainty of reclaiming them were too great to warrant the enterprise. Of late, however, they have been rapidly bought up by capitalists, and their sagacity has been justified by the results on those tracts which have been reclaimed.

These Tule lands—the word is pronounced as though spelled "toola"—are simply deposits of muck, a mixture of the wash or sediment brought down by the Sacramento and San Joaquin rivers with the decayed vegetable matter resulting from an immense growth of various grasses, and of the reed called the "tule," which often grows ten feet high in a season, and decays every year. The Tule lands are in part the low lands along the greater rivers, but in part they are islands, lying in the delta of the Sacramento and San Joaquin rivers, and separated from each other by deep, narrow "sloughs," or "slews" as they are called—branches of these rivers, in fact.   Before reclamation they are over-flowed commonly twice a year—in the winter, when the rains cause the rivers to rise; and again in June, when the melting of the snows on the mountains brings another rise.   You may judge of the extent of this overflowed land by the following list of the principal Tule Islands:

	Acres.
Robert's Island	67,000
Union Island	50,000
Grizzly Island	15,000
Sherman Island	14,000
Grand Island	17,000
Ryer Island	11,800
Staten Island	8,000
Bacon Island	7,000
Brannan Island	7,000
Bouldin Island	5,000
Mandeville Island	5,000
Venice Island	4,000
Tyler Island	4,000
Andros Island	4,000
Twitchell Island	3,600
Sutter Island	3,000
Joyce Island	1,500
Rough and Ready Island	1,500
Long Island	1,000
In all	217,400

These are the largest islands; but you must understand that on the main-land, along the Sacramento and its affluents, there is a great deal of similar land, probably at least twice as much more, perhaps three times.

The swamp and overflowed lands were given by Congress to the State; and the State has, in its turn, virtually given them to private persons.   It has sold them for one dollar per acre, of which twenty per cent. was paid down, or twenty cents per acre; and this money, less some small charges for recording the transfer and for inspecting the reclamation, is returned by the State to the purchaser if he, within three years after the purchase, reclaims his land.   That is to say, the State gives away the land on condition that it shall be reclaimed and brought into cultivation.

During a number of years past enterprising individuals have undertaken to reclaim small tracts on these islands by diking them, but with not encouraging success, and it was not until a law was passed empowering the majority of owners of overflowed lands in any place to form a reclamation district, choose a Board of Reclamation, and levy a tax upon all the land in the district, for

A WATER JAM OF LOGS.

building and maintaining the dikes or levees that these lands really came into use.

Now, this work of draining is going on so fast that this year nearly six hundred miles of levee will be completed among the islands alone, not to speak of reclamation districts on the main-land. There seems to be a general determination to do the work thoroughly, the high floods of 1871–72 having shown the farmers and land-owners that they must build high and strong levees, or else lose all, or at least much, of their labor and outlay. During the spring of 1872 I saw huge breaks in some of the levees, which overflowed lands to the serious damage of farmers, for not only is the crop of the year lost, but orchards and

9

vineyards, which flourish on the Tule lands, perished or were seriously injured by the waters.

Chinese labor is used almost entirely in making the levees. An engineer having planned the work, estimates are made, and thereupon Chinese foremen take contracts for pieces at stipulated rates, and themselves hire their countrymen for the actual labor. This subdivision, to which the perfect organization of Chinese labor readily lends itself, is very convenient. The engineer or master in charge of the work deals only with the Chinese foremen, pays them for the work done, and exacts of them the due performance of the contract.

The levee stuff is taken from the inside; thus the ditch is inside of the levee, and usually on the outside is a space of low marsh, which presently fills with willow and cotton-wood. You may sail along the river or slough, therefore, for miles, and see only occasional evidences of the embankment.

The soil is usually a tough turf, full of roots, which is very cheaply cut out with an instrument called a "tule-knife," and thrown up on the levee, where it seems to bind well, though one would not think it would. At frequent intervals are self-acting tide-gates for drainage; these are made of the redwood of the coast, which does not rot in the water. The rise and fall of the tides is about six feet. The levees have been in some places troubled with beaver, which, however, are now hunted for their fur, and will not long be troublesome. There is no musk-rat—an animal which would do serious damage here. The tule-rat lives on roots on the land, but is not active or strong enough to be injurious.

The levee is usually from six to eight feet broad on top, with the inside sloping; but I was told that experience had shown that the outside should be perpendicular. It is not unusual for parts of a levee to sink down, but I could hear of no case of capsizing. The Levee Board of a district appoints levee-masters, whose duty it is to look after the condition of the work, and on the islands I visited there were gangs of Chinamen engaged in repairing and heightening the embankments.

You land at a wharf, and, standing on top of the levee, you see before you usually the house and other farm buildings, set up on piles, for security against a break and overflow; and beyond a great track of level land, two or three or five feet below the level of the levee, and, if it has but lately been reclaimed, covered with the remnants of tules and of grass sods.

`When the levee is completed, and the land has had opportunity to drain a little, the first operation is to burn it over. This requires time and some care, for it is possible to burn too deep; and in some parts the fire burns deep holes if it is not checked. If the land is covered with dry tules, the fire is set so easily that a single match will burn a thousand acres, the strong trade-wind which blows up the river and across these lands carrying the fire rapidly. If the dry tules have been washed off, a Chinaman is sent to dig holes through the upper sod; after him follows another, with a back-load of straw wisps, who sticks a wisp into each hole, lights it with a match, and goes on. At this rate, I am told, it cost on one island only one hundred dollars to burn fifteen hundred acres.

When this work is done you have an ash-heap, extremely disagreeable to walk over, and not yet solid enough to bear horses or oxen. Accordingly, the first crop is put on with sheep. First the tract is sowed, usually with a coffee-mill sower or hand machine, and, I am told, at the rate of about thirty pounds of wheat to the acre, though I believe it would be better to sow more thickly. Then comes a band or flock of about five hundred sheep. These are driven over the surface in a compact body, and at no great rate of speed, and it is surprising how readily they learn what is expected of them, and how thoroughly they tramp in the seed. Dogs are used in this work to keep the sheep together, and they expect to "sheep in," as they call it, about sixteen acres a day with five hundred animals, giving these time besides to feed on the levee and on spare land.

Tule land thus prepared has actually yielded from forty to sixty bushels of wheat per acre. It does not always do so, because, as I myself saw, it is often badly and irregularly burned over, and probably otherwise mismanaged. The crop is taken off with headers, as is usual in this State.

For the second year's crop the land is plowed. A two-share gang-plow is used, with a seat for the plowman. It is drawn by four horses, who have to be shod with broad wooden shoes, usually made of ash plank, nine by eleven inches, fastened to the iron shoes of the horse by screws.

The soil does not appear to be sour, and no doubt the ashes from the burning off do much to sweeten it where it needs that. But several years are needed to reduce the ground to its best condition for tillage, and the difference in this respect between newly-burned or second-crop lands and such matured farms as that of Mr. Bigelow on Sherman Island—who has been there eight or nine years—is very striking.

It seemed to me that the farmers and land-owners with whom I spoke knew "for certain" but very little about the best ways to manage these lands, and that the advice of a thorough scientific agriculturist, like Professor Johnson of Yale, would be very valuable to them. Now, they know only that the land when burned over will bear large crops of wheat; and, of course, in all practical measures for economically putting in and taking off a wheat crop the Californian needs no instructor.

The soil seemed to me, so far as they dig into it—say six feet deep—to be, not peat, but a mass of undecayed or but partly decayed roots, strongly adhering together, so that the upper part of a levee, taken of course from the lowest part of the ditch, lay in firm sods or tussocks. These, however, seem to decay pretty rapidly on exposure to the air. The drainage is not usually deeper than four feet, and in places the water-level was but three feet below the surface. The newly reclaimed land being very light, suffers from the dry season, and is often irrigated, which, as it lies below the river-level, can be quickly and cheaply done.

Sherman Island was one of the earliest to be reclaimed, and there I visited the fine farm of Mr. Bigelow—a New Hampshire man, I believe, and apparently a thorough farmer. He has lived on tule land ten years, and his fields were consequently in the finest condition. Here I saw a three-hundred-acre field of wheat, as fine as wheat could be. He thought he should get about forty-five bushels per acre this year. He had got, he told me, between sixty-five and seventy bushels per acre, and without any further labor the next year brought him from the same fields fifty-two bushels per acre as a "volunteer" or self-seeded crop.

Here I saw luxuriant red clover and blue grass, and he had also a field of carrots, which do well on this alluvial bottom, it seems. But what surprised me more was to find that apples, pears, peaches, plums, grapes, apricots—all the fruits—do well on this soil. With us I think the pear would not do well on peat; but here it withstood last year's flood, which broke a levee and overflowed Mr. Bigelow's farm, and the trees do not appear to have suffered. He had also wind-breaks of osier willow, which of course grows rapidly, and had been a source of profit to him in yielding cuttings for sale.

Timothy does not do well on tule land, as its roots do not push down deep enough, and the surface of such light soils always dries up rapidly. Mr. Bigelow told me that he once sowed alfalfa in February with wheat, and took off forty-five bushels of wheat per acre, and a ton and a half of alfalfa later; and pastured (in a thirty-acre field) twenty-five head of stock till Christmas on the same land, after the hay was cut.

They have one great advantage on the tule lands—they can put in their crops at any time from November to the last of June.

It was very curious to sit on the veranda at the farm-house, after dinner, with a high levee immediately in front of us almost hiding the Sacramento River, and with a broad canal—the inner ditch—full of fresh water, running along the boundary as far as the eye could reach, the level of the levee broken occasionally by tide-gates. The prospect would have been monotonous had we not had at one side the lovely mountain range of which Mount Diablo is the prominent peak. But the great expanse of clean fields, level as a billiard-table, and in as fine tilth as though this was a model farm, was a delight to the eye, too.

It may interest grape-growers in the East to be told that of what we call "foreign grapes," the Muscat of Alexandria succeeds best in these moist, peaty lands. It is the market grape here. Trees have not grown to a great size on the tule lands, but bees are very fond of the wild-flowers which abound in the unreclaimed marshes, and, having no hollow trees to build in, they adapt them-

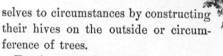

MOUNT HOOD, OREGON.

selves to circumstances by constructing their hives on the outside or circumference of trees.

Fencing costs here about three hundred and twenty dollars per mile. The redwood posts are driven into the ground with mauls. Farm laborers receive in the tules thirty dollars per month and board if they are white men, but one dollar a day and feed themselves, where they are Chinese.

On Twitchell Island I found an experiment making in ramie and jute, Mr. Finch, formerly of Haywards, having already planted twenty-six acres of ramie, and intending to put seven acres into jute, for which he had the plants all ready, raised in a canvas-covered inclosure. He raised ramie successfully last year, and sold, he told me, from one-tenth of an acre, two hundred and sixty three pounds of prepared ramie, for fifteen cents per pound. He used, to dress it, a machine made in California, which several persons have assured me works well and cheaply, a fact which ramie-growers in Louisiana may like to know; for the chief obstacle to ramie culture in this country has been, so far, the lack of a cheap and rapidly-working machine for its preparation. It struck me that Mr. Finch's experiment with ramie and jute would promise better were it not made on new land from which I believe only one crop had been taken.

When these tule lands have been diked and drained, they are sold for from twenty to twenty-five dollars per acre. Considering the crops they bear, and their nearness to market—ships could load at almost any of the islands—I suppose the price is not high; but a farmer ought to be sure that the levees are high enough, and properly made. To levee them costs variously, from three to twelve dollars per acre.

The tule lands which lie on the main-land, and which are equally rich with the islands, are usually ditched and diked for less than six dollars per acre; and this sum is regarded, I believe, by the State Commissioners as the maximum which the owners are allowed to borrow on reclamation land-bonds for the purpose of levee building.

I spoke awhile back of the existence of beavers in the tule country. Elk and grizzly bears used also to abound here, and I am told that on the unreclaimed lands elk are still found, though the grizzlies have gone to the mountains. One of the curiosities hereabouts is the ark, or floating house, used by the hunters, which you see anchored or moored in the sloughs: in these they live, using a small boat when they go ashore to hunt, and floating from place to place with the tide. On one of these arks I saw a magnificent pair of elk horns from an animal recently shot.

COAST VIEW, MENDOCINO COUNTY.

CHAPTER IV.

SHEEP-GRAZING IN NORTHERN CALIFORNIA.

IN the last year I have received a good many letters from persons desirous to try sheep-farming in California, and this has led me to look a little closely into this business as it is conducted in the northern parts of California.

There is no doubt that the climate of California gives some exceptional advantages to the sheep-grazer. He need not, in most parts of the State, make any provision against winter. He has no need for barns or expensive sheds, or for a store of hay or roots. His sheep live out-of-doors all the year round, and it results that those who have been so fortunate as to secure cheaply extensive ranges have made a great deal of money, even though they conducted the business very carelessly.

It ought to be understood, however, by persons who think of beginning with sheep here, that the business has changed considerably in character within two or three years. Land, in the first place, has very greatly risen in price; large ranges are no longer easily or cheaply obtained, and in the coast counties of Southern California particularly large tracts are now too high-priced, considering the quality of the land and its ability to carry sheep, for prudent men to buy.

Moreover, Southern California has some serious disadvantages for sheep-grazing which the northern part of the State—the Sacramento Valley and the adjoining coast-range and Sierra foot-hills—are without, and which begin to tell strongly, now that the wool of this State begins to go upon its merits, and is no longer bought simply as "California wool," regardless of its quality. Southern California has a troublesome burr, which is not found north of Sacramento, except on the lower lands. In Southern California it is often difficult to tide the sheep over the fall months in good order, whereas in the northern part of the State they have a greater variety of land, and do this more easily. The average of southern wool brings less by five or six cents per pound than that of the Sacramento Valley; and this is due in part to the soil and climate, and in part to the fact that sheep are more carefully kept in the northern part of the State.

Many of the sheep farmers in the Sacramento Valley have entirely done away with the mischievous practice of corraling their sheep—confining them at night, I mean, in narrow, crowded quarters—a practice which makes and keeps the sheep scabby. They very generally fence their lands, and thus are able to save their pasture and to manage it much more advantageously. They seem to me more careful about overstocking than sheep farmers generally are in the southern part of the State, though it should be understood that such men as Colonel Hollester, Colonel Diblee, Dr. Flint, and a few others in the South, who, like these, have exceptionally fine ranges, keep always the best sheep in the best manner. But smaller tracks, sown to alfalfa, are found to pay in the valleys where the land can be irrigated.

In Australia and New Zealand sheep inspectors are appointed, who have the duty to examine flocks and force the isolation of scabby sheep; and a careless flock-master who should be discovered driving scabby sheep through the country would be heavily fined; here the law says nothing on this head, but I have found this spring several sheep owners in the Sacramento Valley who assured me that they had eradicated scab so entirely from their flocks that they dealt also by isolation with such few single specimens as they found to have this disease.

Moreover, I find that the best sheep farmers aim to keep, not the largest flocks, but the best sheep. There is no doubt that the sheep deteriorates in this State unless it is carefully and constantly bred up. "We must bring in the finest bucks from Australia, or the East, or our own State," said one very successful sheep farmer to me; "and we must do this all the time, else our flocks will go back." "It is more profitable to keep fewer sheep of the best kind than more not quite so good. It is more profitable to keep a few sheep always in good condition than many with a period of semi-starvation for them in the fall," said another; and added, "I would rather, if I were to begin over again, spend my money on a breed worth six dollars a head, than one worth two or three dollars, and I would rather not keep sheep at all than not fence."

He had his land—about twenty-five thousand acres—fenced off in lots of from four to six thousand acres, and into one of these he turned from six to eight thousand sheep, leaving them to graze as they pleased. He had noticed, he told me, that whereas the sheep under the usual corral system feed the greater part of the day, no matter how hot the sun, his sheep in these large pastures were lying down from nine in the morning to four or five in the afternoon; and he often found them feeding far into the night, and rising again to graze long before daylight. They were at liberty to follow their own pleasure, having water always at hand. An abundant supply of water he thought of great importance.

INDIAN SWEAT-HOUSE.

Of course, where the sheep are turned out into fenced land no shepherds are required, which makes an important saving. One man, with a horse, visits the different flocks, and can look after ten or fifteen thousand head.

The farmer whom I have quoted does not dip his sheep to prevent or cure scab, but mops the sore place, when he discovers a scabby sheep, with a sponge dipped into the scab-mixture.

He gets, he told me, from his flock of ten thousand merinoes, an average of seven pounds per head of wool, and he does not shear any except the lambs, in the fall. It is a common but bad practice here to shear all sheep twice a year; and where, as is too often the case, a flock is very scabby, no doubt this is necessary.

He had long sheds as shelter for his ewes about lambing-time, so as to protect them against fierce winds and cold rain storms; and he saved every year about two hundred tons of hay, cut from the wild pastures, to feed in case the rain should hold off uncommonly late. His aim was to keep the sheep always in good condition, so that there should never be any weak place in the wool. His sheds cost him about one dollar per running foot. The sheep found their own way to them.

I find it is the habit of the forehanded sheep-grazers in the Sacramento Valley to own a range in the foot-hills and another on the bottom-lands. During the summer the sheep are kept in the bottoms, which are then dry and full of rich grasses; in the fall and winter they are taken to the uplands, and there they lamb, and are shorn. Where the range lies too far away from any river, they drive the sheep in May into the mountains, where they have green grass all summer; and about Red Bluff I saw a curious sight—cattle and horses wandering, singly or in small groups, of their own motion, to the mountains, and actually crossing the Sacramento without driving; and I was told that in the fall they would return, each to its master's rancho. I am satisfied that, except, perhaps, for the region north of Redding, where the winters are cold and the summers have rain and green grass, and where long-wooled sheep will do well, the merino is the sheep for this State; and "the finer the better," say the best sheep men. Near Red Bluff I saw some fine Cotswolds, and in the coast valleys north of San Francisco these and Leicesters, I am told, do well.

A great deal of the land which is now used for sheep will, in the next five, or at most ten years, be plowed and cropped. There is a tendency to tax all land at its real value; and, except with good management, it will not pay to keep sheep on land fit for grain and taxed as grain land, which a great deal of the grazing land is. As the State becomes more populous, the flocks will become smaller, and the wool will improve in quality at the same time.

I have seen a good deal of alfalfa in the Sacramento Valley, but I have seen also that the sheep men do not trust to it entirely. They believe that it will be better for sheep as hay than as green food; and this lucerne grows so rankly, and has, unless it is frequently cut, so much woody stalk, that I believe this also. It makes extremely nice hay.

Every man who comes to California to farm ought to keep some sheep; and he can keep them more easily and cheaply here than anywhere in the East.

For persons who want to begin sheep-raising on a large scale and with capital the opportunities are not so good here now; but there are yet fine chances in Nevada, in the valley of the Humboldt, where already thousands of head of cattle, and at least one hundred thousand sheep, are now fed by persons who do not own the land at all. I am told extensive tracts could be bought there at really low prices, and with such credit on much of it as would enable a man with capital enough to stock his tract to pay for the land out of the proceeds of the sheep. The white sage in the Humboldt Valley is very nutritious, and there is also in the subsidiary valleys bunch-grass and other nutritious food for stock. Not a few young men have gone into this Humboldt country with a few hundreds of sheep, and are now wealthy. The winters are somewhat longer than in California, but the sheep find feed all the year round; and they are shorn near the line of the railroad, so that there is no costly transportation of the wool. Mutton sheep, too, are driven to the railroad to be sent to market, and for stock, therefore, this otherwise out-of-the-way region is very convenient.

Riding through the foot-hills near Rocklin—where I had been visiting a well-kept sheep-farm—I saw a curious and unexpected sight. There are still a few wretched Digger Indians in this part of California; and what I saw was a party of these engaged in catching grasshoppers, which they boil and eat. They dig a number of funnel-shaped holes, wide at the top, and eighteen inches deep, on a cleared space, and then, with rags and brush, drive the grasshoppers toward these holes, forming for that purpose a wide circle. It is slow work, but they seem to delight in it; and their excitement was great as they neared the circle of holes and the insects began to hop and fall into them. At last there was a close and rapid rally, and half a dozen bushels of grasshoppers were driven into the holes; whereupon hats, aprons, bags, and rags were stuffed in to prevent the multitudes from dispersing; and then began the work of picking them out by handfuls, crushing them roughly in the hand to keep them quiet, and crowding them into the bags in which they were to be carried to their rancheria.

"Sweet—all same pudding," cried an old woman to me, as I stood looking on. It is not a good year for grasshoppers this year; nothing like the year of which an inhabitant of Roseville spoke to me later in the day, when he said, "they ate up every bit of his garden-truck, and then sat on the fence and asked him for a chew of tobacco."

The sheep ranges of the northern interior counties are less broken up than in the coast counties farther south; and it is better and more profitable, in my judgment, to pay five dollars per acre for grazing lands in the Sacramento Valley than two dollars and a half for grazing lands farther south and among the mountains. The grazier in the northern counties has two advantages over his southern competitor: first, in the ability to buy low-lying lands on the river, where he can graze from three to six or even ten sheep to the acre during the summer months, and where he may plant large tracts in alfalfa; and, secondly, in a safe refuge against drought in the mountain meadows of the Sierras, and in the little valleys and fertile hill-slopes of the Coast Range, where there is much unsurveyed Government land, to which hundreds of thousands of sheep and cattle are annually driven by the graziers of the plain, who thus save their own pastures, and are able to carry a much larger number of sheep than they otherwise would.

Moreover, nearness to the railroad is an important advantage for the sheep-farmer; and I found that the most enterprising and intelligent sheep men in the northern counties send their wool direct by railroad to the Eastern States, instead of shipping it to San Francisco to be sold.

Finally, much of the land now obtainable for grazing in the Sacramento Valley, at prices in some cases not too dear for grazing purposes, is of a quality which will make it valuable agricultural land as soon as the valley begins to fill up; and thus, aside from the profit from the sheep, the owner may safely reckon upon a large increase in the value of his land. This can not be said of much of the grazing land of the southern coast counties, which is mountainous and broken, and fit only for grazing.

Of course I speak here of the average lands only. There are large tracts or ranchos in the southern coast counties, such as the Lampoc rancho of Hollester & Diblee, and lands in the Salinas Valley, which are exceptionally fine, and to which what I have said of the coast ranchos generally does not apply.

ANOTHER COAST VIEW, NORTHERN CALIFORNIA.

CHAPTER V.

THE CHINESE AS LABORERS AND PRODUCERS.

A S I crossed from Oakland to San Francisco on a Sunday afternoon last July, there were on the ferry-boat a number of Chinese. They were decently clad, quiet, clean, sat apart in their places in the lower part of the boat conversing together, and finally walked off the boat when she came to land as orderly as though they had been Massachusetts Christians.

There were also on the boat a number of half-grown and full-grown white boys, some of whom had been fishing, and carried their long rods with them. These were slouchy, dirty, loud-voiced, rude; and, as they passed off the boat, I noticed that with their long rods they knocked the hats of the Chinese off their heads, or punched them in the back, every effort of this kind being rewarded with boisterous laughter from their companions. Nor did they confine their annoyance entirely to the Chinese, for they jostled and pushed their way out through the crowd of men and women very much as a gang of pickpockets on a Third Avenue car in New York conducts itself when its members mean to steal a watch or two.

These rowdies were "Hoodlums;" and it is the Hoodlums chiefly who clamor about the Chinese, and who are "ruined by Chinese cheap labor." The anti-Chinese agitation in San Francisco has led me to look a little closely into this matter, and I declare my belief that there are not a hundred decent men who work for a living in that city engaged in this crusade against the Chinese. If you could to-day assemble there all who join in this persecution, and if then you took from this assemblage all the Hoodlums, all the bar-room loafers, and all the political demagogues, I don't believe you would have a hundred men left on the ground. That is to say, the people who actually earn the bread they eat do not persecute the Chinese.

If an Eastern reader suggests that it argues a lack of public spirit in the decent part of the community to allow the roughs to rule in this matter, I take leave to remind him of the time, not very long ago, when the same combination of Hoodlum and demagogue mobbed negroes in New York, and threatened vengeance if colored people were allowed to ride in the street-cars. Here, as there then, there are unfortunately newspapers which ignorantly pander to this vile class, and help to swell the cry of persecution. And here, as in New York a few years ago, it results that the proscribed race is hardly dealt with, not only by the roughs, but sometimes in the courts, and gets scant and hard justice dealt out to it. The courageous and upright action of Mayor Alvord in veto-ing the inhuman and silly acts of the city supervisors, which, by-the-way, has made him one of the most popular men in California, for the moment shamed the demagogues and silenced the rowdies; but there are means of annoying the Chinese within the law, which are still used. For instance, there is an ordinance declaring a fine for overcrowding tenement-houses, and requiring that in every room there shall be five hundred cubic feet of air for each occu-pant, and for violating this a fine of ten dollars is imposed. This ordinance is enforced only against the Chinese—so I am assured on the best authority, and they only are fined. But justice would seem to demand not only that the law should be enforced against all alike, but that the owner of the prop-erty should be made liable for its misuse as well as the unfortunate and igno-rant occupants.

The Chinese quarter in San Francisco consists, for the most part, of a lot of decayed rookeries which would put our own Five Points to the blush. The Chinese live here very much as the Five Points' population lives in New York. And here, as there, respectable people—or people at any rate who would think themselves insulted if you called their respectability in question—own these filthy and decayed tenements; live in comfort on the rent paid them by the Chinese; perhaps go to church on Sunday, and, no doubt, thank God that they are not as other people. It is very good to fine a poor devil of a Chinaman because he lives in an overcrowded tenement; but what a stir there would be if some enterprising San Francisco journal should give a description of these holes, and the different uses they are put to, and add the names and residences of the owners.

California has, according to Cronise—a good authority—40,000,000 acres of arable land. It has, according to the last census, 560,247 people, of whom 149,473 live in San Francisco, and yet nowhere in the United States have I heard so much complaint of "nothing to do" as in San Francisco. One of the leading cries of the demagogues here is that the Chinese are crowding white men out of employment. But one of the complaints most frequently heard from men who need to get work done is that they can get nobody to do it. A hundred times and more, in my travels through the State, I have found Chinese serving not only as laborers, but holding positions where great skill and faithfulness were required; and almost every time the employer has said to me, "I would rather, of course, employ a white man, but I can not get one whom I can trust, and who will stick to his work." In some cases this was not said, but the employer spoke straight out that he had tried white men, and preferred the Chinese as more faithful and painstaking, more accurate, and less eye-servants.

A gentleman told me that he had once advertised in the San Francisco papers for one hundred laborers; his office was besieged for three days. Three hundred and fifty offered themselves, all presumably ruined by Chinese cheap labor; but all but a dozen refused to accept work when they heard that they were required to go "out of the city."

The charge that the Chinese underbid the whites in the labor market is bosh. When they first come over, and are ignorant of our language, habits, customs, and manner of work, they no doubt work cheaply; but they know very accurately the current rate of wages and the condition of the labor market, and they manage to get as much as any body, or, if they take less in some cases, it is because they can not do a full day's work. It is a fact, however, that they do a great deal of work which white men will not do out here; they do not stand idle, but take the first job that is offered them. And the result is that they are used all over the State, more and more, because they chiefly, of the laboring population, will work steadily and keep their engagements.

Moreover, the admirable organization of the Chinese labor is an irresistible convenience to the farmer, vineyardist, and other employer. "How do you arrange to get your Chinese?" I asked a man in the country who was employing more than a hundred in several gangs. He replied: "I have only to go or send to a Chinese employment office in San Francisco, and say that I need so many men for such work and at such pay. Directly up come the men, with a foreman of their own, with whom alone I have to deal. I tell only him what I want done; I settle with him alone; I complain to him, and hold him alone responsible. He understands English; and this system simplifies things amazingly. If I employed white men I should have to instruct, reprove, watch, and pay each one separately; and of a hundred, a quarter, at least, would be dropping out day after day for one cause or another. Moreover, with my Chinese comes up a cook for every twenty men, whom I pay, and provisions of their own which they buy. Thus I have nobody to feed and care for. They do it themselves."

This is the reply I have received in half a dozen instances where I made inquiry of men who employed from twenty-five to two hundred Chinese. Any one can see that, with such an organization of labor, many things can be easily done which under our different and looser system a man would not rashly undertake. So far as I have been able to learn, such a thing as a gang of Chinese leaving a piece of work they had engaged to do, unless they were cheated or ill-treated, is unknown. Then they don't drink whisky. With all this, any one can see that they need not work cheaply. To a man who wants to get a piece of work done their systematic ways are worth a good deal of money. In point of fact, they are quick enough to demand higher wages.

Of the population of California when the census of 1870 was taken, 49,310 were Chinese, 54,421 were Irish, 29,701 were Germans, and 339,199 were born in the United States. In an official return from the California State-prison, the number of convicts in 1871, the last year reported, is given at 880; of whom 477 were native born, 118 were Chinese, 86 were Irish, 29 were German. This gives, of convicts, one in every 635 of the whole

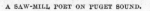

A SAW-MILL PORT ON PUGET SOUND.

population of the State; one in 711 of the native born; one in 417 of the Chinese; one in 632 of the Irish born; and one in 1024 of the Germans. That is to say, of the different nationalities the Germans contribute the fewest convicts, the native born next, the Irish next, and the Chinese the greatest number proportionately.

But pray bear in mind the important fact that the Chinese here are almost entirely grown men; they have no families here, and but a small number of women, almost all of whom are, moreover, prostitutes.

If, then, you would compare these figures rightly you would have to leave out of the count the women and children of all the other nationalities; it would, perhaps, then appear that the Chinese furnish a much smaller proportion of criminals than the above figures show; and this in spite of the well-known fact that Dame Justice commonly turns a very cold shoulder toward a Chinaman. I wonder that the comparison shows so favorably for them.

It is said that they send money out of the country. I wonder who sends the most, the Chinaman or the white foreigner? If one could get at the sums remitted to England, Ireland, and Germany, and those sent to China, I don't know which would be the greater.

But a Chinese, to whom I mentioned this charge, made me an excellent answer. He said: "Suppose you work for me; suppose I pay you; what business I what you do with money? If you work good for me, that all I care. No business my what you do your pay." Surely he was right; the Chinaman may send some part of his wages out of the country, though not much, for he must eat, must be clothed and lodged, must pay railroad and stage fares, must smoke opium, and usually gamble a little. When all this is done, the surplus of a Chinaman's wages is not great. But suppose he sent off all his pay; he does not and can not send off the work he has done for it, the ditches he has dug, the levees he has made, the meals he has cooked, and the clothes he has washed and ironed, the harvest he has helped to sow and gather, and the vegetables he has raised; the cigars, and shoes, blankets, gloves, slippers, and other things he has made. These remain to enrich the country, to make abundance where, but for his help, there would be scarcity, or importation from other States or countries.

But lately it is asserted that the Chinese have brought or will bring the leprosy hither. This is a genuine cry of anguish and terror from the Hoodlums; for, bear in mind that, according to the best medical opinion in the Sandwich Islands, where this disease is most frequent and has been most thoroughly studied, it is communicated only by cohabitation or the most intimate association. If you ask a policeman to pilot you through the Chinese quarter of San Francisco between eight and eleven o'clock any night, you will see the creatures who make this outcry. They are Hoodlums, gangs of whom perambulate the worst alleys, and pass in and out of the vilest kennels.

I was curious to know something about the "Chinese Companies" of which one frequently hears here, and which exercise important powers over their countrymen all over the State. What follows concerning these organizations I derived from conversation with several Chinese who speak English, and with a missionary who labors among them.

There are six of these companies, calling themselves "Yong Wong," "Howk Wah," "Sam Yup," "Yen Wah," "Kong Chow," and "Yong Woh." They are benevolent societies; each looks after the people who come from the province or district for whose behalf it is formed.

When a ship comes into port with Chinese, the agents of the companies board it, and each takes the names of those who belong to his province. These then come into the charge of their proper company. That lodges, and, if necessary, feeds them; as quickly as possible secures them employment; and, if they are to go to a distant point, lends them the needed passage-money. The company also cares for the sick, if they are friendless and without means; and it sends home the bones of those who die here.

Moreover, it settles all disputes between Chinese, levies fines upon offenders; and

CAPE HORN, COLUMBIA RIVER.

when a Chinaman wishes to return home, his company examines his accounts, and obliges him to pay his just debts here before leaving.

The means to do all this are obtained by the voluntary contributions of the members, who are all who land at San Francisco from the province which a company represents.

In the Canton company, "Sam Yup," I was told that the members pay seven dollars each, which sum is paid at any time, but always before they go home.

"Suppose a man does not pay?" I asked a Chinese who speaks English very well. He replied, " Then the company loses it; but all who can, pay. Very seldom any one refuses."

"Suppose," said I, "a Chinaman refuses to respect the company's decision, in case of a quarrel?" He replied, "They never refuse. It is their own company. They are all members."

Naturally there are sometimes losses and a deficit in the treasury. This is made up by levying an additional contribution.

"Do the companies advance money to bring over Chinese?" "No," was the reply, "the company has no money; it is not a business association, but only for mutual aid among the Chinese here." Nor does it act as an employment office, for this is a separate and very well organized business. It sends home the bones of dead men, and this costs fifteen dollars; and wherever the deceased leaves property or money, or the relatives are able to pay, the company exacts this sum.

It is evident that the Chinese in California keep up a very active correspondence with San Francisco as well as with China. They "keep the run" of their people very carefully; and the poorer class, who have probably gone into debt at home for money to get over here, seem to pay their debts with great honesty out of their earnings. It is clear to me that the poorer Chinese command far greater credit among their countrymen than our laboring class usually receives, and this speaks well for their general honesty.

I do not mean to hold up the Chinaman as an entirely admirable creature. He has many excellent traits, and we might learn several profitable lessons from him in the art of organizing labor, and in other matters. But he has grave vices; he does commonly, and without shame, many things which we hold to be wrong and disreputable; and, altogether, it might have been well could we have kept him out.

The extent to which they carry organization and administration is something quite curious. For instance, there are not only organized bands of laborers, submitting themselves to the control and management of a foreman; benevolent societies, administering charity and, to a large extent, justice; employment societies, which make advances to gangs and individuals all over the State; but there is in San Francisco a society or organization for the importation of prostitutes from China. The existence of this organization was not suspected until during last summer some of its victims appealed to a city missionary to save them from a life of vice. Thereupon suit was brought by Chinese in the courts for money which they claimed these women owed; and, on an examination, I was told, no attempt was made to conceal the fact that a regularly formed commercial organization was engaged in either buying or kidnapping young women in China, bringing them to San Francisco, there furnishing them clothing and habitations, and receiving from them a share of the money they gained by prostitution.

But the Chinaman is here; treaty laws made by our Government with his give him the right to come here, and to live here securely. And this is to be said, that if we could to-day expel the Chinese from California, more than half the capital now invested there would be idle or leave the State, many of the most important industries would entirely stop, and the prosperity of California would receive a blow from which it would not recover for twenty years. They are, as a class, peaceable, patient, ingenious, and industrious. That they deprive any white man of work is absurd, in a State which has scarcely half a million of people, and which can support ten millions, and needs at least three millions to develop fairly its abundant natural wealth; and no matter what he is, or what the effect of his presence might be, it is shameful that he should be meanly maltreated and persecuted among a people who boast themselves Christian and claim to be civilized.

SAW-MILL.

CHAPTER VI.

THE MENDOCINO COAST AND CLEAR LAKE—GENERAL VIEW.

SOME of the most picturesque country in California lies on or near the coast north of San Francisco. The coast counties, Marin, Sonoma, Mendocino, Humboldt, Klamath, and Del Norte, are the least visited by strangers, and yet, with Napa, Lake, and Trinity, they make up a region which contains a very great deal of wild and fine scenery, and which abounds with game, and shows to the traveler many varieties of life and several of the peculiar industries of California.

Those who have passed through the lovely Napa Valley, by way of Calistoga, to the Geysers, or who have visited the same place by way of Healdsburg and the pretty Russian River Valley, have no more than a faint idea of what a tourist may see and enjoy who will devote two weeks to a journey along the sea-coast of Marin and Mendocino counties, returning by way of Clear Lake — a fine sheet of water, whose borders contain some remarkable volcanic features.

The northern coast counties are made up largely of mountains, but imbosomed in these lie many charming little, and several quite spacious, valleys, in which you are surprised to find a multitude of farmers living, isolated from the world, that life of careless and easy prosperity which is the lot of farmers in the fat valleys of California.

In such a journey the traveler will see the famous redwood forests of this State, whose trees are unequaled in size except by the gigantic sequoias; he will see those dairy-farms of Marin County whose butter supplies not only the Western coast, but is sent East, and competes in the markets of New York and Boston with the product of Eastern dairies, while, sealed hermetically in glass jars, it is transported to the most distant military posts, and used on long sea-voyages, keeping sweet in any climate for at least a year; he will see, in Mendocino County, one of the most remarkable coasts in the world, eaten by the ocean into the most singular and fantastic shapes; and on this coast saw-mills and logging camps, where the immense redwood forests are reduced to useful lumber with a prodigious waste of wood.

He will see, besides the larger Napa, Petaluma, Bereyessa, and Russian River valleys, which are already connected by railroad with San Francisco, a number of quiet, sunny little vales, some of them undiscoverable on any but the most recent maps, nestled among the mountains, unconnected as yet with the world either by railroad or telegraph, but fertile, rich in cattle, sheep, and grain, where live a people peculiarly Californian in their habits, language, and customs, great horsemen, famous rifle-shots, keen fishermen, for the mountains abound in deer and bear, and the streams are alive with trout.

He may see an Indian reservation—one of the most curious examples of mis-managed philanthropy which our Government can show. And finally, the traveler will come to, and, if he is wise, spend some days on, Clear Lake—a strikingly lovely piece of water, which would be famous if it were not American.

For such a journey one needs a heavy pair of colored blankets and an overcoat rolled up together, and a leather bag or valise to contain the necessary change of clothing. A couple of rough crash towels and a piece of soap also should be put into the bag; for you may want to camp out, and you may not always find any but the public towel at the inn where you dine or sleep. Traveling in spring, summer, or fall, you need no umbrella or other protection against rain, and may confidently reckon on uninterrupted fine weather.

The coast is always cool. The interior valleys are warm, and during the summer quite hot, and yet the dry heat does not exhaust or distress one, and cool nights refresh you. In the valleys and on much-traveled roads there is a good deal of dust, but it is, as they say, "clean dirt," and there is water enough in the country to wash it off. You need not ride on horseback unless you penetrate into Humboldt County, which has as yet but few miles of wag-on-road. In Mendocino, Lake, and Marin, the roads are excellent, and either a public stage, or, what is pleasanter and but little dearer, a private team, with a driver familiar with the country, is always obtainable. In such a journey one element of pleasure is its somewhat hap-hazard nature. You do not travel over beaten ground, and on routes laid out for you; you do not know before-hand what you are to see, nor even how you are to see it; you may sleep in a house to-day, in the woods to-morrow, and in a sail-boat the day after; you dine one day in a logging camp, and another in a farm-house. With the ba-rometer at "set fair," and in a country where every body is civil and obliging,

WOOD-CHOPPER AT WORK.

and where all you see is novel to an Eastern person, the sense of adventure adds a keen zest to a journey which is in itself not only amusing and health-ful, but instructive.

Marin County, which lies across the bay from San Francisco, and of which the pretty village of San Rafael is the county town, contains the most pro-ductive dairy-farms in the State. When one has long read of California as a dry State, he wonders to find that it produces butter at all; and still more to discover that the dairy business is extensive and profitable enough—with butter at thirty-five cents a pound at the dairy—to warrant the employment of several millions of capital, and to enable the dairy-men to send their product to New York and Boston for sale.

For the coast journey the best route, because it shows you much fine scenery on your way, is by way of Soucelito, which is reached by a ferry from San Francisco. From Soucelito either a stage or a private conveyance carries you to Olema, whence you should visit Point Reyes, one of the most rugged capes' on the coast, where a light-house and fog-signal are placed to warn and guide mariners. It is a wild spot, often enveloped in fogs, and where it blows at least half a gale of wind three hundred days in the year.

Returning from Point Reyes to Olema, your road bears you past Tomales Bay, and back to the coast of Mendocino County; and by the time you reach the mouth of Russian River you are in the saw-mill country. Here the road runs for the most part close to the coast, and gives you a long succession of wild and strange views. You pass Point Arena, where is another light-house; and finally land at Mendocino City.

Before the stage sets you down at Mendocino, or " Big River," you will have noticed that the coast-line is broken at frequent intervals by the mouths of small streams, and at the available points at the mouths of these streams saw-mills are placed. This continues up the coast, wherever a river-mouth offers the slightest shelter to vessels loading; for the redwood forests line the coast up to and beyond Humboldt Bay.

When you leave the coast for the interior, you ride through mile after mile of redwood forest. Unlike the firs of Oregon and Puget Sound, this tree does not occupy the whole land. It rears its tall head from a jungle of laurel, madrone, oak, and other trees; and I doubt if so many as fifty large redwoods often stand upon a single acre. I was told that an average tree would turn out about fifteen thousand feet of lumber, and thus even thirty such trees to the acre would yield nearly half a million feet.

The topography of California, like its climate, has decided features. As there are but two seasons, so there are apt to be sharply-drawn differences in natural features, and you descend from what appears to you an interminable mass of mountains suddenly into a plain, and pass from deep forests shading the mountain road at once into a prairie valley, which nature made ready to the farmer's hands, taking care even to beautify it for him with stately and umbrageous oaks. There are a number of such valleys on the way which I took from the coast at Mendocino City to the Nome Cult Indian Reservation, in Round Valley. The principal of these, Little Lake, Potter, and Eden valleys, contain from five to twelve thousand acres; but there are a number of smaller vales, little gems, big enough for one or two farmers, fertile and easily cultivated.

A good many Missourians and other Southern people have settled in this part of the State. The better class of these make good farmers; but the person called "Pike" in this State has here bloomed out until, at times, he becomes, as a Californian said to me about an earthquake, "a little monotonous."

The Pike in Mendocino County regards himself as a laboring-man, and in that capacity he has undertaken to drive out the Indians, just as a still lower class in San Francisco has undertaken to drive out the laboring Chinese. These Little Lake and Potter Valley Pikes were ruined by Indian cheap labor; so they got up a mob and expelled the Indians, and the result is that the work which these poor people formerly performed is now left undone.

As for the Indians, they are gathered at the Round Valley Reservation to the number of about twelve hundred, where they stand an excellent chance to lose such habits of industry and thrift as they had learned while supporting themselves. At least half the men on the reservation, the superintendent told me, are competent farmers, and many of the women are excellent and competent house-servants. No one disputes that while they supported themselves by useful industry in the valleys where were their homes they were peaceable and harmless, and that the whites stood in no danger from them. Why, then, should the United States Government forcibly make paupers of them? Why should this class of Indians be compelled to live on reservations?

Under the best management which we have ever had in the Indian Bureau —let us say under its present management—a reservation containing tame or peaceable Indians is only a pauper asylum and prison combined, a nuisance to the respectable farmers, whom it deprives of useful and necessary laborers, an injury to the morals of the community in whose midst it is placed, an injury to the Indian, whom it demoralizes, and a benefit only to the members of the Indian ring.

Round Valley is occupied in part by the Nome Cult Reservation, and in part by farmers and graziers. In the middle of the valley stands Covelo, one of the roughest little villages I have seen in California, the gathering-place for a rude population, which inhabits not only the valley, but the mountains within fifty miles around, and which rides into Covelo on mustang ponies whenever it gets out of whisky at home or wants a spree.

The bar-rooms of Covelo sell more strong drink in a day than any I have ever seen elsewhere; and the sheep-herder, the vaquero, the hunter, and the wandering rough, descending from their lonely mountain camps, make up as rude a crowd as one could find even in Nevada. Being almost without exception Americans, they are not quarrelsome in their cups. I was told, indeed, by an old resident, that shooting was formerly common, but it has gone out of fashion, mainly, perhaps, because most of the men are excellent shots, and the amusement was dangerous. At any rate, I saw not a single fight or disturbance, though I spent the Fourth of July at Covelo; and it was, on the whole, a surprisingly well-conducted crowd, in spite of a document which I picked up there, and whose directions were but too faithfully observed by a large majority of the transient population. This was called a "toddy time-table," and I transcribe it here from a neat gilt-edged card for the warning and instruction of Eastern topers.

TODDY TIME-TABLE.

6 A.M.	Eye-opener.	3 P.M. Cobbler.
7 "	Appetizer.	4 " Social Drink.
8 "	Digester.	5 " Invigorator.
9 "	Big Reposer.	6 " Solid Straight.
10 "	Refresher.	7 " Chit-chat.
11 "	Stimulant.	8 " Fancy Smile.
12 M.	Ante-lunch.	9 " Entire Acte (*sic*).
1 P.M.	Settler.	10 " Sparkler.
2 "	A la Smythe.	11 " Rouser.

12 P.M. Night-cap.

GOOD-NIGHT.

My impression is that this time-table was not made for the latitude of Covelo, for they began to drink much earlier than 6 A.M. at the bar, near which I slept, and they left off later than midnight. It would be unjust for me not to add that, for the amount of liquor consumed, it was the soberest and the best-natured crowd I ever saw. I would like to write "respectable" also, but it would be ridiculous to apply that term to men whose every word almost is an oath, and whose language in many cases corresponds too accurately with their clothes and persons.

From Round Valley there is a "good enough" horseback trail, as they call it, over a steep mountain into the Sacramento Valley; but a pleasanter journey, and one, besides, having more novelty, is by way of Potter Valley to Lakeport, on Clear Lake. The road is excellent; the scenery is peculiarly Californian. Potter Valley is one of the richest and also one of the prettiest of the minor valleys of this State, and your way to Lakeport carries you along the shores of two pleasant mountain lakelets—the Blue Lakes, which are probably ancient craters.

Two days' easy driving, stopping overnight in Potter Valley, brings you to Lakeport, the capital of Lake County, and the only town I have seen in California where dogs in the square worry strangers as they are entering the place. As the only hotel in the town occupies one corner of this square, and as in Californian fashion the loungers usually sit in the evening on the sidewalk before the hotel, the combined attack of these dogs occurs in their view, and perhaps affords them a pleasing and beneficial excitement. The placid and impartial manner with which the landlord himself regards the contest between the stranger and the town dogs will lead you to doubt whether his house is not too full to accommodate another guest, and whether he is not benevolently letting the dogs spare him the pain of refusing you a night's lodging; but it is gratifying to be assured, when you at last reach the door, that the dogs " scarcely ever bite any body."

Clear Lake is a large and picturesque sheet of water, twenty-five miles long by about seven wide, surrounded by mountains, which in many places rise from the water's edge.   At Lakeport you can hire a boat at a very reasonable price, and I advise the traveler to take his blankets on board, and make this boat his home for two or three days.   He will get food at different farm-houses on the shore; and as there are substantial, good-sized sail-boats, he can sleep on board very enjoyably.   Aside from its fine scenery, and one or two good specimens of small Californian farms, the valley is remarkable for two borax lakes and a considerable deposit of sulphur, all of which lie close to the shore.

At one of the farm-houses, whose owner, a Pennsylvanian, has made himself a most beautiful place in a little valley hidden by the mountains which butt on the lake, I saw the culture of silk going on in that way in which only, as I believe, it can be made successful in California.   He had planted about twenty-five hundred mulberry-trees, built himself an inexpensive but quite sufficient little cocoonery, bought an ounce and a half of eggs for fifteen dollars, and when I visited him had already a considerable quantity of cocoons, and had several thousand worms then feeding.

It was his first attempt; he had never seen a cocoonery, but had read all the books he could buy about the management of the silk-worm; and, as his grain harvest was over, he found in the slight labor attending the management of these worms a source of interest and delight which was alone worth the cost of his experiment.   But he is successful besides; and his wife expressed great delight at the new employment her husband had found, which, as she said, had kept him close at home for about two months.   She remarked that all wives ought to favor the silk culture for their husbands; but the old man added that some husbands might recommend it to their wives.

Certainly I had no idea how slight and pleasant is the labor attending this industry up to the point of getting cocoons.   If, however, you mean to raise eggs, the work is less pleasant.

This farmer, Mr. Alter, had chosen his field of operations with considerable shrewdness.   He planted his mulberry-trees on a dry side-hill, and found that it did not hurt his worms to feed to them, under this condition, even leaves from the little shrubs growing in his nursery rows.   His cocoonery was sheltered from rude winds by a hill and a wood, and thus the temperature was very equal.   He had no stove in his house, the shelves were quite rough, and the whole management might have been called careless if it were not successful.

I believe that the country about Clear Lake and in the Napa and Sonoma valleys will be found very favorable to the culture of the silk-worm; but I believe also that this industry will not succeed except where it is carried on by farmers and their families in a small way.

MOUNT HOOD, OREGON.

Boat life on Clear Lake is as delightful an experience as a traveler or lounger can get anywhere. The lake is placid; there is usually breeze enough to sail about; and you need not fear storms or rainy weather in the dry season. If it should fall calm, and you do not wish to be delayed, you can always hire an Indian to row the boat, and there is sufficient to see on the lake to pleasantly detain a tourist several days, besides fine fishing and hunting in the season, and lovely views all the time.

Going to the Sulphur Banks on a calm morning, I hired an Indian from a rancheria upon Mr. Alter's farm to row for us, and my Indian proved to be a prize. His name was Napoleon, and he was a philosopher. Like his greater namesake, he had had two wives. Of the first one he reported that "Jim catchee him," by which I was to understand that he had tired of her, and had sold her to "Jim;" and he had now taken number two, a moderately pretty Digger girl, of whom he seemed to be uncommonly fond. As he rowed he began to speak of his former life, when he had served a white farmer.

"Him die now," said Napoleon; adding, in a musing tone, "he very good man, plenty money; give Injun money all time. Him very good white man, that man; plenty money all a time."

Napoleon dwelt upon the wealth of his favorite white man so persistently that presently it occurred to me to inquire a little further.

"Suppose a white man had no money," said I, "what sort of a man would you think him?"

My philosopher's countenance took on a fine expression of contempt. "Suppose white man no got money?" he asked. "Eh! suppose he no got money—him dam fool!" And Napoleon glared upon us, his passengers, as though he wondered if either of us would venture to contradict so plain a proposition.

The sulphur bank is a remarkable deposit of decomposed volcanic rock and ashes, containing so large a quantity of sulphur that I am told that at the refining-works, which lie on the bank of the lake, the mass yields eighty per cent. of pure sulphur. The works were not in operation when I was there.

Several large hot springs burst out from the bank, and gas and steam escape with some violence from numerous fissures. The deposit looks very much like a similar one on the edge of the Kilauea crater, on the island of Hawaii, but is, I should think, richer in sulphur. Near the sulphur bank, on the edge of the lake, is a hot borate spring, which is supposed to yield at times three hundred gallons per minute, and which Professor Whitney, the State Geologist, declares remarkable for the extraordinary amount of ammoniacal salts its waters contain—more than any natural spring water that has ever been analyzed.

There is abundant evidence of volcanic action in all the country about Clear Lake. A dozen miles from Lakeport, not far from the shore of the lake, the whole mountain side along which the stage-road runs is covered for several miles with splinters and fragments of obsidian or volcanic glass, so that it looks as though millions of bottles had been broken there in some prodigious revelry; and where the road cuts into the side of the mountain you see the osidian lying in huge masses and in boulders. Joining this, and at one point inter-rupting it, is a tract of volcanic ashes stratified, and the strata thrown up ver-tically in some places, as though after the volcano had flung out the ashes there had come a terrific upheaval of the earth.

The two borax lakes lie also near the shore of Clear Lake; the largest one, which is not now worked, has an area of about three hundred acres. Little Borax Lake covers only about thirty acres, and this is now worked. The ef-florescing matter is composed of carbonate of soda, chloride of sodium, and bi-borate of soda. The object of the works is, of course, to separate the borax, and this is accomplished by crystallizing the borax, which, being the least solu-ble of the salts, is the first to crystallize.

The bottom of the lake was dry when I was there; it was covered all over with a white crust, which workmen scrape up and carry to the works, where it is treated very successfully. My nose was offended by the fetid stench which came from the earth when it was first put in the vats with hot water; and I was told by the foreman of the works that this arose from the immense number of flies and other insects which fly upon the lake and perish in it. Chinese are employed as laborers here, and give great satisfaction; and about eight days are required to complete the operation of extracting the borax in crystals.

Earth containing biborate of lime is brought to this place all the way from Wadsworth, in the State of Nevada—a very great distance, with several tran-shipments—to be reduced at these works; and it seems that this can be more cheaply done here than there, where they have neither wood for the fires nor soda for the operation.

Clear Lake is but twelve hours distant from San Francisco; the journey thither is full of interest, and the lake itself, with the natural wonders on its shores, is one of the most interesting and enjoyable spots in California to a tourist who wishes to breathe fresh mountain air and enjoy some days of free, open-air life.

The visitor to Clear Lake should go by way of the Napa Valley, taking stage for Lakeport at Calistoga, and return by way of the Russian River Valley, taking the railroad at Cloverdale. Thus he will see on his journey two of the richest and most fertile of the minor valleys of California, both abounding in fruit and vines as well as in grain.

As there are two sides to Broadway, so there are two sides to the Bay of San Francisco. On the one side lies the fine and highly-cultivated Santa Clara Valley, filling up fast with costly residences and carefully-kept country places. Opposite, on the other side of the bay, lies the Russian River Valley, as beau-tiful naturally as that of the Santa Clara, and of which Peteluma, Santa Rosa, Healdsburg, and Cloverdale are the chief towns. It is a considerable plain, bounded by fine hills and distant mountains, which open up, as you pass by on the railroad, numerous pretty reaches of subsidiary vales, where farmers live protected by the projecting hills from all harsh sea-breezes, and where frost is seldom if ever felt.

As you ascend the valley, the madrone, one of the most striking trees of California, becomes abundant and of larger growth, and its dark-green foliage and bright cinnamon-colored bark ornament the landscape. The laurel, too, or California bay-tree, grows thriftily among the hills. and the plain and foot-hills are dotted with oak and redwood. This valley is as yet somewhat thinly peopled, but it has the promise of a growth which will make it the equal some day of the Santa Clara, and the superior, perhaps, of the Napa Valley.

INDIANS SPEARING SALMON, COLUMBIA RIVER.

CHAPTER VII.

AN INDIAN RESERVATION.

A PART of Round Valley, in Mendocino County, is set apart and used for an Indian reservation; and, under the present policy of the Government, an attempt has been made to gather and keep all the Indians of the northern coast of California upon this reserve. In point of fact they are not nearly all there. One thousand and eighty-one men, women, and children, according to a census recently taken, or nearly one thousand two hundred according to the Rev. Mr. Burchard, the Indian agent, are actually within the reservation lines; and about four hundred are absent, at work for themselves or for white men, but have the right to come in at any time to be clothed and fed.

Round Valley is a plain surrounded by high mountains. The plain is mostly excellent agricultural land; the mountain slopes are valuable for grazing. The reservation contains, it is said, sixty thousand acres; but only a small part of this is plain, and the reservation occupies about one-third or perhaps only a quarter of the whole valley. The remainder is held by white farmers; and there is a rude little town, Covelo, in the centre of the valley, about a mile and a half from the reservation house.

The reservation has a mill, store-houses, the houses of the agent and his subordinates, two school-houses, and the huts of the Indians; the latter are either rough board one-roomed shanties, or mere wigwams built by the owners of brush, with peculiar low entrances, into which you must creep on all-fours. These they prefer for summer use, and I found that a number of the board-shanties were empty and the doors nailed up, their owners sensibly preferring to live in brush houses during the hot weather.

When I arrived at the agency the Indians were receiving their ration of flour, and, as they gathered in a great court-yard, I had an opportunity to examine them. They are short, dark-skinned, generally ugly, stout, and were dressed in various styles, but always in such clothing as they get from the Government; not in their native costume. Among several hundred women I saw not one even tolerably comely or conspicuously clean or neat; but I saw several men very well dressed. They carried off their rations in baskets which they make, and which are water-tight. The agent or superintendent, Mr. Burchard, very obligingly showed me through the camp, and answered my questions, and what follows of information I gained in this way.

The Indian shanties contain a fire-place, a bed-place, and sometimes a table; once I saw a small store-room; and on the walls hung dresses, shoes, fishing-nets, and other property of the occupants. The agent pointed out to me that in most of the houses there were bags of flour and meal stowed away, and remarked, " Whatever they may say against the President, no one can say that he does not make the Indians comfortable ;" and it is true that I saw everywhere in the camp the evidence of abundant supplies of food and sufficient clothing in the possession of the Indians. The superintendent said to me, " They have plenty of every thing ; they have often several bags of flour in the house at once; no man can say they are wronged."

The earthern floors of the houses were usually cleanly swept; there are wells at which the people get water; the school-houses are well furnished, and as good as the average country-school, and the Indians seem to suffer no hardship of the merely physical kind. The agent, Mr. Burchard, seems to be a genuinely kind person, simple - hearted, and, I should think, honest; and his assistants, whom I saw, struck me as respectable men. Indeed, several persons in the valley, unconnected with the reservation, told me that under Mr. Burchard's rule the Indians were much better treated than by his predecessor. I suppose, therefore, that I saw one of the most favorable examples of the reservation system.

In what follows, then, I criticise the reservation system, so far, at least, as it applies to the Indians of California, and not the management at Round Valley; and I say that it is a piece of cruel and stupid mismanagement and waste for which there is no excuse except in the ignorance of the President who continues it.

11

Most of the Indians of these northern coast counties, as well as those of Southern California, have for some years been a valuable laboring force for the farmers. They were employed to clear land, to make hay, and in many other avocations about the farm; they lived usually in little rancherias, or collections of huts, near the farm-houses; the women washed and did chores for the whites about the houses; and there has been, for at least half a dozen years, no pretense even that their presence among the whites was dangerous to these. Mr. Burchard told me himself that more than half the Indian men at Round Valley were competent farmers, and that the Indian women were used at the agency houses as servants, and made excellent and competent house-help.

Scattered through Potter, Little Lake, Ukiah, and other valleys, they were earning their living, and a number of farmers of that region have assured me that it was a serious disadvantage to them to lose the help of these Indians. Nor was it even necessary to speak their language in order to use their labor, for the agent told me that, of the Potter Valley tribe, nine-tenths speak English; of the Pitt Rivers, four-fifths; of the Little Lakes, two-thirds; of the Redwoods, three-quarters; of the Concows and Capellos, two-thirds. The Wylackies and Ukies speak less; they have been, I believe, longer on the reservation. As I walked through the Indian camp, English was as often spoken in my hearing as Indian.

The removal of the useful and self-supporting part of the Indian population to the reservation was brought about by means which are a disgrace to the United States Government. There is in all this northern country a class of mean whites, ignorant, easily led to evil, and extremely jealous of what they imagine to be their rights. Among these somebody fomented a jealousy of the Indians. It was said that they took the bread out of white men's mouths, that their labor interfered with the white men, and so forth. In fact, I suspect that the Indians were too respectable for these mean whites; and you can easily find people in California who say that it is to the interest of the Indian Bureau to make the whites hate the Indians.

The Indians were an industrious and harmless people; even the squaws worked; the Indian men had learned to take contracts for clearing land, weeding fields, and so forth; and many of them were so trustworthy that the farmers made them small advances where it was necessary. They were not turbulent, and I was surprised to be told that drunkenness was rare among them.

After secret deliberations among the mean whites, incited by no one knows who, and headed by the demagogues who are never found wanting when dirty work is to be done, a petition was sent to the State Superintendent of Indian Affairs at San Francisco for the removal of the Indians; but the more decent people immediately prepared and sent up a counter-petition, stating the whole case. This was in the spring of 1872.

I do not know the State Indian agent, but I am told that he hesitated, did not act, and, in May of the same year, a mob, without authority from him or from any body else, without notice to the Indians, and without even giving these poor creatures time to gather up their household goods or to arrange their little affairs, drove them out of their houses, and sixty miles, over a cruel road, to the reservation.

CHINOOK WOMAN AND CHILD.

Against this act of lawless violence toward peaceable and self-supporting men and women, who are, I notice, officially called "the nation's unfortunate wards," the proper officer of the United States Government, the Superintendent of Indian Affairs, did not protest, and for it no one has ever been punished.

But this was not all. The Indians being thus driven out, a meeting was called, at which it was announced that if they dared to return they would be killed; and, in fact, three unfortunates, who ventured back after some months to see their old homes, were shot down in cold blood; and, though the men are known who did this, for it no one has ever been punished.

Why should they be? The mob was only carrying out the prevailing "Indian policy," and the United States Government looked on with its hands folded.

It happens that the Indians of these little valleys are a mild race, not prone to war. When the white settlers first came to this region they lived unmolested by the Indians, who were numerous then, and might easily have "wiped out," to use a California phrase, the intruding white men. It happens that the Indians of the interior are braver and more warlike; and, accordingly, among them there were forty-five resolute Modocs, unwilling to be driven to a reservation, defying the United States for half a year. But from what I have written one can see how the Modoc war came about; for it arose from an attempt to force Captain Jack on to the Klamath Reservation—an attempt made, not by United States troops, as it ought to have been if it was to be done, but in their absence, and by men who purposely and carefully kept the military ignorant of what they intended to do; for there exists the utmost jealousy on the part of the Indian agents, of the War Department and the military authorities; and I repeat that the removal of the Modocs was planned and attempted to be carried out by the Indian Bureau officers, they keeping the military in careful ignorance of their designs.

I do not say too much when I say that if General Schofield had been informed and consulted beforehand, there would have been no Modoc war, and General Canby and Mr. Thomas might have been alive to-day.

Accordingly, these "unfortunate wards of the nation" are driven on the reservation. If their agent happens to be honest and kindly, like Mr. Burchard, they get enough to eat and to wear. If he is not, they do not fare quite so well. Captain Jack said he was "tired of eating horse-meat."

But if you are a guardian, and have a ward, you are not satisfied if your ward, presumedly an ignorant person in a state of pupilage, merely has enough to eat and to wear. You endeavor to form his manners and morals. Well, the Indian camp at Round Valley is in a deplorable state of disorder. No attempt is made to teach our wards to be clean or orderly, or to form in them those habits which might elevate, at least, their children. The plain around the shanties is full of litter, and overgrown with dog-fennel. As Mr. Burchard, the superintendent, walked about with me, half-grown boys sat on the grass, and even on the school-house steps, gambling with cards for tobacco, and they had not been taught manners enough to rise or move aside at the superintendent's approach. As we sat in the school-house, one, two, three Indian men came in to prefer a request, but not one of them took off his hat. We entered a cabin and found a big he-Indian lying on his bed. "Are you sick?" inquired Mr. Burchard, and the lazy hound, without offering to rise, muttered "No; me lying down."

The agent, in reply to my questions, said that they gambled a good deal for money and beads during the week, but he had forbidden it on Sundays; and he would not allow them to gamble away their clothing, as they formerly did.

There are about eighty scholars on the school-list, and about fifty attend school. Was there any compulsion used? I asked, and he said No. Now surely here, if anywhere, one might begin with a compulsory school-law.

Did he attempt to regulate the conduct of the growing boys and girls? No.

Do the Indians marry on the reservation? No. One chief has two wives; men leave their wives, or change them as they please.

What if children are born irregularly? Well, the reservation feeds and supports all who are on it. Nobody suffers.

Are the women often diseased? Yes, nearly all of them.

Have you a hospital, or do you attempt to isolate those who are diseased? No; the families all take care of their sick. The doctor visits them in their shanties. (Bear in mind this reservation was established, and has had Indians on it since 1860.)

Do the Indians have to ask permission to go to the town? No; they go when they please.

Is there much drunkenness? No; singularly little.

Do you attempt to make them rise at any specified hour in the morning? No.

Have you a list or roster of the Indians who belong on the reservation? No.

How many Indians own horses? I do not know.

On Sunday there is preaching; the audience varies; and those who do not come to church—where the preaching is in English—play shinny.

Is not all this deplorable? Here is a company of ignorant and semi-barbarous people, forcibly gathered together by the United States Government (with the help of a mob), under the pretense that they are the "unfortunate wards of the nation;" and the Government does not require the officers it sets over them to control them in any single direction where a conscientious guardian would feel bound to control his ward. How can habits of decency, energy, order, thrift, virtue, grow up—nay, how can they continue, if in the beginning they existed, with such management? Captain Jack and his forty-five Modocs were at least brave and energetic men. Can any one blame them, if they were bored to desperation by such a life as this, and preferred death to remaining on the reservation?

Nor is this all. Of the two thousand acres of arable land on the reservation, about five hundred are kept for grazing, and one thousand acres are in actual cultivation this year—seven hundred in grain and hay, one hundred and ninety-five in corn, and one hundred and nine in vegetables. A farmer, assistant-farmer, and gardener manage this considerable piece of land. When they need laborers they detail such men or women as they require, and these go out to work. They seldom refuse; if they do, they are sent to the military post, where they are made to saw wood. Not one of the cabins has about it a garden spot; all cultivation is in common; and thus the Indian is deprived of the main incentive to industry and thrift — the possession of the actual fruits of his own toil; and, unless he were a deep-thinking philosopher, who had studied out for himself the problems of socialism, he must, in the nature of things, be made a confirmed pauper and shirk by such a system, in which he sees no direct reward for his toil, and neither receives wages nor consciously eats that which his own hands have planted.

In the whole system of management, as I have described it, you will see that there is no reward for, or incentive to, excellence; it is all debauching and demoralizing; it is a disgrace to the Government, which consents to maintain at the public cost what is, in fact, nothing else but a pauper shop and house of prostitution.

And what is true of this reservation is equally true of that on the Tule River, in Southern California, which I saw in 1872. In both, to sum up the story, the Government has deprived the farmers of an important laboring force by creating a pauper asylum, called a reservation; and, having thus injured the community, it further injures the Indian by a system of treatment which ingeniously takes away every incentive to better living, and abstains from controlling him on those very points wherein an upright guardian would most rigidly and faithfully control and guide his ward.

To force a population of laboring and peaceable Indians on a reservation is a monstrous blunder. For wild and predatory or unsettled Indians, like the Apaches, or many tribes of the plains, the reservation is doubtless the best place; but even then the Government, acting as guardian, ought to control and train its wards; it ought to treat them like children, or at least like beasts; it ought not only to feed and clothe them, but also to teach them, and enforce upon them order, neatness, good manners, and habits of discipline and steady labor. This seems plain enough, but it will never be done by "Indian agents," selected from civil life, be these ministers or laymen.

An army officer, methodical, orderly, and having the habit of command, is the proper person for superintendent of a reservation; for drill and discipline, regular hours, regular duties, respectful manners, cleanliness, method — these are the elements of civilization that are needed, and which an army officer knows how to impress without harshness, because they are the essence of his own life. But under our present Indian policy the army is the mere servant of the Indian agent. If it were not for the small military force at Camp Wright, Mr. Burchard, the agent, could not keep an Indian on his reservation. But the intelligent, thoroughly-trained, and highly-educated soldier who commands there has neither authority nor influence at the reservation. He is a mere policeman, to whom an unruly Indian is sent for punishment, and who goes out at the command of the superintendent, a person in every way his inferior except in authority, to catch Indians when no mob is at hand to drive them in.

A true and humane Indian policy would be to require all peaceable Indians to support themselves as individuals and families among the whites, which would at once abolish the Round Valley and Tule River reservations; to place all the nomads on reservations, under the control of picked and intelligent army officers, and to require these to ignore, except for expediency's sake, all tribal distinctions and the authority of chiefs; to form every reservation into a military camp, adopting and maintaining military discipline, though not the drill, of course; to give to every Indian family an acre of ground around its hut, and require it to cultivate that, demanding of the male Indians at the same time two or three days of labor every week in the common fields, or on roads and other public improvements within the reservation during the season when no agricultural labor is required; to curb their vices, as a parent would those of his children; to compel the young to attend schools; to insist upon a daily morning muster, and a daily inspection of the houses and grounds; to establish a hospital for the sick; and thus gradually to introduce the Indian to civilization by the only avenue open to savages—by military discipline.

Under such a system a reserve like that of Round Valley would not to-day, after thirteen years of occupation, be a mass of weeds and litter, with bad roads, poor fences, and an almost impassable corduroy bridge over a little ditch. On the contrary, in half the time it would be a model of cleanliness and order; it would have the best roads, the neatest cottages, the cleanest grounds, the most thorough culture; and when the Indians had produced this effect, they would not fail to be in love with it.

Nor is it impossible to do all this with Indians. But it needs men used to command, well educated, and with habits of discipline—the picked men of the army. At present, an Indian reservation differs from an Indian rancheria or village only in that it contains more food, more vice, and more lazy people.

VIEW ON THE COLUMBIA RIVER.

CHAPTER VIII.

THE REDWOODS AND THE SAW-MILL COUNTRY OF MENDOCINO.

SOME years ago, before there was a wagon-road between Cloverdale and
Mendocino City, or Big River, as it is more commonly called up here on
the northern coast, the mail was carried on horse—or, more usually, on mule—
back; and the mail-rider was caught, on one stormy and dark night, upon the
road, and found himself unable to go farther.   In this dilemma he took refuge,
with his mule and the United States mails, in a hollow redwood, and man
and mule lay down comfortably within its shelter.   They had room to spare
indeed, as I saw when the stage-driver pointed out the tree to me and kindly
stopped until I examined it.

At a road-side inn I found they had roofed over a hollow stump, and used
it as a capacious store-room.

All these were large trees, of course; but there is no reason to believe that
they were the biggest of their kind; and when you have traveled for two or

three days through the redwood forests of the northern coast of California you will scarcely be surprised at any story of big trees.

The redwood seems to be found only near the coast of California; it needs the damp air which comes from the sea and which blows against the mountain slopes, which the tree loves. The coast, from fifty miles north of San Francisco to the northern border of Humboldt County, is a dense redwood forest; it is a mountainous and broken country, and the mountains are cut at frequent intervals by streams, some but a few miles in length, others penetrating into the interior by narrow cañons forty or fifty miles, and dividing in their upper waters into several branches.

The man who wondered at the wisdom of Providence in causing great rivers to flow past large cities would be struck with admiration at the convenient outflow of these streams; for upon them depends the accessibility of the redwood forests to the loggers and saw-mill men who are busily turning these forests into lumber. At the mouth of every stream is placed a saw-mill; and up these little rivers, many of which would hardly aspire to the dignity of creeks in Missouri or Mississippi, loggers are busy chopping down huge trees, sawing them into lengths, and floating them down to the mills.

The redwood has the color of cedar, but not its fragrance; it is a soft wood, unfit for ship-building, but easily worked and extraordinarily durable. It is often used in California for water-pipes, and makes the best fence posts, for it never rots below ground. Moreover, it is excellent material for houses. When varnished, it keeps its fine red color, but without this protection it slowly turns black with exposure to the air. It is a most useful lumber, and forms a not unimportant part of the natural wealth of California.

The saw-mills are mostly on so large a scale that about every one grows up a village or town, which usually contains several saloons or grog-shops, one or two billiard-rooms, a rude tavern or two, a doctor or two, several stores, and, in some cases, a church. There are, besides, the houses of those mill-men who have families, shanties for the bachelors, and usually one or two houses of greater pretensions, inhabited by the owners or local superintendents.

Not easily accessible, these little saw-mill ports are rarely visited by strangers, and the accommodations are somewhat rude; but the people are kindly, and the country is wonderfully picturesque, and well repays a visit.

The absolute coast is almost barren, by reason of the harsh, strong winds which prevail during the greater part of the year. The redwood forests begin a mile or two back from the sea. The climate of this part of the coast is remarkably equal, cool but not cold, all the year round; they have fires in the evening in July, and don't shut their doors, except in a storm, in December. They wear the same clothing all the year round, and seldom have frost. But when you get out of the reach of the sea, only a mile back, you find hot weather in July; and in winter they have snow, quite deep sometimes, in the redwoods.

Where the little saw-mill rivers enter the sea, there is usually a sort of road-stead—a curve of the shore, not enough to make a harbor, but sufficient to give anchorage and a lee from the prevailing north-west wind, which makes it possible, by different devices, to load vessels. There are rivers in Humboldt County where nature has not provided even this slight convenience, and there —it being impossible to ship the lumber—no saw-mills have been established.

Vessels are frequently lost, in spite of all precautions; for, when the wind changes to south-west, the whole Pacific Ocean rolls into these roadsteads; and, when a gale is seen approaching, the crews anchor their ships as securely as they can, and then go ashore. It has happened in Mendocino harbor, that a schooner has been capsized at her anchorage by a monstrous sea; and Captain Lansing told me that in the last twenty years he had seen over a hundred persons drowned in that port alone, in spite of all precautions.

The waves have cut up the coast in the most fantastic manner. It is rock-bound, and the rock seems to be of varying hardness, so that the ocean, trying every square inch every minute of the day for thousands of years, has eaten out the softer parts, and worked out the strangest caverns and passages. You scarcely see a headland or projecting point through which the sea has not forced a passage, whose top exceeds a little the mark of high tide; and there are caves innumerable, some with extensive ramifications. I was shown one such cave at Mendocino City, into which a schooner, drifting from her anchors, was sucked during a heavy sea. As she broke from her anchors the men hoisted sail, and the vessel was borne into the cave with all sail set. Her masts were snapped off like pipe-stems, and the hull was jammed into the great hole in the rock, where it began to thump with the swell so vehement-ly that two of the frightened crew were at once crushed on the deck by the overhanging ceiling of the cave. Five others hurriedly climbed out over the stern, and there hung on until ropes were lowered to them by men on the cliff above, who drew them up safely. It was a narrow escape; and a more terri-fying situation than that of this crew, as they saw their vessel sucked into a cave whose depth they did not know, can hardly be imagined outside of a hash-eesh dream. The next morning the vessel was so completely broken to pieces that not a piece the size of a man's arm was ever found of her hull.

I suppose all saw-mills are pretty much alike; those on this coast not only saw lumber of different shapes and sizes, but they have also planing and fin-ishing apparatus attached; and in some the waste lumber is worked up with a good deal of care and ingenuity. But in many of the mills there is great waste. It is probably a peculiarity of the saw-mills on this coast, that they must provide a powerful rip-saw to rip in two the larger logs before they are small enough for a circular saw to manage. Indeed, occasionally the huge logs

LUMBERING IN WASHINGTON TERRITORY—PREPARING LOGS.

are split with wedges, or blown apart with gunpowder, in the logging camps, because they are too vast to be floated down to the mill in one piece. The expedients for loading vessels are often novel and ingenious. For instance, at Mendocino the lumber is loaded on cars at the mill, and drawn by steam up a sharp incline, and by horses off to a point which shelters and affords anchorage for schooners. This point is, perhaps, one hundred feet above the water-line, and long wire-rope stages are projected from the top, and suspended by heavy derricks. The car runs to the edge of the cliff; the schooner anchors under the shipping stage one hundred feet below, and the lumber is slid down to her, a man standing at the lower end to check its too rapid descent with a kind of brake. When a larger vessel is to be loaded, they slide the lumber into a lighter, and the ship is loaded from her. The redwood is shipped not only to California ports, but also to China and South America; and while I was at Mendocino, a bark lay there loading for the Navigator Islands.

A large part of the lumbering population consists of bachelors, and for their accommodation you see numerous shanties erected near the saw-mills and lumber piles. At Mendocino City there is quite a colony of such shanties, two long rows, upon a point or cape from which the lumber is loaded.

I had the curiosity to enter one of these little snuggeries, which was unoccupied. It was about ten by twelve feet in area, had a large fire-place (for fuel is shamefully abundant here), a bunk for sleeping, with a lamp arranged for reading in bed, a small table, hooks for clothes, a good board floor, a small window, and a neat little hood over the door-way, which gave this little hut quite a picturesque effect. There was, besides, a rough bench and a small table.

It seemed to me that in such a climate as that of Mendocino, where they wear the same clothes all the year round, have evening fires in July, and may keep their doors open in January, such a little kennel as this meets all the real wants of the male of the human race.

This, I suspect, is about as far as man, unaided by woman, would have carried civilization anywhere. Whatever any of us have over and above such a snuggery as this we owe to womankind; whatever of comfort or elegance we possess, woman has given us, or made us give her. I think no wholesome, right-minded man in the world would ever get beyond such a hut; and I even suspect that the occupant of the shanty I inspected must have been in love, and thinking seriously of marriage, else he would never have nailed the pretty little hood over his door-way. So helpless is man! And yet there are people who would make of woman only a kind of female man!

As you travel along the coast, the stage-road gives you frequent and satisfactory views of its curiously distorted and ocean-eaten caves and rocks. It has a dangerous and terrible aspect, no doubt, to mariners, but it is most wonderful, viewed from the shore. At every projection you see that the waves have pierced and mined the rock; if the sea is high, you will hear it roar in the caverns it has made, and whistle and shriek wherever it has an outlet above through which the waves may force the air.

The real curiosity of this region is a logging camp. The redwood country is astonishingly broken; the mountain sides are often almost precipitous; and on these steep sides the redwood grows tall and straight and big beyond the belief of an Eastern man. The trees do not occupy the whole ground, but share it with laurels, dogwood, a worthless kind of oak, occasionally pine, and smaller wood. It is a kind of jungle; and the loggers, when they have felled a number of trees, set fire to the brush in order to clear the ground before they attempt to draw the logs to the water.

VICTORIA HARBOR, VANCOUVER'S ISLAND.

A logging camp is an assemblage of rude redwood shanties, gathered about one larger shanty, which is the cook-house and dining-hall, and where usually two or three Chinamen are at work over the stove, and setting the table. The loggers live well; they have excellent bread, meat, beans, butter, dried apples, cakes, pies, and pickles; in short, I have dined in worse places.

A camp is divided into "crews;" a crew is composed of from twenty to twenty-six men, who keep one team of eight or ten oxen busy hauling the logs to water.

A "crew" consists of teamsters, choppers, chain-tenders, jack-screw men (for these logs are too heavy to be moved without such machinery), swampers, who build the roads over which the logs are hauled, sawyers, and barkers. A teamster, I was told, receives seventy dollars per month, a chopper fifty dollars, chain-tenders and jack-screw men the same, swampers forty-five dollars, sawyers forty dollars, and barkers, who are usually Indians, one dollar a day and board besides, for all. The pay is not bad, and as the chances to spend money in a logging camp are not good, many of the men lay up money, and by-and-by go to farming or go home. They work twelve hours a day.

A man in Humboldt County got out of one redwood tree lumber enough to make his house and barn, and to fence in two acres of ground.

A schooner was filled with shingles made from a single tree.

One tree in Mendocino, whose remains were shown to me, made a mile of railroad ties.

Trees fourteen feet in diameter have been frequently found and cut down; the saw-logs are often split apart with wedges, because the entire mass is too large to float in the narrow and shallow streams; and I have even seen them blow a log apart with gunpowder.

A tree four feet in diameter is called undersized in these woods; and so skillful are the wood-choppers that they can make the largest giant of the forest fall just where they want it, or, as they say, they "drive a stake with the tree."

To chop down a redwood-tree, the chopper does not stand on the ground, but upon a stage sometimes twelve feet above the ground. Like the sequoia, the redwood has a great bulk near the ground, but contracts somewhat a few feet above. The chopper wants only the fair round of the tree, and his stage is composed of two stout staves, shod with a pointed iron at one end, which is driven into the tree. The outer ends are securely supported; and on these staves he lays two narrow, tough boards, on which he stands, and which spring at every blow of his axe. It will give you an idea of the bulk of these trees, when I tell you that in chopping down the larger ones two men stand on the stage and chop simultaneously at the same cut, facing each other.

They first cut off the bark, which is from four to ten, and often fifteen inches thick. This done, they begin what is called the "undercut"—the cut on that, side toward which the tree is meant to fall; and when they have made a little progress, they, by an ingenious and simple contrivance, fix upon the proper direction of the cut, so as to make the tree fall accurately where they want it. This is necessary, on account of the great length and weight of the trees, and the roughness of the ground, by reason of which a tree carelessly felled may in its fall break and split into pieces, so as to make it entirely worthless. This happens not unfrequently, in spite of every care.

So skillful are they in giving to the tree its proper direction that they are able to set a post or stake in the ground a hundred feet or more from the root of the tree, and drive it down by felling the tree on top of it.

"Can you really drive a stake with a tree?" I asked, and was answered, "Of course, we do it every day."

The "under-cut" goes in about two-thirds the diameter. When it is finished the stage is shifted to the opposite side, and then it is a remarkable sight to see the tall, straight mass begin to tremble as the axe goes in. It usually gives a heavy crack about fifteen minutes before it means to fall. The chopper thereupon gives a warning shout, so that all may stand clear—not of the tree, for he knows very well where that will go, and in a cleared space men will stand within ten feet of where the top of a tree is to strike, and watch its fall; his warning is against the branches of other trees, which are sometimes torn off and flung to a distance by the falling giant, and which occasionally dash out men's brains.

At last the tree visibly totters, and slowly goes over; and as it goes the chopper gets off his stage and runs a few feet to one side. Then you hear and see one of the grandest and most majestic incidents of forest life. There is a sharp crack, a crash, and then a long, prolonged, thunderous crash, which, when you hear it from a little distance, is startlingly like an actual and severe thunder-peal. To see a tree six feet in diameter, and one hundred and seventy-five feet high, thus go down, is a very great sight, not soon forgotten.

The choppers expressed themselves as disappointed that they could not just then show me the fall of a tree ten or twelve feet in diameter, and over two hundred feet high. In one logging camp I visited there remained a stump fourteen feet high. At this height the tree was fourteen feet in diameter, perfectly round and sound, and it had been sawn into seventeen logs, each twelve feet long. The upper length was six feet in diameter. Probably the tree was three hundred feet long, for the top for a long distance is wasted.

So many of the trees and so many parts of trees are splintered or broken in the fall, that the master of a logging camp told me he thought they wasted at least as much as they saved; and as the mills also waste a good deal, it is probable that for every foot of this lumber that goes to market two feet are lost. A five-foot tree occupies a chopper from two and a half to three and a half hours, and to cut down a tree eight feet in diameter is counted a day's work for a man.

When the tree is down the sawyers come. Each has a long saw; he removes the bark at each cut with an axe, and then saws the tree into lengths. It is odd enough to go past a tree and see a saw moving back and forward across its diameter without seeing the man who moves it, for the tree hides him completely from you, if you are on the side opposite him. Then come the barkers, with long iron bars to rip off the thick bark; then the jack-screw men, three or four of whom move a log about easily and rapidly which a hundred men could hardly budge. They head it in the proper direction for the teamsters and chain-men, and these then drag it down to the water over roads which are watered to make the logs slide easily; and then, either at high tide or during the winter freshets, the logs are run down to the mill.

The Maine men make the best wood-choppers, but the logging camp is a favorite place also for sailors; and I was told that Germans are liked as workmen about timber. The choppers grind their axes once a week—usually, I was told, on Sunday—and all hands in a logging camp work twelve hours a day.

The Government has lately become very strict in preserving the timber on Congress land, which was formerly cut at random, and by any body who chose. Government agents watch the loggers, and if these are anywhere caught cutting timber on Congress land their rafts are seized and sold. At present prices, it pays to haul logs in the redwood country only about half a mile to water;

all trees more distant than this from a river are not cut; but the rivers are in many places near each other, and the belt of timber left standing, though considerable, is not so great as one would think.

Redwood lumber has one singular property — it shrinks endwise, so that where it is used for weather-boarding a house, one is apt to see the butts shrunk apart. I am told that across the grain it does not shrink perceptibly.

Accidents are frequent in a logging camp, and good surgeons are in demand in all the saw-mill ports, for there is much more occasion for surgery than for physic. Men are cut with axes, jammed by logs, and otherwise hurt, one of the most serious dangers arising from the fall of limbs torn from standing trees by a falling one. Often such a limb lodges or sticks in the high top of a tree until the wind blows it down, or the concussion of the wood-cutter's axe, cutting down the tree, loosens it. Falling from such a height as two hundred or two hundred and fifty feet, even a light branch is dangerous, and men sometimes have their brains dashed out by such a falling limb.

When you leave the coast for the interior, you ride through mile after mile of redwood forest. Unlike the firs of Oregon and Puget Sound, this tree does not occupy the whole land. It rears its tall head from a jungle of laurel, madrone, oak, and other trees; and I doubt if so many as fifty large redwoods often stand upon a single acre. I was told that an average tree would turn out about fifteen thousand feet of lumber, and thus even thirty such trees to the acre would yield nearly half a million feet.

PORT TOWNSEND, WASHINGTON TERRITORY.

CHAPTER IX.

DAIRY-FARMING IN CALIFORNIA.

THE great valleys of California do not produce much butter, and probably never will, though I am told that cows fed on alfalfa, which is a kind of lucerne, yield abundant and rich milk, and, when small and careful farming comes into fashion in this State, there is no reason why stall-fed cows should not yield butter, even in the San Joaquin or Sacramento valleys. Indeed, with irrigation and stall-feeding, as one may have abundance of green food all the year round in the valleys, there should be excellent opportunity for butter-making.

But it is not necessary to use the agricultural soil for dairy purposes. In the foot-hills of the Sierras, and on the mountains, too, for a distance of more than a hundred miles along and near the line of the railroad, there is a great deal of country admirably fitted for dairying, and where already some of the most prosperous butter ranchos, as they call them here, are found. And as they are near a considerable population of miners and lumber-men, and have access by railroad to other centres of population, both eastward and westward,

12

the business is prosperous in this large district, where, by moving higher up into the mountains as summer advances, the dairy-man secures green food for his cows the summer through, without trouble, on the one condition that he knows the country and how to pick out his land to advantage.

Another dairy district lies on the coast, where the fogs brought in by the prevailing north-west winds keep the ground moist, foster the greenness and succulence of the native grasses during the summer, at least in the ravines, and keep the springs alive.

Marin County, lying north of San Francisco, is the country of butter ranchos on the coast, though there are also many profitable dairies south of the bay, in Santa Cruz and Monterey counties. In fact, dry as California is commonly and erroneously supposed to be, it exports a considerable quantity of butter, and a dairy-man said to me but recently that, to make the business really prosperous, the State needed a million or two more inhabitants, which means that the surplus product is now so great that it keeps down the price. No small quantity of this surplus goes East, as far as New York; and it is one of the curiosities of production and commerce that, while California can send butter to the Atlantic, it buys eggs of Illinois. One would have thought the reverse more probable.

Marin County offers some important advantages to the dairy-farmer. The sea-fogs which it receives cause abundant springs of excellent soft water, and also keep the grass green through the summer and fall in the gulches and ravines. Vicinity to the ocean also gives this region a very equal climate. It is never cold in winter nor hot in summer. In the milk-houses I saw usually a stove, but it was used mainly to dry the milk-room after very heavy fogs or continued rains; and in the height of summer the mercury marks at most sixty-seven degrees, and the milk keeps sweet without artificial aids for thirty-six hours.

The cows require no sheds nor any store of food, though the best dairy-men, I noticed, raised beets; but more, they told me, to feed to their pigs than for the cows. These creatures provide for themselves the year round in the open fields; but care is taken, by opening springs and leading water in iron pipes, to provide an abundance of this for them.

The county is full of dairy-farms; and, as this business requires rather more and better buildings than wheat, cattle, or sheep farming, as well as more fences, this gives the country a neater and thriftier appearance than is usual among farming communities in California. The butter-maker must have good buildings, and he must keep them in the best order.

But, besides these smaller dairy-farms, Marin County contains some large "butter ranchos," as they are called, which are a great curiosity in their way. The Californians, who have a singular genius for doing things on a large scale which in other States are done by retail, have managed to conduct even dairying in this way, and have known how to "organize" the making of butter in a way which would surprise an Orange County farmer. Here, for instance—and to take the most successful and complete of these experiments—is the rancho of Mr. Charles Webb Howard, on which I had the curiosity to spend a couple of days. It contains eighteen thousand acres of land well fitted for dairy purposes. On this he has at this time nine separate farms, occupied by nine tenants engaged in making butter. To let the farms outright would not do, because the tenants would put up poor improvements, and would need, even then, more capital than tenant-farmers usually have. Mr. Howard, therefore, contrived a scheme which seems to work satisfactorily to all concerned, and which appears to me extremely ingenious.

POINT REYES.

He fences each farm, making proper subdivisions of large fields; he opens springs, and leads water through iron pipes to the proper places, and also to the dwelling, milk-house, and corral. He builds the houses, which consist of a substantial dwelling, twenty-eight by thirty-two feet, a story and a half high, and containing nine rooms, all lathed and plastered; a thoroughly well-arranged milk-house, twenty-five by fifty feet, having a milk-room in the centre twenty-five feet square, with a churning-room, store-room, wash-room, etc.; a barn, forty by fifty feet, to contain hay for the farm-horses; also a calf-shed, a corral, or inclosure for the cows, a well-arranged pig-pen; and all these buildings are put up in the best manner, well painted, and neat.

The tenant receives from the proprietor all this, the land, and cows to stock it. He furnishes, on his part, all the dairy utensils, the needed horses and wagons, the furniture for the house, the farm implements, and the necessary labor. The tenant pays to the owner twenty-seven dollars and a half per annum for each cow, and agrees to take the best care of the stock and of all parts of the farm; to make the necessary repairs, and to raise for the owner annually one-fifth as many calves as he keeps cows, the remainder of the calves being killed and fed to the pigs. He agrees also to sell nothing but butter and hogs from the farm, the hogs being entirely the tenant's property.

Under this system fifteen hundred and twenty cows are now kept on nine separate farms on this estate, the largest number kept by one man being two hundred and twenty-five, and the smallest one hundred and fifteen. Mr. Howard has been for years improving his herd; he prefers short-horns, and he saves every year the calves from the best milkers in all his herd, using also bulls from good milking strains. I was told that the average product of butter on the whole estate is now one hundred and seventy-five pounds to each cow; many cows give as high as two hundred, and even two hundred and fifty pounds per annum.

Men do the milking, and also the butter-making, though on one farm I found a pretty Swedish girl superintending all the indoor work, with such skill and order in all the departments, that she possessed, so far as I saw, the model dairy on the estate.

Here, said I to myself, is now an instance of the ability of women to compete with men which would delight Mrs. Stanton and all the Woman's Rights people; here is the neatest, the sweetest, the most complete dairy in the whole region; the best order, the most shining utensils, the nicest butter-room—and not only butter, but cheese also, made, which is not usual; and here is a rosy-faced, white-armed, smooth-haired, sensibly-dressed, altogether admirable, and, to my eyes, beautiful Swedish lass presiding over it all; commanding her men-servants, and keeping every part of the business in order.

Alas! Mrs. Stanton, she has discovered a better business than butter-making. She is going to marry—sensible girl that she is—and she is not going to marry a dairy-farmer either.

I doubt if any body in California will ever make as nice butter as this pretty Swede; certainly, every other dairy I saw seemed to me commonplace and uninteresting, after I had seen hers. I don't doubt that the young man who has had the art to persuade her to love him ought to be hanged, because butter-making is far more important than marrying.   Nevertheless, I wish him joy in advance, and, in humble defiance of Mrs. Stanton and her brilliant companions in arms, hereby give it as my belief that the pretty Swede is a sensible girl— that, to use a California vulgarism, "her head is level."

The hogs are fed chiefly on skim-milk, and belong entirely to the tenant. The calves, except those which are raised for the proprietor, are, by agreement, killed and fed to the pigs.   The leases are usually for three years.

The cows are milked twice a day, being driven for that purpose into a corral, near the milk-house.   I noticed that they were all very gentle; they lay down in the corral with that placid air which a good cow has; and whenever a milkman came to the beast he wished to milk, she rose at once, without waiting to be spoken to.   One man is expected to milk twenty cows in the season of full milk.   On some places I noticed that Chinese were employed in the milk-house, to attend to the cream and make the butter.

The tenants are of different nationalities, American, Swedes, Germans, Irish, and Portuguese.   A tenant needs about two thousand dollars in money to undertake one of these dairy-farms; the system seems to satisfy those who are now engaged in it.   The milkers and farm hands receive thirty dollars per month and "found;" and good milkers are in constant demand.   Every thing is conducted with great care and cleanliness, the buildings being uncommonly good for this State, water abundant, and many labor-saving contrivances used.

At one end of the corral or yard in which the cows are milked is a platform, roofed over, on which stands a large tin, with a double strainer, into which the milk is poured from the buckets.   It runs through a pipe into the milk-house, where it is again strained, and then emptied from a bucket into the pans ranged on shelves around.   The cream is taken off in from thirty-six to forty hours; and the milk keeps sweet thirty-six hours, even in summer. The square box-churn is used entirely, and is revolved by horse-power.   They usually get butter, I was told, in half an hour.

The butter is worked on an ingenious turn-table, which holds one hundred pounds at a time, and can, when loaded, be turned by a finger; and a lever, working upon a universal joint, is used upon the butter.   When ready, it is put up in two-pound rolls, which are shaped in a hand-press, and the rolls are not weighed until they reach the city.   It is packed in strong, oblong boxes, each of which holds fifty-five rolls.

The cows are not driven more than a mile to be milked; the fields being so arranged that the corral is near the centre.   When they are milked, they stray back of themselves to their grazing places.

COLUMBIA RIVER SCENE.

CHAPTER X.

TEHAMA AND BUTTE, AND THE UPPER COUNTRY.

GENERAL BIDWELL, of Butte County, raised last year on his own estate, besides a large quantity of fruit, seventy-five thousand bushels of wheat. Dr. Glenn, of Colusa County, raised and sent to market from his own estate, two hundred thousand bushels. Mr. Warner, of Solano County, produced nine thousand gallons of cider from his own orchards. A sheep-grazer in Placer County loaded ten railroad cars with wool, the clip of his own sheep. For many weeks after harvest you may see sacks of wheat stacked along the railroad and the river for miles, awaiting shipment; for the farmers have no rain to fear, and the grain crop is thrashed in the field, bagged, and stacked along the road, without even a tarpaulin to cover it.

In 1855, California exported about four hundred and twenty tons of wheat; in 1873, the export was but little less than six hundred thousand tons. In 1857, six casks and six hundred cases of California wine were sent out of the State; in 1872, about six hundred thousand gallons were exported. In 1850, California produced five thousand five hundred and thirty pounds of wool; in 1872, this product amounted to twenty-four million pounds. Thirty million pounds of apples, ten million pounds of peaches, four and a half million pounds of apricots, nearly two million pounds of cherries, are part of the product of the State, in which the man is still living who brought across the Plains the first fruit-trees to set out a nursery; while four and a half million of oranges, and a million and a half of lemons, shipped from the southern part of the State, show the rapid growth of that culture.

In the northern counties, of which Tehama and Butte are a sample, they are usually fortunate in the matter of late as well as early rains; but close under the coast range the country is dryer, as is natural, the high mountain range absorbing the moisture from the north-westerly winds. They begin to plow as soon as it rains, usually in November, and sow the grain at once. Formerly the higher plains were thought to be fit only for grazing; but even the red lands, which are somewhat harder to break up, and were thought to be infertile, are found to bear good crops of grain; and this year these lands bear the drought better than some that were and are preferred. Lambing takes place here in February, and they shear in April. The grazing lands abound in wild oats, very nutritious, but apt to run out where the pastures are overstocked. Alfilleria is not found so far north as this; alfalfa has been sown all over the valley in proper places, and does well. They cut it three times in the year, and turn stock in on it after the last cutting; and all who grow it speak well of it.

Red Bluff is one of the oldest towns in the valley; it stands at the head of navigation on the Sacramento, and was, therefore, a place of importance before the railroad was built. The river here is narrow and shoal, and it is crossed by one of those ferries common where the rapid current, pushing against the ferry-boat, drives it across the stream, a wire cable preventing it from floating down stream. The main street of the town consists mainly of bar-rooms, livery-stables, barber-shops, and hotels, with an occasional store of merchandise sandwiched between; and, if you saw only this main street, you would conceive but a poor opinion of the people. But other streets contain a number of pleasant, shady cottages; and, as I drove out into the country, the driver pointed with pride to the school-house, a large and fine building, which had just been completed at a cost of thirty thousand dollars, and seemed to me worth the money. The town has also water-works; and the people propose to bridge the Sacramento at a cost of forty thousand dollars, and to build a new jail, to cost fifteen thousand dollars. Such enterprises show the wealth of the people in this State, and astonish the traveler, who imagines, in driving over the great plain, that it is almost uninhabited, but sees, in a thirty-thousand dollar school-house in a little town like Red Bluff, that not only are there people, but that they have the courage to bear taxation for good objects, and the means to pay.

From Red Bluff two of the great mountain peaks of Northern California are magnificently seen—Lassen's Peaks and Shasta. The latter, still one hundred and twenty miles off to the north, rears his great, craggy, snow-covered summit high in the air, and seems not more than twenty miles away. Lassen's Peaks are twins, and very lonely indeed. They are sixty miles to the east, and are also, at this season, glistening with snow. Between Lassen's and the Sacramento, some thirty miles up among the mountains, there is a rich timber country, whose saw-mills supply the northern part of the valley with lumber, sugar-pine being the principal tree sawed up. The valley begins to narrow above Red Bluff, and the foot-hills and mountains still abound in wild game. Hunters bring their peltries hither for sale; and this has occasioned the establishment at this point of a thriving glove factory, which turned out— from an insignificant looking little shop—not less than forty thousand dollars' worth of gloves last year. Two enterprising young men manage it, and they employ, I was told, from fifty to eighty women in the work, and turn out very excellent buckskin gloves, as well as some finer kinds. Such petty industries are too often neglected in California, where every body still wants to conduct his calling on a grand scale, and where dozens of ways to prosperity, and even wealth, are constantly neglected, because they appear too slow.

This whole country is only about four years in advance of the lower or San Joaquin Valley, and the influence of climate and soil in bringing trees to bear early was shown to me in several thrifty orchards, already beginning to bear, on ground which four years ago was bought for two dollars and fifty cents per acre. The habit of raising wheat is so strong here, that almost every thing else is neglected; and I remember a farm where the wheat field extended, unbroken, except by a narrow path leading to the road, right up to the veranda of the farmer's house. His family lived on canned fruits and vegetables; and except here and there a brilliant poppy, which stubborn Dame Nature had inserted among his wheat, wife and children had not a flower to grace mantle or table. I confess that it pleased me to hear this farmer complain of hard times, because, as he said, the speculators in San Francisco made more money from his wheat than he did. If the speculators in San Francisco teach the farmers in California to grow something besides wheat, they will deserve well of the State.

The upper waters of the Sacramento run through mountain passes, and between banks so steep that for miles at a time the river is inaccessible, except by difficult and often dangerous descents; and an old miner told me that when this part of the river, between where Redding now lies and its source, near Mount Shasta, was first "prospected" for gold, the miners or explorers had to build boats and descend by water, trying for gold by the way, because they could not get down by land. In those days, he said, if a company of miners could not make twenty dollars a day each, the "prospect" was too poor to detain them; and they made but a short stay at most points on the Upper Sacramento.

The country was then full of Indians; and it was very strange, indeed, to hear this miner—a thoroughly kind-hearted man he was, and now the father of a family of children—tell with the utmost unconcern, and as a matter of course, how they used to shoot down these Indians, who waylaid them at favoring spots on the river, and tried to pick them off with arrows.

I remember hearing a little boy ask a famous general once how many men he had killed in the course of his wars, and being disappointed when he heard that the general, so far as he knew, had never killed any body. I suppose a soldier in battle but rarely knows that he has actually shot a man. But one

STREET IN OLYMPIA, WASHINGTON TERRITORY.

of these old Indian fighters sits down after dinner, over a pipe, and relates to you, with quite horrifying coolness, every detail of the death which his rifle and his sure eye dealt to an Indian; and when this one, stroking meantime the head of a little boy who was standing at his knees, described to me how he lay on the grass and took aim at a tall chief who was, in the moonlight, trying to steal a boat from a party of gold-seekers, and how, at the crack of his rifle, the Indian fell his whole length in the boat and never stirred again, I confess I was dumb with amazement. The tragedy had not even the dignity of an event in this man's life. He shot Indians as he ate his dinner, plainly as a mere matter of course. Nor was he a brute, but a kindly, honest, good fellow, not in the least blood-thirsty.

The poor Indians have rapidly melted away under the fervent heat of forty-rod whisky, rifles, and disease. This whole Northern country must have been populous a quarter of a century ago; General Bidwell and other old Californians have told me of the surprisingly rapid disappearance of the Indians, after the white gold-seekers came in. It was, I do not doubt, a pleasant land for the red men. They lived on salmon, clover, deer, acorns, and a few roots which are abundant on mountain and plain, and of all this food there is the greatest plenty even yet. If you travel toward Oregon, by stage, in June, July, or August, you will see at convenient points along the Sacramento parties of Indians spearing and trapping salmon. They build a few rude huts of brush, gather sticks for the fire, which is needed to cook and dry the salmon meat; and then, while the men, armed with long two-pronged spears, stand at the end of logs projecting over the salmon pools, and spear the abundant fish, the squaws clean the fish, roast them to dryness among the hot stones of their rude fire-place, and finally rub the dried meat to a powder between their hands, or by the help of stones, when it is packed away in bags for winter use.

What you thus see on the Sacramento is going on at the same time on half a dozen other rivers; and I am told that these Indians come from considerable distances to this annual fishing, which was practiced by them doubtless a long time before the white men came in. Not unfrequently in these mountains you will find a castaway white man with a half-breed family about him; "squaw-men" they are called, as a term of contempt, by the more decent class.

As you drive by the farm-houses on the road, you may commonly see venison hanging on the porch; and every farmer has a supply of fishing-rods and lines, so that you can not go amiss for trout and venison. Few of them know, however, that a trout ought to be cooked as quickly as possible after he is caught; and if you do not take care, your afternoon fish will appear on the table next day as corned trout, in which shape I have no liking for it.

The Shasta Valley contains a good deal of excellent farming land, but it is used now chiefly for cattle and sheep, and in many parts of it the grazing is very fine. There are a number of lesser valleys scattered through the mountains hereabouts. Indeed, the two ranges seem to open out for a while, and Scott's Valley on the west, and the Klamath Lake country to the east and north-east from Yreka, are favorite grazing regions. Here there is occasional snow in the winter, and some cold weather; the spring opens later and the rains last longer. The streams in all this region bear gold, and miners are busy in them. Yreka, in the Shasta Valley, is the centre of a considerable mining district, and therefore a busy place, even without the Modoc war, which gave it a temporary renown during the winter and spring. Now that the Modoc war is closed, no doubt the famous lava beds will attract curious visitors from afar. They can be reached in thirty-six hours from Yreka; and that place is distant thirty-six hours from San Francisco.

Aside from the public lands still open in small tracts of eighty and one hundred and sixty acres to pre-emption by actual settlers, under the homestead law, and the railroad lands, to be had in sections of six hundred and forty acres, the Sacramento Valley contains a number of considerable Spanish grants; and the following account of these, which I take from the San Francisco *Bulletin*, will give an Eastern reader some idea of the extent of such grants, their value, and how they are used:

"The first large tract of land north and west of Marysville is the Neal grant, containing about seventeen thousand acres. This grant is owned by the Durham estate and Judge C. F. Lott, though Gruelly owns a large slice of it also. The Neal grant is mostly composed of rich bottom-lands; nearly all of it is farmed under lease; the lessees pay one-quarter to one-third of the crops as rent. They do very well under this arrangement.

"The next grant on the north is that of Judge O. C. Pratt. It contains twenty-eight thousand acres of bottom-land. Butte Creek skirts it on one side for a distance of seventeen miles, and a branch of that creek runs through the centre. Nearly six thousand acres are covered with large oak-trees. There are about one hundred miles of fences on this rancho; there are about ten thousand sheep, twelve hundred head of cattle, and two hundred horses on it; the land has been cultivated or used as pasturage for about fourteen years. About ten thousand acres of it, I am informed, would readily sell in subdivisions for fifty dollars per acre; ten thousand acres would sell for about thirty dollars, and eight thousand acres at twenty dollars per acre. There are many tenants on this tract, having leases covering periods of three to five years; rent, one-fourth of the crop raised; the owner builds fences and houses for the lessees. The average quantity of wool annually grown on this rancho is sixty thousand pounds; beef cattle, two hundred and fifty head; value of produce received as rent from tenants, twelve thousand dollars per year. Judge Pratt is willing to sell farms of one hundred and sixty to three hundred and twenty acres at about the rates named, and on easy terms.

"The Hensley grant, lying north of Judge Pratt's rancho, contains five leagues. It was rejected by the United States Courts, and was taken up by, and is covered with, settlers, who own one hundred and sixty to three hundred and twenty acres each, worth forty to sixty dollars per acre. Little or none of that land is for sale, the owners being too well satisfied with their farms to sell them, even at the highest ruling rates.

"General Bidwell's rancho adjoins Judge Pratt's. It contains about twenty thousand acres, of which about one-quarter is of the best quality, and would readily sell at fifty to sixty dollars per acre. About five thousand acres more, lying along the Sacramento River, are subject to overflow. That portion is very rich grazing land, and is worth fifteen to twenty dollars per acre. The other ten thousand acres lie near the foot-hills; they are extremely well adapted to grape culture, and are worth five to twelve dollars per acre. General Bidwell is not willing to sell.

"The next rancho on the west is owned by John Parrot. It contains about seventeen thousand acres, and lies on the east bank of the Sacramento River. It contains about four thousand acres of first-class wheat or corn land; the remainder is composed of excellent pasturage; there are only a few thousand sheep, and a few cattle and horses on this rancho. It has for several years been cultivated by Morehead and Griffith, under a private arrangement with the owner. It is understood that Parrot would sell, either in a body or in small tracts, to desirable purchasers; his prices would probably range from fifteen to fifty dollars per acre.

"The next large rancho is that of Henry Gerke, living twenty miles above Chico. It now contains about eighteen thousand acres, of which a large portion is suitable for wheat or corn growing, and grazing purposes. One of the largest and finest vineyards in the State is on this rancho; and the wine it produces has a large sale in the State. The most of Gerke's land is devoted to wheat raising; eighteen hundred tons of wheat were raised on it last year, and about twenty-two hundred tons this year. It is mostly tilled by tenants. The land is worth from twenty to fifty dollars per acre. The owner would sell the whole rancho, but it is not known whether he would sell in small tracts or not. He has a standing offer of six hundred and seventy-five thousand dollars for the land, vineyards, and improvements.

"General Wilson owns several thousand acres of the original Gerke grant. His land is altogether devoted to wheat growing, and is worth forty dollars per acre.

"A. G. Towne's grant adjoins Gerke's on the north and west. It now contains about twelve thousand acres; much of it is devoted to wheat growing, and is worth fifteen to forty dollars per acre, or an average all round of twenty-five dollars.

"At Tehama, on the west side of the Sacramento River, is Thorne's grant. It contains about twenty thousand acres, one-third of which is of the very best quality of wheat land, the remainder good grazing. It is understood that this land can be bought either as a whole or in small farms. The best of it is worth about forty-five dollars an acre; the body of it about twenty dollars.

"The next grant, on the north, is that of William G. Chard. It is nearly all cut up and owned in small farms. Colonel E. J. Lewis, a well-known politician, is one of the largest owners on the Chard tract. He is extensively engaged in wheat raising.

"Ide's grant is adjacent, on the north; it is also mostly divided and owned in small tracts of one hundred and sixty to four hundred acres each.

"The Dye grant lies east of and opposite to Red Bluff. It was originally a large grant, but has been partially subdivided. It contains some good bottom-land, but is mostly adapted to grazing.

"The most northerly grant in the State is that formerly owned by the late

Major Redding. It is partially subdivided. Like the Dye grant, it contains some rich bottom-land, but, like it, is mostly adapted for grazing and grape growing. Haggin and Tevis lately bought (or hold for debt) about fifteen thousand acres of this rancho, which are worth about one hundred thousand dollars, or about seven dollars per acre. It is understood from inquiries made from the owners of these two last named tracts, that they are willing to sell grain lands at about an average of thirty dollars per acre."

Of course these grants make up, in the aggregate, but a small part of the arable land of the Sacramento Valley.

"TACOMA," OR MOUNT RAINIER.

CHAPTER XI.

TOBACCO CULTURE—WITH A NEW METHOD OF CURING THE LEAF.

THE manufacture of cigars is one of the largest industries of San Francisco. Last year the Government received taxes on 78,000,000 cigars made in the State of California, and in September alone taxes were paid on 8,000,000. But, though the State has thousands of acres of land well fitted to produce tobacco, and though the "weed" has been grown here for twenty years or more with great success, so far as getting a heavy crop is concerned, I doubt if even 1,000,000 of cigars have, until this fall, been made of tobacco raised in California.

There has, however, been no lack of efforts to produce here tobacco fit to manufacture into cigars and for smoking and chewing purposes. The soil in many parts of the State is peculiarly adapted to this plant; the climate, mild and regular, favored its growth and hastened its perfection. The best seed was procured from Connecticut, Kentucky, Virginia, Florida, and Cuba. But for many years the product was rank, coarse, and fitter for sheep-wash than for any other purpose.

Meantime, however, not a few men familiar with the old processes of raising and curing the plant have tried their best ingenuity to improve the quality. It was thought that the soil was too rich, because the tobacco makes a rapid and heavy growth; but planting on thinner or older soil did not answer. Several methods of curing were contrived, and there is now reason to believe that the one known as the Culp process, from the name of its patentee, will produce the desired result. I had heard and read so much about it, and about the merit of the tobacco produced by it, that I went down to Gilroy, seventy or eighty miles south of San Francisco, to see what had really been accomplished. The account I give below will probably interest many tobacco growing and manufacturing readers, while it will, I fear, painfully affect the spirits of the anti-tobacconists; for there is reason to believe that tobacco will become presently one of the most important and valuable crops of this State.

I must premise that I am not an expert in tobacco, nor familiar with the methods pursued in the East. I have seen a tobacco-field and the inside of a Connecticut curing-house, and that is about all. I give, therefore, not opinions, but facts.

Gilroy stands in a long and broad plain, a very rich piece of alluvial bottom, with water so abundant that artesian wells are easily bored and very common. At the depth of one hundred and thirty feet they get flowing wells, and it happened in one case of which I heard that the water came up with such force as to prevent the casing going down into the well, and the pressure of the water broke away the ground, enlarged the bore of the well, and threatened to flood a considerable area, so that the farmers gathered in force, and by means of an iron caisson loaded with stones, and with many cart-loads of stones besides, plugged up the dangerous hole.

The land is a deep alluvial loam, easily worked, and here, and in some neighboring valleys, many tobacco growers have been engaged for the last ten or twelve years. Mr. Culp, who was a tobacco grower, and, if I understood him rightly, also a manufacturer in New York for some years before he came here, and who appears, at any rate, to be a very thorough farmer and a lover of clean fields, has planted tobacco here for fifteen years. He has a farm of about seven hundred acres, four hundred of which have this year been in tobacco. From him and others I learned the following particulars of the way in which they cultivate the plant in California.

They sow the seed from the 1st to the 10th of January, and sometimes even in December. The beds are prepared and sown as in the East, except that they do not always burn the ground over, which, if I remember rightly, is invariably done in Missouri and Kentucky. In this season, the days are always warm enough for the little plants; but there are light frosts at night, and they are protected against these by frames covered with thin cotton cloth.

The fields are plowed—by the best growers—ten inches deep; cross-plowed and harrowed until the soil is fine, and then ridged—that is to say, two furrows are thrown together. This saves the plants from harm by a heavy rain, and also makes the ground warmer, and is found to start the plants more quickly.

Planting in the fields begins about the 8th of April; and the plants are set a foot apart in the rows, the rows being three feet apart, if they are from Havana seed; if Connecticut or Florida, they stand eighteen inches or two feet apart in the rows.

They had grown, besides Havana and Florida, for their crop, Latakia, Hungarian, Mexican, Virginia, Connecticut-seed Standard, Burleigh, White Leaf, and some other kinds, by way of experiment.

Cultivators and shovel-plows are used to keep the soil loose and clean; if the weather should prove damp and cold, the shovel-plow is used to make the ridges somewhat higher. They go over the fields twice in the season with these tools, using the hoe freely where weeds get into the rows. Last year, in twenty-six days after they were done planting, they had gathered two bales of tobacco. This, however, is not common, and was done by very close management, and on a warm soil.

All the tobacco growers with whom I spoke assert that they are not troubled with that hideous creature, "the worm." They attribute this in part to the excellence of their soil, and partly to the abundance of birds and yellow jackets. They do not "worm" their crop, it seems, which must give them an enviable advantage over Eastern growers.

They do not always "top" the Havana, and they do very little "suckering." If the ground is clean, they let the suckers from the root grow, and these become as large and heavy as the original plant. They believe that the soil is strong enough to bear the plants and suckers, and that they get a better leaf and finer quality without suckering.

The planting is continued from April until the latter part of July, so as to let the crop come in gradually; the last planting may be caught by an early frost, but whatever they plant before the 1st of July is safe in any season. Cutting begins about the 4th of June, and this year they were cutting still on the 19th of October. The earlier cut plants sprout again at once, and mature a second and even a third crop. Mr. Culp told me that he had taken four crops of Havana in one year from the same field, and I saw considerable fields of third crop just cut or standing; but in some cases the frost had caught this. "If the soil is in perfect order, we can here make a crop of Havana in forty days from the planting," said he.

One man can prepare and take care of ten acres here, keeping it in good order. For planting and cutting, of course, an extra force is used. One man can set out or plant three thousand plants in a day of Havana; of the other kinds from fifteen hundred to two thousand.

The tobacco is cut with a hatchet; if it is Havana, the toppers usually go just ahead of the cutters in the field, or they may be a day ahead. Florida is topped ten days or two weeks before cutting. You must remember that after April they have no rain here, so that all field work goes on without interruption from the weather, and crops can be exposed in the field as a planter would not dare do in the East. Up to the cutting, the methods here differ from those used in the East, only so far as climate and soil are different.

When the plant lies in the field Mr. Culp's peculiar process begins; and this

I prefer to describe to you as nearly as I can in his own words. He said that tobacco had long been grown in California even before the Americans came. He had raised it as a crop for fifteen years; and before he perfected his new process, he was able usually to select the best of his crop for smoking-tobacco, and sold the remainder for sheep-wash. One year two millions of pounds were raised in the State, and, as it was mostly sold for sheep-wash, it lasted several years, and discouraged the growers. Tobacco always grew readily, but it was too rank and strong. They used Eastern methods, topping and suckering, and as the plant had here a very long season to grow and mature, the leaf was thick and very strong.

The main features of the Culp process are, he said, to let the tobacco, when cut, wilt on the field; then take it at once to the tobacco-house and pile it down, letting it heat on the piles to 100° for Havana. It must, he thinks, come to 100°, but if it rises to 102° it is ruined. Piling, therefore, requires great judgment. The tobacco-houses are kept at a temperature of about 70°; and late in the fall, to cure a late second or third crop, they sometimes use a stove to maintain a proper heat in the house, for the tobacco must not lie in the pile without heating.

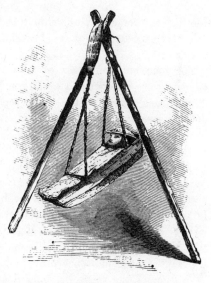

INDIAN CRADLE, WASHINGTON TERRITORY.

When it has had its first sweat, it is hung up on racks; and here Mr. Culp's process is peculiar. He places the stalk between two battens, so that it sticks out horizontally from the frame; thus each leaf hangs independently from the stalk; and the racks or frames are so arranged that all the leaves on all the stalks have a separate access to the air.

The tobacco-houses are frame buildings, 100 × 60 feet, with usually four rows of racks, and two gangways for working. On the rack the surface moisture dries from the leaf; and at the proper time it is again piled, racked, and so on for three or even four times. The racks are of rough boards, and the floor of the house is of earth.

After piling and racking for three weeks, the leaves are stripped from the stalk and put into "hands," and they are then "bulked," and lie thus about three months, when the tobacco is boxed. From the time of cutting, from four to six months are required to make the leaf ready for the manufacturer.

"Piling" appears to be the most delicate part of the cure, and they have often to work all night to save tobacco that threatens to overheat. Mr. Culp thinks the dryness of the climate no disadvantage. I was told that they find it useful sometimes to sprinkle the floors of the tobacco-houses.

I saw racks, too, in the fields—portable, and easily carried anywhere; and on these a great quantity of Florida tobacco, used for chewing and smoking, had been or was getting cured. It was piled in the field where it was cut, and the whole curing process, up to "bulking," is carried on in the open air. Havana "fillers." they also cure in the field, as the fine color is not needed for that.

Mr. Culp thought his method of horizontal suspension allowed the juices from the stalk to be carefully distributed among the leaves. He told me that a fair average crop was about 1500 pounds of Havana, or 2500 pounds of Florida, per acre, of merchantable leaf. In favorable localities this was considerably exceeded, he said. For chewing-tobacco, the cut plant is piled but once.

For four hundred acres of tobacco, about one hundred and twenty-five Chinese were employed in cutting and curing. After planting and up to the cutting season they had but fifty men employed. The Chinese receive one dollar a day and board themselves, living an apparently jolly life in shanties near the fields.

They get their Havana seed from Cuba. The Patent Office seed did not do well. They do not like to risk seed of their own plants. He used home-grown seed for nine years; he could not say that there was a serious deterioration or change in the quality of the tobacco, but a singular change in the form of the leaf took place. That from home-grown seed gets longer, and the veins or ribs, which in Havana tobacco stand out at right angles from the leaf stalk, take an acute angle, and thus become longer and make up a greater part of the leaf. Of Florida tobacco the home-grown seed comes true.

In summer the roads get very dusty in California, and this dust is a disadvantage to the tobacco planter. On the Culp farm I found they were planting double rows of shade trees along the main roads, and graveling the interior roads; also, they seem to feel the high winds which sweep through the California valleys, and were planting almonds and cotton-woods for windbreaks in the fields. It seemed odd to see long rows of almond-trees used for this purpose.

This process has so far won the confidence of experts in tobacco in this State, that a company with large capital has undertaken not only the raising of tobacco by its method, but also the manufacture into cigars, and plug, smoking, and fine-cut chewing-tobacco. They are just beginning operations in Gilroy, on a scale which will enable them to manufacture all the tobacco grown this year on about six hundred acres, and they mean to plant next year one thousand acres, and expect that from fifteen hundred to two thousand acres will be planted and cured by others under licenses from the patentee. Commercially, of course, their undertaking is yet an experiment, though excellent cigars and tobacco have been made already; but the year 1874 will decide the result; and if it should prove as successful as is hoped, and as there is good cause to believe it will, a new and very profitable branch of agriculture will be opened for the farmers of this State; for tobacco will grow in almost all parts of it.

RUNNING THE ROOKERIES—GATHERING MURRE EGGS.

CHAPTER XII.

THE FARALLON ISLANDS.

IF you approach the harbor of San Francisco from the west, your first sight of land will be a collection of picturesque rocks known as the Farallones, or, more fully, the Farallones de los Frayles. They are six rugged islets, whose peaks lift up their heads in picturesque masses out of the ocean, twenty-three and a half miles from the Golden Gate, the famous entrance of San Francisco Bay. Farallon is a Spanish word, meaning a small pointed islet in the sea.

These rocks, probably of volcanic origin, and bare and desolate, lie in a line from south-east to north-west—curiously enough the same line in which the islands of the Hawaiian or Sandwich Island group have been thrown up. Geologists say they are the outcrop of an immense granite dike.

The southernmost island, which is the largest—just as Hawaii, the southernmost of the Sandwich Island group, is also the biggest—extends for nearly a mile east and west, and is three hundred and forty feet high. It is composed of broken and water-worn rocks, forming numerous angular peaks, and having several caves; and the rock, mostly barren and bare, has here and there a few weeds and a little grass. At one point there is a small beach, and at another a depression; but the fury of the waves makes landing at all times difficult, and for the most part impossible.

The Farallones are seldom visited by travelers or pleasure-seekers. The wind blows fiercely here most of the time; the ocean is rough; and, to persons subject to sea-sickness, the short voyage is filled with the misery of that disease. Yet they contain a great deal that is strange and curious. On the highest point of the South Farallon the Government has placed a light-house, a brick tower seventeen feet high, surmounted by a lantern and illuminating apparatus. It is a revolving white light, showing a prolonged flash of ten seconds duration once in a minute. The light is about three hundred and sixty feet above the sea, and with a clear atmosphere is visible, from a position ten feet high, twenty-five and a half miles distant; from an elevation of sixty feet, it can be seen nearly thirty-one miles away; and it is plainly visible from Sulphur Peak on the main-land, thirty-four hundred and seventy-one feet high, and sixty-four and a half miles distant. The light-house is in latitude 37° 41′ 8″ north, and longitude 122° 59′ 05″ west.

On our foggy Western coast it has been necessary to place the light-houses low, because if they stood too high their light would be hidden in fog-banks and low clouds. The tower on the South Farallon is, therefore, low; and this, no doubt, is an advantage also to the light-keepers, who are less exposed to the buffetings of the storm than if their labor and care lay at a higher elevation.

As the Farallones lie in the track of vessels coming from the westward to San Francisco, the light is one of the most important, as it is also one of the most powerful on our Western coast; and it is supplemented by a fog-whistle, which is one of the most curious contrivances of this kind in the world. It is a huge trumpet, six inches in diameter at its smaller end, and blown by the rush of air through a cave or passage connecting with the ocean.

One of the numerous caves worn into the rocks by the surf had a hole at the top, through which the incoming breakers violently expelled the air they carried before them. Such spout-holes are not uncommon on rugged, rocky coasts. There are several on the Mendocino coast, and a number on the shores of the Sandwich Islands. This one, however, has been utilized by the ingenuity of man. The mouth-piece of the trumpet or fog-whistle is fixed against the

LIGHT-HOUSE ON THE SOUTH FARALLON.

aperture in the rock, and the breaker, dashing in with venomous spite, or the huge bulging wave which would dash a ship to pieces and drown her crew in a single effort, now blows the fog-whistle and warns the mariner off. The sound thus produced has been heard at a distance of seven or eight miles. It has a peculiar effect, because it has no regular period; depending upon the irregular coming in of the waves, and upon their similarly irregular force, it is blown somewhat as an idle boy would blow his penny trumpet. It ceases entirely for an hour and a half at low water, when the mouth of the cave or passage is exposed.

The life of the keepers of the Farallon light is singularly lonely and monotonous. Their house is built somewhat under the shelter of the rocks, but they live in what to a landsman would seem a perpetual storm; the ocean roars in their ears day and night; the boom of the surf is their constant and only

ARCH AT WEST END, FARALLON ISLANDS.

music; the wild scream of the sea-birds, the howl of the sea-lions, the whistle and shriek of the gale, the dull, threatening thunder of the vast breakers, are the dreary and desolate sounds which lull them to sleep at night, and assail their ears when they awake. In the winter months even their supply vessel, which, for the most part, is their only connection with the world, is sometimes unable to make a landing for weeks at a time. Chance visitors they see only occasionally, and at that distance at which a steamer is safe from the surf, and at which a girl could not even recognize her lover. The commerce of San Francisco passes before their eyes, but so far away that they can not tell the ships and steamers which sail by them voiceless and without greeting; and of the events passing on the planet with which they have so frail a social tie they learn only at long and irregular intervals. The change from sunshine to fog is the chief variety in their lives; the hasty landing of supplies the great event in their months. They can not even watch the growth of trees and plants; and to a child born and reared in such a place, a sunny lee under the shelter of rocks is probably the ideal of human felicity.

Except the rock of Tristan d'Acunha in the Southern Atlantic Ocean, I have never seen an inhabited spot which seemed so utterly desolate, so entirely separated from the world, whose people appeared to me to have such a slender hold on mankind. Yet for their solace they know that a powerful Government watches over their welfare, and — if that is any comfort — that, thirty miles away, there are lights and music and laughter and singing, as well as crowds, and all the anxieties and annoyances incidental to what we are pleased to call civilization.

But though these lonely rocks contain but a small society of human beings— the keepers and their families—they are filled with animal life; for they are the home of a multitude of sea-lions, and of vast numbers of birds and rabbits.

The rabbits, which live on the scanty herbage growing among the rocks, are descended from a few pair brought here many years ago, when some speculative genius thought to make a huge rabbit-warren of these rocks for the supply of the San Francisco market. These little animals are not very wild. In the dry season they feed on the bulbous roots of the grass, and sometimes they suffer from famine. In the winter and spring they are fat, and then their meat is white and sweet. During summer and fall they are not fit to eat.

They increase very rapidly, and at not infrequent intervals they overpopulate the island, and then perish by hundreds of starvation and the diseases which follow a too meagre diet. They are of all colors, and though descended from some pairs of tame white rabbits, seem to have reverted in color to the wild race from which they originated.

The Farallones have no snakes.

The sea-lions, which congregate by thousands upon the cliffs, and bark, and howl, and shriek and roar in the caves and upon the steep sunny slopes, are but little disturbed, and one can usually approach them within twenty or thirty yards. It is an extraordinarily interesting sight to see these marine monsters, many of them bigger than an ox, at play in the surf, and to watch the superb skill with which they know how to control their own motions when a huge wave seizes them, and seems likely to dash them to pieces against the rocks. They love to lie in the sun upon the bare and warm rocks; and

SEA-LIONS.

here they sleep, crowded together, and lying upon each other in inextricable confusion.

The bigger the animal, the greater his ambition appears to be to climb to the highest summit; and when a huge, slimy beast has with infinite squirming attained a solitary peak, he does not tire of raising his sharp-pointed, maggot-like head, and complacently looking about him. They are a rough set of brutes —rank bullies, I should say; for I have watched them repeatedly as a big one shouldered his way among his fellows, reared his huge front to intimidate some lesser seal which had secured a favorite spot, and first with howls, and if this did not suffice, with teeth and main force, expelled the weaker from his lodgment. The smaller sea-lions, at least those which have left their mothers, appear to have no rights which any one is bound to respect. They get out of the way with an abject promptness which proves that they live in terror of the stronger members of the community; but they do not give up their places without harsh complaints and piteous groans.

Plastered against the rocks, and with their lithe and apparently boneless shapes conformed to the rude and sharp angles, they are a wonderful, but not a graceful or pleasing sight. At a little distance they look like huge maggots, and their slow, ungainly motions upon the land do not lessen this resemblance. Swimming in the ocean, at a distance from the land, they are inconspicuous objects, as nothing but the head shows above water, and that only at intervals. But when the vast surf which breaks in mountain waves against the weather side of the Farallones with a force which would in a single sweep dash to pieces the biggest Indiaman—when such a surf, vehemently and with apparently irresistible might, lifts its tall white head, and with a deadly roar lashes the rocks half-way to their summit—then it is a magnificent sight to see a dozen or half a hundred great sea-lions at play in the very midst and fiercest part of the boiling surge, so completely masters of the situation that they allow themselves to be carried within a foot or two of the rocks, and at the last and imminent moment, with an adroit twist of their bodies, avoid the shock, and, diving, re-appear beyond the breaker.

As I sat, fascinated with this weird spectacle of the sea-lions, which seemed to me like an unhallowed prying into some hidden and monstrous secret of nature, I could better realize the fantastic and brutal wildness of life in the earlier geological ages, when monsters and chimeras dire wallowed about our unripe planet, and brute force of muscles and lungs ruled among the populous hordes of beasts which, fortunately for us, have perished, leaving us only this great wild sea-beast as a faint reminiscence of their existence. I wondered what Dante would have thought—and what new horrors his gloomy imagination would have conjured, could he have watched this thousand or two of sea-lions at their sports.

The small, sloping, pointed head of the creature gives it, to me, a peculiarly horrible appearance. It seems to have no brain, and presents an image of life with the least intelligence. It is in reality not without wits, for one needs only to watch the two or three specimens in the great tank at Woodward's Gardens, when they are getting fed, to see that they instantly recognize their keeper, and understand his voice and motion. But all their wit is applied to the basest uses. Greed for food is their ruling passion, and the monstrous lightning-like lunges through the water, the inarticulate shrieks of pleasure or of fury as he dashes after his food or comes up without it, the wild, fierce eyes, the eager and brutal vigor with which he snatches a morsel from a smaller fellow - creature, the reliance on strength alone, and the abject and panic-struck submission of the weaker to the stronger—all this shows him a brute of the lowest character.

Yet there is a wonderful snake-like grace in the lithe, swift motions of the animal when he is in the surf. You forget the savage blood-shot eyes, the receding forehead, the clumsy figure and awkward motion, as he wriggles up the steep rocks, the moment you see him at his supurb sport in the breakers. It seemed to me that he was another creature. The eye looks less baleful, and even joyous; every movement discloses conscious power; the excitement of the sport sheds from him somewhat of the brutality which re-appears the moment he lands or seeks his food.

So far as I could learn, the Farallon sea-lions are seldom disturbed by men seeking profit from them. In the egging season one or two are shot to supply oil to the lamps of the eggers; and occasionally one is caught for exhibition on the main-land. How do they catch a sea-lion? Well, they lasso him, and, odd as it sounds, it is the best and probably the only way to capture this beast. An adroit Spaniard, to whom the lasso or reata is like a fifth hand, or like the trunk to the elephant, steals up to a sleeping congregation, fastens his eye on the biggest one of the lot, and, biding his time, at the first motion of the animal, with unerring skill flings his loose rawhide noose, and then holds on for dear life. It is the weight of an ox and the vigor of half a dozen that he has tugging at the other end of his rope, and if a score of men did not stand ready to help, and if it were not possible to take a turn of the reata around a solid rock, the seal would surely get away.

Moreover, they must handle the beast tenderly, for it is easily injured. Its skin, softened by its life in the water, is quickly cut by the rope; its bones are easily broken; and its huge frame, too rudely treated, may be so hurt that the life dies out of it. As quickly as possible the captured sea-lion is stuffed into a strong box or cage, and here, in a cell too narrow to permit movement, it roars and yelps in helpless fury, until it is transported to its tank. Wild and fierce as it is, it seems to reconcile itself to the tank life very rapidly. If the narrow space of its big bath-tub frets it, you do not perceive this, for hunger is its chief passion, and with a moderately full stomach the animal does well in captivity, of course with sufficient water.

The South Farallon is the only inhabited one of the group. The remainder are smaller; mere rocky points sticking up out of the Pacific. The Middle Farallon is a single rock, from fifty to sixty yards in diameter, and twenty or thirty feet above the water. It lies two and a half miles north-west by west from the light-house. The North Farallon consists, in fact, of four pyramidal rocks, whose highest peak, in the centre of the group, is one hundred and sixty feet high; the southern rock of the four is twenty feet high. The four have a diameter of one hundred and sixty, one hundred and eighty - five, one hundred and twenty-five, and thirty-five yards respectively, and the most northern of the islets bears north 64° west from the Farallon light, six and three-fifths miles distant.

All the islands are frequented by birds; but the largest, the South Farallon, on which the light-house stands, is the favorite resort of these creatures, who come here in astonishing numbers every summer to breed; and it is to this island that the eggers resort at that season to obtain supplies of sea - birds' eggs for the San Francisco market, where they have a regular and large sale.

The birds which breed upon the Farallones are gulls, murres, shags, and sea-parrots, the last a kind of penguin. The eggs of the shags and parrots are not

THE GULL'S NEST.

used, but the eggers destroy them to make more room for the other birds. The gull begins to lay about the middle of May, and usually ten days before the murre. The gull makes a rude nest of brush and sea-weed upon the rocks; the murre does not take even this much trouble, but lays its eggs in any convenient place on the bare rocks.

The gull is soon through, but the murre continues to lay for about two months. The egging season lasts, therefore, from the 10th or 20th of May until the last of July. In this period the egg company which has for eighteen years worked this field gathered in 1872 seventeen thousand nine hundred and fifty-two dozen eggs, and in 1873 fifteen thousand two hundred and three dozen. These brought last year in the market an average of twenty-six cents per dozen. There has been, I was assured by the manager, no sensible decrease in the number of the birds or the eggs during twenty years.

From fifteen to twenty men are employed during the egging season in collecting and shipping the eggs. They live on the island during that time in rude shanties near the usual landing-place. The work is not amusing, for the birds seek out the least accessible places, and the men must follow, climbing often where a goat would almost hesitate. But this is not the worst. The gull sits on her nest, and resists the robber who comes for her eggs, and he must take care not to get bitten. The murre remains until her enemy is close upon her; then she rises with a scream which often startles a thousand or two of birds, who whirl up into the air in a dense mass, scattering filth and guano over the eggers.

Nor is this all. The gulls, whose season of breeding is soon past, are extravagantly fond of murre eggs; and these rapacious birds follow the egg-gatherers, hover over their heads, and no sooner is a murre's nest uncovered than the bird swoops down, and the egger must be extremely quick, or the gull will snatch the prize from under his nose. So greedy and eager are the gulls that they sometimes even wound the eggers, striking them with their

SHAGS, MURRES, AND SEA-GULLS.

beaks. But if the gull gets an egg, he flies up with it, and, tossing it up, swallows what he can catch, letting the shell and half its contents fall in a shower upon the luckless and disappointed egger below.

Finally, so difficult is the ground that it is impossible to carry baskets. The egger therefore stuffs the eggs into his shirt bosom until he has as many as he can safely carry, then clambers over rocks and down precipices until he comes to a place of deposit, where he puts them into baskets, to be carried down to the shore, where there are houses for receiving them. But so skillful and careful are the gatherers that but few eggs are broken.

The gathering proceeds daily, when it has once begun, and the whole ground

CONTEST FOR THE EGGS.

is carefully cleared off, so that no stale eggs shall remain. Thus if a portion of the ground has been neglected for a day or two, all the eggs must be flung into the sea, so as to begin afresh. As the season advances, the operations are somewhat contracted, leaving a part of the island undisturbed for breeding; and the gathering of eggs is stopped entirely about a month before the birds usually leave the island, so as to give them all an opportunity to hatch out a brood.

The murre is not good to eat. If undisturbed it lays two eggs only; when robbed, it will keep on laying until it has produced six or even eight eggs; and the manager of the islands told me that he had found as many as eight eggs forming in a bird's ovaries when he killed and opened it in the beginning of the season. The male bird regularly relieves the female on the nest, and also watches to resist the attacks of the gull, which not only destroys the eggs, but also eats the young. The murre feeds on sea-grass and jelly-fish, and I was assured that though some hundreds had been examined at different times, no fish had ever been found in a murre's stomach.

The bird is small, about the size of a half-grown duck, but its egg is as large as a goose egg. The egg is brown or greenish, and speckled. When quite fresh it has no fishy taste, but when two or three days old the fishy taste becomes perceptible. They are largely used in San Francisco by the restaurants and bakers, and for omelets, cakes, and custards.

During the height of the egging season the gulls hover in clouds over the rocks, and when a rookery is started, and the poor birds leave their nests by hundreds, the air is presently alive with gulls flying off with the eggs, and the eggers are sometimes literally drenched.

There is thus inevitably a considerable waste of eggs. I asked some of the eggers how many murres nested on the South Farallon, and they thought at least one hundred thousand. I do not suppose this an extravagant estimate, for, taking the season of 1872, when seventeen thousand nine hundred and fifty-two dozen eggs were actually sold in San Francisco, and allowing half a dozen to each murre, this would give nearly thirty-six thousand birds; and adding the proper number for eggs broken, destroyed by gulls, and not gathered, the number of murres and gulls is probably over one hundred thousand. This on an island less than a mile in its greatest diameter, and partly occupied by the light-house and fog-whistle and their keepers, and by other birds and a large number of sea-lions!

When they are done laying, and when the young can fly, the birds leave the island, usually going off together. During the summer and fall they return in clouds at intervals, but stay only a few days at a time, though there are generally a few to be found at all times; and I am told that eggs in small quantities can be found in the fall.

The murre does not fly high, nor is it a very active bird, or apparently of long flight. But the eggers say that when it leaves the island they do not know whither it goes, and they assert that it is not abundant on the neighboring coast. The young begin to fly when they are two weeks old, and the parents usually take them immediately into the water.

The sea-parrot has a crest, and somewhat resembles a cockatoo. Its numbers on the South Farallon are not great. It makes a nest in a hole in the rocks, and bites if it is disturbed. The island was first used as a sealing station; but this was not remunerative, there being but very few fur seal, and no sea-otters. This animal, which abounds in Alaska, and is found occasionally on the southern coast of California, frequents the masses of kelp which line the shore; but there is no kelp about the Farallones.

In the early times of California, when provisions were high-priced, the egg-gatherers sometimes got great gains. Once, in 1853, a boat absent but three days brought in one thousand dozen, and sold the whole cargo at a dollar a dozen; and in one season thirty thousand dozen were gathered, and brought an average of but little less than this price.

THE GREAT ROOKERY.

Of course there was an egg war. The prize was too great not to be struggled for; and the rage of the conflicting claimants grew to such a pitch that guns were used and lives were threatened, and at last the Government of the United States had to interfere to keep the peace. But with lower prices the strife ceased; the present company bought out, I believe, all adverse claims, and for the last fifteen or sixteen years peace has reigned in this part of the county of San Francisco—for these lonely islets are a part of the same county with the metropolis of the Pacific.

INDIAN GIRLS AND CANOE, PUGET SOUND.

CHAPTER XIII.

THE COLUMBIA RIVER AND PUGET SOUND—HINTS TO TOURISTS.

IN less than forty-eight hours after you leave San Francisco you find yourself crossing the bar which lies at the mouth of the Columbia River, and laughing, perhaps, over the oft-told local tale of how a captain, new to this region, lying off and on with his vessel, and impatiently signaling for a pilot, was temporarily comforted by a passenger, an old Californian, who "wondered why Jim over there couldn't take her safe over the bar."

"Do you think he knows the soundings well enough?" asked the anxious skipper; and was answered,

"I don't know about that, captain; but he's been taking all sorts of things 'straight' over the bar for about twenty years, to *my* knowledge, and I should think he might manage the brig."

The voyage from San Francisco is almost all the way in sight of land; and as you skirt the mountainous coast of Oregon you see long stretches of forest, miles of tall firs killed by forest fires, and rearing their bare heads toward the sky like a vast assemblage of bean-poles—a barren view which you owe to the noble red man, who, it is said, sets fire to these great woods in order to produce for himself a good crop of blueberries.

When, some years ago, Walk - in - the - Water, or Red Cloud, or some other Colorado chief, asserted in Washington the right of the Indian to hunt buffalo, on the familiar ground that he *must* live, a journalist given to figures demolished the Indian position by demonstrating that a race which insisted on living on buffalo meat required about sixteen thousand acres of land per head for its subsistence, which is more than even we can spare. One wonders, re-

14

membering these figures, how many millions of feet of first-class lumber are sacrificed to provide an Indian rancheria in Oregon with huckleberries.

On the second morning of your voyage you enter the Columbia River, and stop, on the right bank, near the mouth, at a place famous in history and romance, and fearfully disappointing to the actual view — Astoria. When you have seen it, you will wish you had passed it by unseen. I do not know precisely how it ought to have looked to have pleased my fancy, and realized the dreams of my boyhood, when I read Bonneville's " Journal " and Irving's "Astoria," and imagined Astoria to be the home of romance and of picturesque trappers. Any thing less romantic than Astoria is to-day you can scarcely imagine; and what is worse yet, your first view shows you that the narrow, broken, irreclaimably rough strip of land never had space for any thing picturesque or romantic.

Astoria, in truth, consists of a very narrow strip of hill-side, backed by a hill so steep that they can shoot timber down it, and inclosed on every side by dense forests, high, steep hills, and mud flats. It looks like the rudest Western clearing you ever saw. Its brief streets are paved with wood; its inhabitants wear their trowsers in their boots; if you step off the pavement you go deep into the mud; and ten minutes' walk brings you to the "forest primeval," which, picturesque as it may be in poetry, I confess to be dreary and monotonous in the extreme in reality.

There are but few remains of the old trapper station—one somewhat large house is the chief relic; but there is a saw-mill, which seems to make, with all its buzz and fuzz, scarcely an appreciable impression upon the belt of timber which so shuts in Astoria that I thought I had scarcely room in it to draw a full breath; and over to the left they pointed out to me the residence of a gentleman—a general, I think he was—who came hither twenty-six years ago in some official position, and had after a quarter of a century gained what looked to me from the steamer's deck like a precarious ten-acre lot from the "forest primeval," about enough room to bury himself and family in, with a probability that the firs would crowd them into the Columbia River if the saw-mill should break down.

On the voyage up I said to an Oregonian, "You have a good timber country, I hear?" and his reply seemed to me at the time extravagant. "Timber?" he said; "timber—till you can't sleep." When I had spent a day and a half at anchor abreast of Astoria, the words appeared less exaggerated. Wherever you look you see only timber; tall firs, straight as an arrow, big as the California redwoods, and dense as a Southern canebrake. On your right is Oregon —its hill-sides a forest so dense that jungle would be as fit a word for it as timber; on the left is Washington Territory, and its hill-sides are as densely covered as those of the nearer shore. This interminable, apparently impenetrable, thicket of firs exercised upon my mind, I confess, a gloomy, depressing influence. The fresh lovely green of the evergreen foliage, the wonderful arrowy straightness of the trees, their picturesque attitude where they cover headlands and reach down to the very water's edge, all did not make up to me for their dreary continuity of shade.

Astoria, however, means to grow. It has already a large hotel, which the timber has crowded down against the tide-washed flats; a saw-mill, which is sawing away for dear life, because if it stopped the forest would doubtless push it into the river, on whose brink it has courageously effected a lodgment; some tan-yards, shops, and "groceries;" and if you should wish to invest in real estate here, you can do so with the help of a "guide," which is distributed on the steamer, and tells you of numerous bargains in corner lots, etc.; for here, as in that part of the West which lies much farther east, people live apparently only to speculate in real estate.

An occasional flash of broad humor enlivens some of the land circulars and advertisements. I found one on the hotel table headed "Homes," with the following sample:

221 ACRES,

Four miles east of Silverton; frame house and a log house (can live in either); log barn; 20 acres in cultivation; 60 acres timber land; balance pasture land; well watered. We will sell this place for $1575. Will throw in a cook stove and all the household furniture, consisting of a frying-pan handle and a broomstick; also a cow and a yearling calf; also one bay heifer; also 8400 lbs. of hay, minus what the above-named stock have consumed during the winter; also 64 bushels of oats, subject to the above-mentioned diminution. If sold, we shall have left on our hands one of the driest and ugliest-looking old bachelors this side of the grave, which we will cheerfully throw in if at all acceptable to the purchaser. Old maids and rich widows are requested to give their particular attention to this special offer. Don't pass by on the other side.

HOME, SWEET HOME!

Be it ever so humble, there's no place like Home!
We still have a few more "Sweet Homes" for sale, consisting of,
etc., etc., etc.

☞ Title perfect—a Warrantee Deed from the hub of the earth to the top of the skies,
and Uncle Sam's Patent to back us!

A further-reaching title one could scarcely require.

I don't know where I got the belief that the Columbia was a second-rate river. There must have been some blunder in the geographies out of which I got my lessons and my notions of the North-west coast at school. Possibly, too, the knowledge that navigation is interrupted by rapids at the Cascades and Dalles contributed to form an impression conspicuously wrong. In fact, the Columbia is one of the great rivers of the world. It seems to me larger, as it is infinitely grander, than the Mississippi.

Between Astoria and the junction of the Willamette its breadth, its depth, its rapid current, and the vast body of water it carries to sea reminded me of

SALEM, CAPITAL OF OREGON.

descriptions I had read of the Amazon; and I suspect the Columbia would rank with that stream were it not for the unlucky obstructions at the Cascades and Dalles, which divide the stream into two unequal parts.

For ten miles above Astoria the river is so wide that it forms really a vast bay. Then it narrows somewhat, and the channel approaches now one and then the other of its bold, picturesque shores, which often for miles resemble the Palisades of the Hudson in steepness, and exceed them in height. But even after it becomes narrower the river frequently widens into broad, open, lake-like expanses, which are studded with lovely islands, and wherever the shore lowers you see, beyond, grand mountain ranges snow-clad and amazingly fine.

The banks are precipitous nearly all the way to the junction of the Willamette, and there is singularly little farming country on the immediate river. Below Kalama there are few spots where there is even room for a small farmstead. But along this part of the river are the "salmon factories," whence come the Oregon salmon, which, put up in tin cans, are now to be bought not only in our Eastern States, but all over the world. The fish are caught in weirs, in gill nets, as shad are caught on the Hudson, and this is the only part of the labor performed by white men. The fishermen carry the salmon in boats to the factory—usually a large frame building erected on piles over the water—and here they fall into the hands of Chinese, who get for their labor a dollar a day and their food.

The salmon are flung up on a stage, where they lie in heaps of a thousand at a time, a surprising sight to an Eastern person, for in such a pile you may see many fish weighing from thirty to sixty pounds. The work of preparing them for the cans is conducted with exact method and great cleanliness, water being abundant. One Chinaman seizes a fish and cuts off his head; the next slashes off the fins and disembowels the fish; it then falls into a large vat, where the blood soaks out—a salmon bleeds like a bull—and after soaking and repeated washing in different vats, it falls at last into the hands of one of a gang of Chinese whose business it is, with heavy knives, to chop the fish into chunks of suitable size for the tins. These pieces are plunged into brine, and presently stuffed into the cans, it being the object to fill each can as full as possible with fish, the bone being excluded.

The top of the can, which has a small hole pierced in it, is then soldered on, and five hundred tins set on a form are lowered into a huge kettle of boiling water, where they remain until the heat has expelled all the air. Then a Chinaman neatly drops a little solder over each pin-hole, and after another boiling, the object of which is, I believe, to make sure that the cans are hermetically sealed, the process is complete, and the salmon are ready to take a journey longer and more remarkable even than that which their progenitors took when, seized with the curious rage of spawning, they ascended the Columbia, to deposit their eggs in its head waters, near the centre of the continent.

I was assured by the fishermen that the salmon do not decrease in numbers or in size, yet in this year, 1873, more than two millions of pounds were put up in tin cans on the Lower Columbia alone, besides fifteen or twenty thousand barrels of salted salmon.

From Astoria to Portland is a distance of one hundred and ten miles, and as the current is strong, the steamer requires ten or twelve hours to make the trip. As you approach the mouth of the Willamette you meet more arable land, and the shores of this river are generally lower, and often alluvial, like the Missouri and Mississippi bottoms; and here you find cattle, sheep, orchards, and fields; and one who is familiar with the agricultural parts of California notices here signs of a somewhat severer climate, in more substantial houses; and the evidence of more protracted rains, in green and luxuriant grasses at a season when the pastures of California have already begun to turn brown.

Portland is a surprisingly well-built city, with so many large shops, so many elegant dwellings, and other signs of prosperity, as will make you credit the assertion of its inhabitants, that it contains more wealth in proportion to its population than any other town in the United States. It lies on the right bank of the Willamette, and is the centre of a large commerce. Its inhabitants seemed to me to have a singular fancy for plate-glass fronts in their shops and hotels, and even in the·private houses, which led me at first to suppose that there must be a glass factory near at hand. It is all, I believe, imported.

From Portland, which you can see in a day, and whose most notable sight is a fine view of Mount Hood, obtainable from the hills back of the city, the sight-seer makes his excursions conveniently in various directions; and as the American traveler is always in a hurry, it is perhaps well to show what time is needed:

SEATTLE, WASHINGTON TERRITORY.

To the Dalles and Celilo, and return to Portland, three days.

To Victoria, Vancouver's Island, and return to Portland, including the tour of Puget Sound, seven days.

To San Francisco, overland, by railroad to Roseburg, thence by stage to Redding, and rail to San Francisco, seventy - nine hours.

Thus you may leave San Francisco by steamer for Portland, see the Dalles, the Cascades, Puget Sound, Victoria, the Willamette Valley, and the magnificent mountain scenery of Southern Oregon and Northern California, and be back in San Francisco in less than three weeks, making abundant allowance for possible though not probable detentions on the road. The time absolutely needed for the tour is but seventeen days.

Of course he who "takes a run over to California" from the East, predetermined to be back in his office or shop within five or six weeks from the day he left home, can not see the Columbia River and Puget Sound. But travelers are beginning to discover that it is worth while to spend some months on the Pacific coast; some day, I do not doubt, it will be fashionable to go across the continent; and those whose circumstances give them leisure should not leave the Pacific without seeing Oregon and Washington Territory. In the few pages which follow, my aim is to smooth the way for others by a very simple account of what I myself saw and enjoyed.

And first as to the Cascades and the Dalles of the Columbia. You leave Portland for Dalles City in a steamboat at five o'clock in the morning. The better way is to sleep on board this steamer, and thus avoid an uncomfortably early awakening. Then when you do rise, at six or half past, you will find yourself on the Columbia, and steaming directly at Mount Hood, whose splendid snow-covered peak seems to bar your way but a short distance ahead. It lies, in fact, a hundred miles off; and when you have sailed some hours toward it the river makes a turn, which leaves the snowy peak at one side, and presently hides it behind the steep bank.

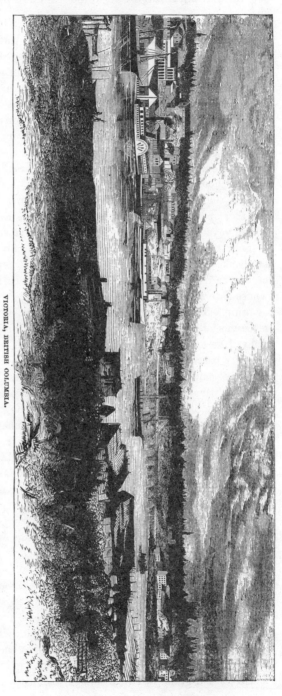

VICTORIA, BRITISH COLUMBIA.

The little steamer, very clean and comfortable, affords you an excellent breakfast, and some amusement in the odd way in which she is managed. Most of the river steamers here have their propelling wheel at the stern; they have very powerful engines, which drive them ahead with surprising speed. I have gone sixteen miles an hour in one, with the current; and when they make a landing the pilot usually runs the boat's head slantingly against the shore, and passengers and freight are taken in or landed over the bow. At the wood-pile on the shore you may generally see one of the people called "Pikes," whom you will recognize by a very broad-brimmed hat, a frequent squirting of tobacco-juice, and the possession of two or three hounds, whom they call hereabouts "hound-dogs," as we say "bull-dog." And this reminds me that in Oregon the country people usually ask you if you will eat an "egg-omelet;" and they speak of pork—a favorite food of the Pike—as "hog-meat."

The voyage up the river presents a constant succession of wild and picturesque scenery; immense rocky capes jut out into the broad stream; for miles the banks are precipitous, like the Hudson River Palisades, only often much higher, and for other miles the river has worn its channel out of the rock, whose face looks bare and clean cut, as though it had been of human workmanship. The first explorer of the Columbia, even if he was a very commonplace mortal, must have passed days of the most singular exhilaration, especially if he ascended the stream in that season when the skies are bright and blue, for it seems to me one of the most magnificent sights in the world. I am not certain that the wildness does not oppress one a little after a while, and there are parts of the river where the smoothly cut cliffs, coming precipitously down to the water's edge, and following down, sheer down, to the river's bottom, make you think with terror of the unhappy people who might here be drowned, with this cold rock within their reach, yet not affording them even a momentary support. I should like to have seen the rugged cliffs relieved here and there by the softness of smooth lawns, and some evidences that man had conquered even this rude and resisting nature.

But for a century or two to come the traveler will have to do without this relief; nor need he grumble, for, with all its rugged grandeur, the scenery has many exquisite bits where nature has a little softened its aspect. Nor is it amiss to remember that but a little way back from the river there are farms, orchards, cattle, and sheep. At one point the boat for a moment turned her bow to the shore to admit a young man, who brought with him a wonderful bouquet of wild flowers, which he had gathered at his home a few miles back; and here and there, where the hill-sides have a more moderate incline, you will see that some energetic pioneer has carved himself out a farm.

Nevertheless it is with a sense of relief at the change that you at last approach a large island, a flat space of ten or twelve hundred acres, with fences and trees and grain fields and houses, and with a gentle and peaceful aspect, doubly charming to you when you come upon it suddenly, and fresh from the preceding and somewhat appalling grandeur. Here the boat stops; for you are here at the lower end of the famous Cascades, and you tranship yourself into cars which carry you to the upper end, a distance of about six miles, where again you take boat for Dalles City.

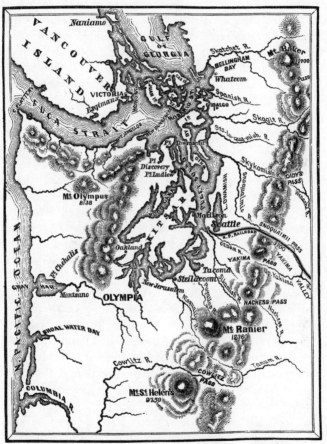

MAP OF PUGET SOUND AND VICINITY.

The Cascades are rapids. The river, which has ever a swift and impetuous current, is nearly two miles wide just above these rapids. Where the bed shoals it also narrows, and the great body of water rushes over the rocks, roaring, tumbling, foaming — a tolerably wild sight. There is nowhere any sudden descent sufficient to make a water-fall; but there is a fall of a good many feet in the six miles of cascades.

These rapids are considered impassable, though I believe the Indians used sometimes to venture down them in canoes; and it was my good fortune to shoot down them in a little steamer — the *Shoshone* — the third only, I was told, which had ever ventured this passage. The singular history of this steamboat shows the vast extent of the inland navigation made possible by the Columbia and its tributaries. She was built in 1866 on the Snake River, at a point ninety miles from Boise City, in Idaho Territory, and was employed in the upper waters of the Snake, running to near the mouth of the Bruneau, within one hundred and twenty-five miles of the head of Salt Lake.

When the mining excitement in that region subsided there ceased to be business for her, and her owner determined to bring her to Portland. She passed several rapids on the Snake, and at a low stage of water was run over the Dalles. Then she had to wait nearly a year until high water on the Cascades, and finally passed those rapids, and carried her owner, Mr. Ainsworth, who was also for this passage of the Cascades her pilot, and myself safely into Portland.

We steamed from Dalles City about three o'clock on an afternoon so windy as to make the Columbia very rough. When we arrived at the head of the Cascades we found the shore lined with people to watch our passage through the rapids. As we swept into the foaming and roaring waters the engine was slowed a little, and for a few minutes the pilots had their hands full; for the fierce currents, sweeping her now to one side and then to the other, made the steering extraordinarily difficult. At one point there seemed a probability that we should be swept on to the rocks; and it was very curious to stand, as General Sprague and I, the only passengers, did, in front of the pilot-house, and watch the boat's head swing against the helm and toward the rocks, until at last, after half a minute of suspense, she began slowly to swing back, obedient to her pilot's wish.

We made six miles in eleven minutes, which is at the rate of more than thirty miles per hour, a better rate of speed than steamboats commonly attain. Of course it is impossible to drive a vessel up the Cascades, and a steamboat which has once passed these rapids remains forever below.

At the upper end of the Cascades a boat awaits you, which carries you through yet more picturesque scenery to Dalles City, where you spend the night. This is a small place, remarkable to the traveler chiefly for the geological collection which every traveler ought to see, belonging to the Rev. Mr. Condon, a very intelligent and enthusiastic geologist, the Presbyterian minister of the place. You have also at Dalles City a magnificent view of Mount Hood, and Mr. Condon will tell you that he has seen this old crater emit smoke since he has lived here.

There is no doubt that both Mount Hood and Mount St. Helens have still internal fires, though both their craters are now filled up with ashes. There is reason to believe that at its last period of activity Mount Hood emitted only ashes; for there are still found traces of volcanic ashes, attributable, I am told, to this mountain, as far as one hundred miles from its summit. Of Mount St. Helens it is probable that its slumbering fires are not very deeply buried. A few years ago two adventurous citizens of Washington Territory were obliged, by a sudden fog and cold storm, to spend a night near its summit, and seeking for some cave among the lava where to shelter themselves from the storm, found a fissure from which came so glowing and immoderate a heat that they could not bear its vicinity, and, as they related, were alternately frozen and scorched all night—now roasting at the volcanic fire, and again rushing out to cool themselves in the sleet and snow.

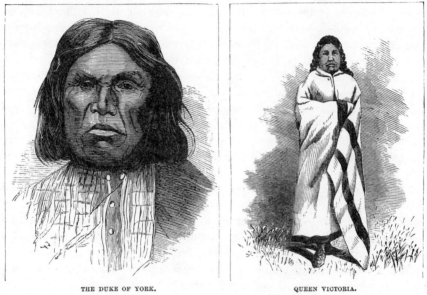

THE DUKE OF YORK. QUEEN VICTORIA.

Puget Sound Chiefs.

The rocks are volcanic from near the mouth of the Willamette to and above the Dalles, and geologists suppose that there have been great convulsions of nature hereabouts in recent geological times. The Indians have a tradition, indeed, that the river was originally navigable and unobstructed where now are the Cascades, and that formerly there was a long, natural tunnel, through which the Columbia passed under a mountain. They assert that a great earthquake broke down this tunnel, the site of which they still point out, and that the débris formed the present obstructions at the Cascades.

Oregon, if one may judge by the fossil remains in Mr. Condon's collection, seems once to have been inhabited by a great number and variety of pre-adamite beasts; but the most singular object he has to show is a very striking ape's head, carved with great spirit and vigor out of hard lava. This object was found upon the shore of the Columbia by Indians, after a flood which had washed away a piece of old alluvial bank. The rock of which it is composed is quite hard; the carving is, as I said, done with remarkable vigor; and the top of the head is hollowed out, precisely as the Indians still make shallow depressions in figures and heads which they carve out of slate, in which to burn what answers in their religious ceremonies for incense.

But supposing this relic to belong to Oregon—and there is, I was told, no reason to believe otherwise—where did the Indian who carved it get his idea of an ape? The Indians of this region, poor creatures that they are, have still the habit of carving rude figures out of slate and other soft rocks. They have also the habit of cutting out shallow, dish-like depressions in the heads of such figures, wherein to burn incense. But they could not give Mr. Condon any account of the ape's head they brought him, nor did they recognize its features as resembling any object or creature familiar to them even by tradition.

The Dalles of the Columbia are simply a succession of falls and rapids, not reaching over as great a distance as the Cascades, but containing one feature much more remarkable than any thing which the Cascades afford, and indeed, so far as I know, found nowhere else.

The Columbia above the Dalles is still a first-class river, comparable in depth and width, and in the volume of its water, only with the Lower Mississippi or the Amazon. It is a deep, rapidly-flowing stream, nearly a mile wide. But at one point in the Dalles the channel narrows until it is, at the ordinary height of the river, not over a hundred yards wide; and through this narrow gorge the whole volume of the river rushes for some distance. Of course water is not subject to compression; the volume of the river is not diminished; what happens, as you perceive when you see this singular freak of nature, is that the river is suddenly turned up on its edge. Suppose it is, above the Dalles, a mile wide and fifty feet deep; at the narrow gorge it is but a hundred yards wide — how deep must it be? Certainly it can be correctly said that the stream is turned up on its edge.

The Dalles lie five or six miles above Dalles City; and you pass these rapids in the train which bears you to Celilo early the next morning after you arrive at Dalles City. Celilo is not a town; it is simply a geographical point; it is the spot where, if you were bound to the interior of the continent by water, you would take steamboat. There is here a very long shed to shelter the goods which are sent up into this far-away and, to us Eastern people, unknown interior; there is a wharf where land the boats when they return from a journey of perhaps a thousand miles on the Upper Columbia or the Snake; there are two or three laborers' shanties—and that is all there is of Celilo; and your journey thither has been made only that you may see the Dalles, and Cape Horn, as a bold promontory on the river is called.

What I advise you to do is to take a hearty lunch with you, and, if you can find one, a guide, and get off the early Celilo train at the Dalles. You will have a most delightful day among very curious scenery; will see the Indians spearing salmon in the pools over which they build their stages; and can examine at leisure the curious rapids called the Dalles. A party of three or four persons could indeed spend several days very pleasantly picnicking about the Dalles; and in the season they would shoot hare and birds enough to supply them with meat. The weather in this part of Oregon, east of the Cascade range, is as settled, as that of California, so that there is no risk in sleeping out-of-doors in summer.

There is a singularly sudden climatic change between Western and Eastern Oregon; and if you ask the captain or pilot on the boat which plies between the Cascades and Dalles City, he can show you the mountain range on one side of which the climate is wet, while on the other side it is dry. The Cascade range is a continuation northward of the Sierra Nevada; and here, as farther south, it stops the water-laden winds which rush up from the sea. Western Oregon, lying between the Cascades and the ocean, has so much rain that its people are called "Web-feet;" Eastern Oregon, a vast grazing region, has comparatively little rain. Western Oregon, except in the Willamette and Rogue River valleys, is densely timbered; Eastern Oregon is a country of boundless plains, where they irrigate their few crops, and depend mainly on stock-grazing. This region is as yet sparsely settled; and when we in the East think of Oregon, or read of it even, it is of that part of the huge State which lies west of the Cascades, and where alone agriculture is carried on to a considerable extent.

You will spend a day in returning from the Dalles to Portland, and arriving there in the evening can set out the next morning for Olympia, on Puget Sound, by way of Kalama, which is the Columbia River terminus for the present of the Northern Pacific Railroad. It is possible to go by steamer from Portland to Victoria, and then return down Puget Sound to Olympia; but to most people the sea-voyage is not enticing, and there are but slight inconveniences in the short land journey. The steamer leaving Portland at six A.M. lands you at Kalama about eleven; there you get dinner, and proceed about two by rail to Olympia. It is a good plan to telegraph for accommodations on the pretty and comfortable steamer *North Pacific*, and go directly to her on your arrival at Olympia.

Puget Sound is one of the most picturesque and remarkable sheets of water in the world; and the voyage from Olympia to Victoria, which shows you the greater part of the Sound, is a delightful and novel excursion, specially to be recommended to people who like to go to sea without getting sea-sick; for these land-encircled waters are almost always smooth.

When, at Kalama, you enter Washington Territory, your ears begin to be assailed by the most barbarous names imaginable. On your way to Olympia

NANAIMO, VANCOUVER'S ISLAND.

by rail you cross a river called the Skookum-Chuck; your train stops at places named Newaukum, Tumwater, and Toutle; and if you seek further, you will hear of whole counties labeled Wahkiakum, or Snohomish, or Kitsap, or Klikatat; and Cowlitz, Hookium, and Nenolelops greet and offend you. They complain in Olympia that Washington Territory gets but little immigration; but what wonder? What man, having the whole American continent to chose from, would willingly date his letters from the county of Snohomish, or bring up his children in the city of Nenolelops? The village of Tumwater is, as I am ready to bear witness, very pretty indeed; but surely an emigrant would think twice before he established himself either there or at Toutle. Seattle is sufficiently barbarous; Steilacoom is no better; and I suspect that the Northern Pacific Railroad terminus has been fixed at Tacoma —if it is fixed there—because that is one of the few places on Puget Sound whose name does not inspire horror and disgust.

Olympia, which lies on an arm of Puget Sound, and was once a town of great expectations, surprises the traveler by its streets, all shaded with magnificent maples. The founder of the town was a man of taste; and he set a fashion which, being followed for a few years in this country of abundant rains, has given Olympia's streets shade trees by the hundred which would make it famous were it an Eastern place.

Unluckily, it has little else to charm the traveler, though it is the capital of the Territory; and when you have spent half an hour walking through the streets you will be quite ready to have the steamer set off for Victoria. The voyage lasts but about thirty-six hours, and would be shorter were it not that the steamer makes numerous landings. Thus you get glimpses of Seattle, Steilacoom, Tacoma, and of the so-called saw-mill ports—Port Madison, Port Gamble, Port Ludlow, and Port Townsend—the last named being also the boundary of our Uncle Samuel's dominions for the present, and the port of entry for this district, with a custom-house which looks like a barn, and a collector and inspectors, the latter of whom examine your trunk as you return from Victoria to save you from the sin of smuggling.

From Port Townsend your boat strikes across the straits of San Juan de Fuca to Victoria; and just here, as you are crossing from American to English territory, you get the most magnificent views of the grand Olympian range of mountains and of Mount Regnier. Also, the captain will point out to you in the distance that famous island of San Juan which formed the subject or object, or both, of our celebrated boundary dispute with great Britain, and you will wonder how small an object can nearly make nations go to war, and for what a petty thing we set several kings and great lords to studying geography and treaties and international law, and boring themselves, and filling enterprising newspapers with dozens of columns of dull history; and you will wonder the more at the stupid pertinacity of these English in clinging to the little island of San Juan when you reach Victoria, and see that we shall presently take that dull little town too, not because we want it or need it, but to save it from perishing of inanition.

It is something to have taste and a sense of the beautiful. Certainly the English, who discovered the little landlocked harbor of Victoria and chose it as the site of a town, displayed both. It is by natural advantages one of the loveliest places I ever saw, and I wonder, remote as it is, that it is not famous. The narrow harbor, which is not so big as one of the big Liverpool docks, is surrounded on both sides by the prettiest little miniature bays, rock-bound, with grassy knolls, and here and there shady clumps of evergreens; a river opening out above the town into a kind of lake, and spanned by pretty bridges, invites you to a boating excursion; and the fresh green of the lawn-like expanses of grass which reach into the bay from different directions, the rocky little promontories with boats moored near them, the fine snow-covered mountains in the distance, and the pleasantly winding roads leading in different directions into the country, all make up a landscape whose soft and gay aspect I suppose is the more delightful because one comes to it from the somewhat oppressive grandeur of the fir forests in Washington Territory.

In the harbor of Victoria the most conspicuous object is the long range of warehouses belonging to the Hudson Bay Company, with their little trading steamers moored alongside. These vessels bear the signs of traffic with a savage people in the high boarding nettings which guard them from stem to stern, and which are in their more solid parts pierced for musketry. Here, too, you see a queer little old steamboat, the first that ever vexed the waters of the Pacific Ocean with its paddle-wheels. And as your own steamer hauls up to the wharf, you will notice, arrayed to receive you, what is no doubt the most shocking and complete collection of ugly women in the world.

These are the Indians of this region. They are very light-colored; their complexion has an artificial look; there is something ghastly and unnatural in the yellow of the faces, penetrated by a rose or carmine color on the cheeks. They are hideous in all the possible aspects and varieties of hideousness—undersized, squat, evil-eyed, pug-nosed, tawdry in dress, ungraceful in every motion; they really mar the landscape, so that you are glad to escape from them to your hotel, which you find a clean and comfortable building, where, if you are as fortunate as the traveler who relates this, you may by-and-by catch a glimpse or two of a fresh, fair, girlish English face, which will make up to you for the precedent ugliness.

Victoria hopes to have its dullness enlivened by a railroad from the mainland one of these days, which may make it more prosperous, but will probably destroy some of the charm it now has for a tourist. It can hardly destroy the excellent roads by which you may take several picturesque drives and walks in the neighborhood of the town, nor the pretty views you have from the hills near by, nor the excursions by boat, in which you can best see how much Nature has done to beautify this place, and how little man has done so far to mar her work.

Silks and cigars are said to be very cheap in Victoria; and those who consume these articles will probably look through the shops and make a few purchases, not enough to satisfy, though sufficient to arouse the suspicions of the Collector of Customs at Port Townsend. If you use your time well, the thirty-six hours which the steamer spends at Victoria will suffice you to see all that is of interest there to a traveler, and you can return in her down the Sound, and make more permanent your impressions of its scenery.

You will perhaps be startled, if you chance to overhear the conversation of your fellow-passengers, to gather that it concerns itself chiefly with millions, and these millions run to such extraordinary figures that you may hear one man pitying another for the confession that he made no more than a hundred millions last year. It is feet of lumber they are speaking of; and when you see the monstrous piles of sawdust which encumber the mill ports, the vast quantities of waste stuff they burn, and the huge rafts of timber which are towed down to the mills, as well as the ships which lie there to load for South America, Tahiti, Australia, and California, you will not longer wonder that they talk of millions.

Some of these mills are owned by very wealthy companies, who have had the good fortune to buy at low rates large tracts of the best timber lands lying along the rivers and bays. A saw-mill is the centre of quite a town—and a very rough town too, to judge from the appearance of the men who come down to the dock to look at the steamer, and the repute of the Indian women who go from port to port and seem at home among the mill men.

Having gone by sea to Oregon, I should advise you to return to California overland. The journey lies by rail through the fertile Willamette Valley, for the present the chief agricultural country of Oregon, to Roseburg, and thence by stage over and through some of the most picturesque and grand scenery in America, into California. If you are curious in bizarre social experiments, you may very well stop a day at Aurora, thirty miles below Portland, and look at some of the finest orchards in the State, the property of a strange German community which has lived in harmony and acquired wealth at this point.

Salem, too, the capital of Oregon, lying on the railroad fifty miles below Portland, is worth a visit, to show you how rich a valley the Willamette is. And as you go down by stage toward California you will enjoy a long day's drive through the Rogue River Valley, a long, narrow, winding series of nooks, remote, among high mountains, looking for all the world as though in past ages a great river had swept through here, and left in its dry bed a fertile soil, and space enough for a great number of happy and comfortable homes.

May and June are the best months in which to see Oregon and Puget Sound. With San Francisco as a starting-point, one may go either to Portland or to Victoria direct. If you go first to Victoria, you save a return journey across Puget Sound, and from Olympia to Kalama, but you miss the sail up the Columbia from Astoria to Portland. The following table of fares will show you the cost of traveling in the region I have described:

	Time.	Fare.
From San Francisco to Portland	3 days	$30 00
From San Francisco to Victoria	3 "	30 00
From Portland to Celilo	1 day	7 00
Excursion tickets, good from Portland to Celilo and back	3 days	10 00
From Portland by Olympia to Victoria	3 "	12 25
From Portland to San Francisco by railroad and stage	79 hours	42 00

Meals on these journeys are extra, and cost from half a dollar to seventy-five cents. They are generally good. All these rates are in coin. On the steamer from San Francisco to Portland or Victoria meals are included in the fare.

When you are once in Portland, a vast region opens itself to you, if you are

15

an adventurous tourist. You may take boat at Celilo, above the Dalles, and steam up to Wallula, where you take stage for Elkton, a station on the Pacific Railroad, in Utah; this journey shows you the heart of the continent, and is said to abound in magnificent scenery. I have not made it, but it is frequently done. If you have not courage for so long an overland trip, a journey up to the mouth of Snake River and back to Portland, which consumes but a week, will give you an intelligent idea of the vastness of the country drained by the main body of the great Columbia River.

The great plains and table-lands which lie east of the Cascades, and are drained by the Columbia, the Snake, and their affluents, will some day contain a vast population. Already enterprising pioneers are pushing into the remotest valleys of this region. As you sail up the Columbia, you will hear of wheat, barley, sheep, stock, wool, orchards, and rapidly growing settlements, where, to our Eastern belief, the beaver still builds his dams, unvexed even by the traps and rifle of the hunter.

ANCIENT HAWAIIAN IDOL.

APPENDIX.

CONTRIBUTIONS OF A VENERABLE SAVAGE TO THE ANCIENT HISTORY OF THE HAWAIIAN ISLANDS.*

TRANSLATED FROM THE FRENCH OF M. JULES REMY, BY WILLIAM T. BRIGHAM.

[I am indebted to Mr. William T. Brigham, of Boston, the translator of the following "Contributions of a venerable Savage," and the author of a valuable treatise on the volcanoes of the Sandwich Islands, as well as of several memoirs on the natural history of the Islands, for his kind permission to use this very curious fragment, with his additions, in my volume. The original I have not been able to lay my hands on. It gives a picturesque account of the Hawaiian people before they came into relations with foreigners. It should be remembered by the reader that Mr. Remy is a Frenchman, and that his relations with the Roman Catholic missionaries somewhat colored his views of the labors of the American missionaries on the Islands.

The "contributions" in this translation of Mr. Brigham were privately printed by him some years ago, and the following note by him explains their origin. It will be seen that Mr. Brigham translated the Mele, or chant of Kawelo, from the original.]

ONE evening, in the month of March, 1853, I landed at Hoopuloa, on the western shore of Hawaii. Among the many natives collected on the beach to bid me welcome and draw my canoe up over the sand, I noticed an old man of average size, remarkably developed chest, and whose hairs, apparently once flaxen, were hoary with age. The countenance of this old man, at once savage and attractive, was furrowed across the forehead with deep and regular wrinkles. His only garment was a shirt of striped calico.

A sort of veneration with which his countrymen seemed to me to regard him only increased the desire I at first felt to become acquainted with the old islander. I was soon

---

* The original *Récits d'un Vieux Sauvage pour servir a l'histoire ancienne de Hawaii* was read on the 15th of December, 1857, to the Society of Agriculture, Commerce, Science, and Arts of the Department of the Marne, of which M. Remy was a corresponding member, and published at Chalons-sur-Marne in 1859. The translation is perfectly literal, and the Mele of Kawelo has been translated directly from the Hawaiian, M. Remy's translation being often too free. A portion of this work was translated several years since by President W. D. Alexander, of Oahu College, and published in *The Friend*, at Honolulu, by William T. Brigham.

told that his name was Kanuha, that he was already a lad when Alapai[1] died (about 1752), that he had known Kalaniopuu, Cook, and Kamehameha the Great. When I learned his name and extraordinary age, I turned toward Kanuha, extending my hand. This attention flattered him, and disposed him favorably toward me. So I resolved to take advantage of this lucky encounter to obtain from an eye-witness an insight into Hawaiian customs before the arrival of Europeans.

A hut of pandanus had been prepared for me upon the lava by the care of a missionary. I made the old man enter, and invited him to partake of my repast of poi,[2] cocoanut, raw fish, and roast dog. While eating the poi with full fingers, Kanuha assured me that he had lived under King Alapai, and had been his runner, as well as the courier of Kalaniopuu, his successor. So great had been Kanuha's strength in his youth that, at the command of his chiefs, he had in a single day accomplished the distance from Hoopuloa to Hilo, more than forty French leagues. When Cook died, in 1779, the little children of Kanuha's children had been born. When I spoke of Alapai to my old savage, he told me that *it seemed to him a matter of yesterday;* of Cook, *it was a thing of to-day*.

From these facts it may be believed that Kanuha was not less than one hundred and sixteen years old when I met him on this occasion. This remarkable example of longevity was by no means unique at the Hawaiian Islands a few years since. Father Maréchal knew at Ka'u, in 1844, an aged woman who remembered perfectly having seen Alapai. I had occasion to converse at Kauai with an islander who was already a grandfather when he saw Captain Cook die. I sketched, at this very Hoopuloa, the portrait of an old woman, still vigorous, Meawahine, who told any who would hear her that her breasts were completely developed when her chief gave her as wife to the celebrated English navigator.

Old Kanuha was the senior of all these centenaries. I took advantage of his willing disposition to draw from him the historical treasures with which his memory was stored. Here, in my own order, is what he told me during a night of conversation, interrupted only by the Hawaiian dances (*hulahula*), and by some pipes of tobacco smoked in turn, in the custom of the country.

OF GOVERNMENT AND SOCIETY WITH THE ANCIENT HAWAIIANS.

The soil was the property of the king, who reserved one part of it for himself, assigning another to the nobles, and left the rest to the first occupant. Property, based on a possession more or less ancient, was transmitted by heritage; but the king could always dispose, according to his whims, of property of chiefs and subjects, and the chiefs had the same privilege over the people.

Taxes were not assessed on any basis. The king levied them whenever it seemed good to him, and almost always in an arbitrary way. The chiefs also, and the priests, received a tribute from the people. The tax was always in kind, and consisted of:

Kalo, raw and made into poi;

Potatoes (*Convolvulus batatas*, L.) many varieties;

Bananas (*maia*) of different kinds;

Cocoa-nuts (called *niu* by the natives);

Dogs (destined for food);[3]

Hogs;

Fowls;

Fish, crabs, cuttle-fish, shell-fish;

Kukui nuts (*Aleurites moluccana*) for making relishes, and for illumination;

Edible sea-weed (*limu*);

Edible ferns (several species, among others the *hapuu*);

Awa (*Piper methysticum*, Forst.);

Ki roots (*Cordyline ti*, Schott.), a very saccharine vegetable;

Feathers of the *Oo* (*Drepanis pacifica*), and of the *Iiwi* (*Drepanis coccinea*): these birds were taken with the glue of the *ulu* or bread-fruit (*Artocarpus incisa*);

Fabrics of beaten bark (*kapa*) and fibre of the *olona* (*Bœhmeria*), of *wauke* (*Broussonetia papyrifera*), of *hau* (*Hibiscus tiliaceus*), etc.;

Mats of Pandanus and of Scirpus;

Pili (grass to thatch houses with);

Canoes (*waa*);

Wood for building;

Calabashes (serving for food vessels, and to hold water);

Wooden dishes;

Arms and instruments of war, etc., etc.

A labor tax was also enforced, and it was perhaps the most onerous, because it returned almost regularly every moon for a certain number of days. The work was principally cultivating the *loi*, or fields of kalo, which belonged to the king or chiefs.

The Hawaiian people were divided into three very distinct classes; these were:

1. The nobility (*Alii*), comprising the king and the chiefs of whatever degree;

2. The clergy (*Kahuna*), comprising the priests, doctors, prophets, and sorcerers;

3. Citizens (*Makaainana*), comprising laborers, farmers, proletaries, and slaves.

THE NOBILITY. NA'LII.

The chiefs or nobles were of several orders. The highest chief bore the title of *Moi*, which may best be rendered by the word majesty. In a remote period of Hawaiian history, this title was synonymous with *Ka lani*, heaven. This expression occurs frequently in ancient poems: *Auhea oe, e ka lani? Eia ae.* This mode of address is very poetic, and quite pleasing to the chiefs.

The Moi was still called *kapu* and *aliinui*. To tread on his shadow was a crime punished with death: *He make ke ee malu.* The chief next the throne took the title of *Wohi*. He who ranked next, that of *Mahana*. These titles could belong at the same time to several chiefs of the blood-royal, who were called *Alii kapu, Alii wohi.* The ordinary nobility furnished the king's aids-de-camp, called *Hulumanu* (plumed officers).

By the side of the nobility were the *Kahu alii*, literally guardians of the chiefs, of noble origin by the younger branch, but who dared not claim the title of chief in the presence of their elders. The Kahu alii of the male sex might be considered born chamberlains; of the female, ladies of the bed-chamber.

There were five kinds of Kahu alii, which are: Iwikuamoo, Ipukuha, Paakahili, Kiaipoo, Aipuupuu.

These titles constituted as many hereditary charges reserved for the lesser nobility. The functions of the Iwikuamoo (backbone of the chief) were to rub his lord on the back, when stretched on his mat. The Ipukuha had charge of the royal spittoons. The Paakahili carried a very long plume (*kahili*), which he waved around the royal person to drive away the flies and gnats. The duties of this officer were continual and most fatiguing, for he must constantly remain near the person of his master, armed with his ka-hili, whether the king was seated or reclining, eating or sleeping. The Kiaipoo's special charge was to watch at the side of his august chief during sleep. The Aipuupuu was the chief cook, and, besides, performed functions similar to those of steward or pur-veyor.

There were, besides, other inferior chiefs, as the *Puuku*, attendants of the house or palace; *Malama ukana*, charged with the care of provisions in traveling; *Aialo*, who had the privilege of eating in the presence of the chief; and, at the present day, the *Muki baka*, who had the honor of lighting the king's pipe and carrying his tobacco-pouch.

Although the people considered these last four orders as belonging to the nobility, it seems that they were of lower rank than the citizens favored by the chiefs.

Finally, the king had always in his service the *Hula*, who, like the buffoon or jester of the French kings, must amuse his majesty by mimicry or dancing. The *Kahu alii*, or *Kaukaualii*, as they are now styled, are attendants or followers of the high chiefs by right of birth. They accompany their masters everywhere, almost in the same manner that a governess follows her pupil.[4] From the throne down nobility was heredita-ry. The right of primogeniture was recognized as natural law. Nobility transmitted through the mother was considered far superior to that on the father's side only, even if he were the highest of chiefs. This usage was founded on the following proverb: *Maopopo ka makuahine, aole maopopo ka makuakane* (It is always evident who the mother is, but one is never sure about the father). Agreeably to this principle, the high chiefs, when they could not find wives of a sufficiently illustrious origin, might espouse their sisters and their nieces, or, in default of either of these, their own mother. Nevertheless, history furnishes us several examples of kings who were not noble on the maternal side.[5]

THE CLERGY. NA KAHUNA.

The priests formed three orders:
1. The *Kahuna* proper.
2. The *Kaula*, or prophets.
3. The *Kilo*, diviners or magicians.

The priesthood, properly so called (*Kahuna maoli, Kahuna pule*), was hereditary. The priests received their titles from their fathers, and transmitted them to their offspring, male and female, for the Hawaiians had priestesses as well. The priest was the peer of the nobility; he had a portion of land in all the estates of the chiefs, and sometimes ac-quired such power as to be formidable to the alii. In religious ceremonies, the priests were clothed with absolute power, and selected the victims for the sacrifices. This privilege gave them an immense and dangerous influence in private life, whence the Hawaiian proverb: The priest's man is inviolable, the chief's man is the prey of death, *Aole e make ko ke kahuna kanaka, o ko ke 'lii kanaka ke make.*

The kahuna, being clothed with supreme power in the exercise of his functions, alone could designate the victim suitable to appease the anger of the gods. The people feared him much for this prerogative, which gave the power of life and death over all, and the result was that the priest had constantly at his service an innumerable crowd of men and women wholly devoted to him. It was not proper for him to choose victims from a people who paid him every imaginable attention. But among the servants of the alii, if there were any who had offended the priest or his partisans, nothing more was neces-sary to condemn to death such or such an attendant of even the highest chief. From this it may be seen how dangerous it was not to enjoy the good graces of the kahuna, who, by his numerous clan, might revolutionize the whole country. History affords us an example in the Kahuna Kaleihokuu of Laupahoehoe, who had in his service so considerable a body of retainers that he was able in a day, by a single act of his will, to put to death the great chief Hakau, of Waipio, and substitute in his place Umi, the bastard son (*poolua*) of King Liloa, who had, however, been adopted by Kaleihokuu. Another example of this remarkable power is seen in the Kahuna of Ka'u, who massacred the high chief Kohookalani, in the neighborhood of Ninole, tumbling down upon him a huge tree from the top of the *pali* (precipice) of Hilea.

The *Kahuna*, especially those of the race of Paao, were the natural depositaries of history, and took the revered title of *Mooolelo*, or historians. Some individuals of this stock still exist, and they are all esteemed by the natives, and regarded as the chiefs of the historical and priestly caste. The sacerdotal order had its origin in Paao, whose descendants have always been regarded as the *Kahuna maoli*.[6] Paao came from a distant land called Kahiki. According to several chiefs, his genealogy must be more correct than that of the kings. Common tradition declares that Paao came from foreign countries, landing on the north-west shore of Hawaii (Kohala), at Puuepa, in the place where, to this day, are seen the ruins of the Heiau (temple) of Mokini, the most ancient of all the temples, and which he is said to have built. The advent of Paao and his erection of this heiau are so ancient, according to the old men, that Night helped the priest raise the temple: *Na ka po i kukulu ae ia Mokini, a na Paao nae.* These sayings, in the native tongue, indicate the high antiquity of Paao.[7]

To build the temple of Mokini, which also served as a city of refuge, Paao had stones brought from all sides, even from Pololu, a village situated four or five leagues from Mokini or Puuepa. The Kanakas formed a chain the whole length of the route, and passed the stones from one to another—an easy thing in those times—from the immense population of the neighborhood.

Paao has always been considered as the first of the Kahuna. For this reason his descendants, independently of the fact that they are regarded as *Mookahuna*, that is, of the priesthood, are more like nobles in the eye of the people, and are respected by the chiefs themselves. There are, in the neighborhood of Mokini, stones which are considered petrifactions of the canoe, paddles, and fish-hooks of Paao.

At Pololu, toward the mountain, are found fields of a very beautiful verdure. They are called the pastures, or grass-plots, of Paao (*Na mauu a Paao*). The old priest cultivated these fields himself, where no one since his time has dared to use spade or mattock. If an islander was impious enough to cultivate the meadow of Paao, the people believe that a terrible punishment would be the inevitable consequence of that profanation. Disastrous rains, furious torrents, would surely ravage the neighboring country.

Some Hawaiians pretend that there exists another sacerdotal race besides that of Paao, more ancient even than that, and whose priests belonged at the same time to a race of chiefs. It is the family of Maui, probably of Maui-hope, the last of the seven children of Hina,[8] the same who captured the sea-monster Piimoe. The origin of this race, to which Naihe of Kohala pretends to belong, is fabulous. Since the reign of Kamehameha, the priests of the order of Maui have lost favor.

The second class of the clergy was composed of the prophets (*Kaula*), an inoffensive and very respectable people, who gave vent to their inspiration from time to time in unexpected and uncalled-for prophesies.

The third order of the clergy is that of *Kilo,* diviners or magicians. With these may be classed the *Kilokilo,* the *Kahunalapaau* and *Kahunaanaana,* a sort of doctors regarded as sorcerers, to whom was attributed the power of putting to death by sorcery and witchcraft.[9] The Kahunaanaana and the Kahunalapaau have never been considered as belonging to the high caste of Kahuna maoli.

The Kahunaanaana, or sorcerers, inherited their functions. They were thoroughly detested, and the people feared them, and do to this day. When the chiefs were dissatisfied with a sorcerer, they had his head cut off with a stone axe (*koipohaku*), or cast him from the top of a pali.

The doctors were of two kinds. The first, the Kahunalapaau proper, comprised all who used plants in the treatment of disease. Just as the sorcerers understood poisonous vegetables, so the doctors knew the simples which furnished remedies to work cures. The second kind comprised the spiritual doctors, who had various names, and who seem to have been intermediate between priests and magicians, sharing at once in the attributes of both. They were:

Kahuna uhane, the doctors of ghosts and spirits;

Kahuna makani, doctors of winds;

Kahuna hoonohonoho akua, who caused the gods to descend on the sick;

Kahuna aumakua, doctors of diseases of the old;

Kahuna Pele, doctors or priests of Pele, goddess of volcanoes.

All the doctors of the second kind are still found in the islands,[10] where they have remained idolaters, although they have been for the most part baptized. There is hardly a Kanaka who has not had recourse to them in his complaints, preferring their cures and their remedies to those of the foreign physicians. Laws have been enacted to prohibit these charlatans from exercising their art; but under the rule of Kamehameha III., who protected them, these laws have not been enforced.

THE CITIZENS. NA MAKAAINANA.

The class of *Makaainana* comprises all the inhabitants not included in the two preceding classes; that is to say, the bulk of the people.

There were two degrees of this cast: the *kanaka wale,* freemen, private citizens, and the *kauwa* or servants. The Hawaiian saying, *O luna, o lalo, kai, o uka a o ka hao pae, ko ke 'lii* (All above, all below, the sea, the land, and iron cast upon the shore, all belong to the king), exactly defines the third class of the nation, called makaainana, the class that possesses nothing, and has no right save that of sustenance.

The Hawaiians honored canoe-builders and great fishers as privileged citizens. The chiefs themselves granted them some consideration; but it must be confessed that the honorable position they occupied in society was due to their skill in their calling rather than to any thing else. These builders were generally deeply in debt. They ate in advance the price of their labor, which usually consisted of hogs and fowls, and they died of starvation before the leaves ceased to sprout on the tree their adze had transformed into a canoe.

The *kauwa,* servants, must not be confounded with the *kauwa maoli,* actual slaves. A high chief, even a wohi, would call himself without dishonor *ke kauwa a ke 'lii nui,* the servant of the king. At present, their excellencies the ministers and the nobles do not hesitate to sign their names under the formula *kou kauwa,* your servant; but it is none the less true, for all that, that formerly there were among the common people a class, few in number, of slaves, or serfs, greatly despised by the Hawaiians, and still to our days so lowered in public opinion that a simple peasant refuses to associate with the descendants of this caste.

They point the finger at people of kauwa extraction, lampoon them, and touch the soles of their feet when they speak of them, to mark the lowness of their origin. If they were independent, and even rich, an ordinary islander would deem himself disgraced to marry his daughter to one of these pariahs.

The slaves were not permitted to cross the threshold of the chiefs' palace. They could do no more than crawl on hands and knees to the door. In spite of the many changes infused into Hawaiian institutions, the kauwa families remain branded with a stigma, in the opinion of the natives, and the laws, which accord them the same rights as other citizens, can not reinstate them.

It seems certain that the origin of slavery among the Hawaiians must be sought in conquests. The vanquished, who were made prisoners, became slaves, and their posterity inherited their condition.

From time immemorial the islanders have clothed themselves, the men with the *malo*, the women with the *pau*. The malo is bound around the loins, after having passed between the legs, to cover the pudenda. The pau is a short skirt, made of bark cloth or of the ki leaves, which reaches from the waist half down to the knees. The old popular songs show clearly that this costume has always been worn by the natives. To go naked was regarded as a sign of madness, or as a mark of divine birth. Sometimes the kings were attended by a man sprung from the gods, and this happy mortal alone had the right to follow, *puris naturalibus*, his august master. The people said, in speaking of him, *He akua ia*, he is a god.

Kapa, a kind of large sheet in which the chiefs dressed themselves, was made of the soaked and beaten bark of several shrubs, such as the wauke, olona, hau, oloa. Fine varieties were even made of the kukui (*Aleurites moluccana*). In ancient times it was an offense punishable with death for a common man to wear a double kapa or malo.

The Hawaiians have never worn shoes. In certain districts where lava is very abundant, they make sandals (*kamaa*) with the leaves of the ki and pandanus. They always go bare-headed, except in battle, where they like to exhibit themselves adorned with a sort of helmet made of twigs and feathers.

The women never wear any thing but flowers on their heads. Tattooing was known, but less practiced than at the Marquesas, and much more rudely.

The Hawaiians are not cannibals. They have been upbraided in Europe as eaters of human flesh, but such is not the case. They have never killed a man for food. It is true that in sacrifices they eat certain parts of the victim, but there it was a religious rite, not an act of cannibalism. So, also, when they ate the flesh of their dearest chiefs, it was to do honor to their memory by a mark of love: they never eat the flesh of bad chiefs.

The Hawaiians do not deny that the entrails of Captain Cook were eaten; but they insist that it was done by children, who mistook them for the viscera of a hog, an error easily explained when it is known that the body had been opened and stripped of as much flesh as possible, to be burned to ashes, as was due the body of a god. The officers of the distinguished navigator demanded his bones, but as they were destroyed,*

---

* This was not true. Liholiho carried some to England, and the rest were probably hidden in some of the many caverns on the shores of Kealakeakua Bay.—*Trans.*

those of a Kanaka were surrendered in their stead, receiving on board the ships of the expedition the honors intended for the unfortunate commander.

The condition of the women among the ancient Hawaiians was like that of servants well treated by their masters. The chiefesses alone enjoyed equal rights with men. It is a convincing proof that women were regarded as inferior to men, that they could in no case eat with their husbands, and that the kapu was often put upon their eating the most delicious food. Thus bananas were prohibited on pain of death. Their principal occupations consisted in making kapa, the malo and pau, and in preparing food.

Marriage was performed by cohabitation with the consent of the relations. Polygamy was only practiced by the chiefs. Children were very independent, and although their parents respected them so much as seldom to dare lay hands on them, they were quite ready to part with them to oblige a friend who evinced a desire for them. Often an infant was promised before birth. This singular custom still exists, but is much less frequent.

They had little regard for old men who had become useless, and even killed them to get them out of the way. It was allowable to suffocate infants to avoid the trouble of bringing them up. Women bestowed their affection upon dogs and pigs, and suckled them equally with their children. Fleas, lice, and grasshoppers were eaten, but flies inspired an unconquerable horror; if one fell into a calabash of poi, the whole was thrown away.[11]

The Hawaiians practiced a sort of circumcision, differing from that of the Jews, but having the same sanitary object. This operation (*mahele*) consisted in slitting the prepuce by means of a bamboo. The mahele has fallen into disuse, but is still practiced in some places, unbeknown to the missionaries, upon children eight or ten years old. A sort of priest (kahuna) performs the operation.[12]

The Hawaiian women are always delivered without pain, except in very exceptional cases. The first time they had occasion to witness, in the persons of the missionaries' wives, the painful childbirths of the white race, they could not restrain their bursts of laughter, supposing it to be mere custom, and not pain, that could thus draw cries from the wives of the Haole (foreigners).

The ancient Hawaiians cared for their dead. They wrapped them in kapa with fragrant herbs, such as the flowers of the sugar-cane, which had the property of embalming them. They buried in their houses, or carried their bodies to grottoes dug in the solid rock. More frequently they were deposited in natural caves, a kind of catacombs, where the corpses were preserved without putrefaction, drying like mummies. It was a sacred duty to furnish food to the dead for several weeks. Sometimes the remains were thrown into the boiling lava of the volcanoes, and this mode of sepulture was regarded as homage paid to the goddess Pele, who fed principally on human flesh.

THE STORY OF UMI: HIS BIRTH AND YOUTH.

Liloa reigned over the island of Hawaii. In the course of one of his journeys through the province of Hamakua, he met a woman of the people named Akahikameainoa, who pleased him, and whose favors he claimed as supreme chief.

Akahikameainoa was then in her menses, so that the malo of the king was soiled with the discharge. Liloa said to the woman: "If you bring into the world a man-child, it shall belong to me; if a girl, it shall be yours. I leave with you as tokens of my sovereign will my *niho palaao* (whale's tooth), and my *lei*. Conceal these things from all eyes; they will one day be a souvenir of our relation, a proof of the paternity of the child who shall be born from our loves."

That would, indeed, be an unexceptionable testimony, for by the law of kapu a wife could not, under pain of death, approach her husband while in her courses. The soiled malo and the time of the child's birth would give certain indications.

Akahikameainoa carefully concealed the royal tokens of her adultery, saying nothing to any one, not even to her husband. The spot where she hid them is known to this day as *Huna na niho*, the hiding-place of the teeth.

Liloa then held his court at Waipio in all the splendor of the time. Besides a considerable troop of servants, he had in attendance priests (kahuna), prophets (kaula), nobles, and his only son, Hakau. The palace was made merry night and day by the licentious motions of the dancers, and by the music of the resounding calabashes.

Nine moons after her meeting with the king, Akahikameainoa gave birth to a man-child, which she called Umi, and brought up under the roof of her husband, who believed himself the father. The child developed rapidly, became strong, and acquired a royal stature. In his social games, in the sports of youth, he always bore away the palm. He was, moreover, a great eater: *Hao wale i ka ai a me ka ia.*[13] In a word, Umi was a perfect Kanaka, and a skillful fighter, who made his comrades suffer for it. At this time he conceived a strong affection for two peasants of the neighborhood, Koi of Kukui-haole and Omakamau, who became his *aikane*.

One day his supposed father, angry at his conduct, was about to punish him: "Strike him not," exclaimed Akahikameainoa, "he is your lord and chief! Do not imagine that he is the son of us two: he is the child of Liloa, your king." Umi was then about fifteen or sixteen years old.

His mother, after this declaration, startling as a thunder-bolt, went and uncovered the tokens Liloa had left as proof, and placed them before her husband, who was motionless with fear at the thought of the high treason he had been on the point of committing.

In the mean time, Liloa had grown old, and Akahikameainoa, deeming the moment had arrived, invested Umi with the royal malo, the niho palaoa, and the lei, emblems of power, which high chiefs alone had the right to wear. "Go," said she to him then; "go, my son, present yourself at Waipio to King Liloa, your father. Tell him you are his child, and show him, in proof of your words, these tokens which he left with me."

Umi, proud enough of the revelation of his mother, at once departs, accompanied by Koi and Omakamau.

The palace of Liloa was surrounded by guards, priests, diviners, and sorcerers. The kapu extended to the edge of the outer inclosure, and no one might pass on penalty of death. Umi advanced boldly and crossed the threshold. Exclamations and cries of death sounded in his ears from all sides. Without troubling himself, he passed on and entered the end door. Liloa was asleep, wrapped in his royal mantle of red and yellow feathers. Umi stooped, and, without ceremony, uncovered his head. Liloa, awakening, said, "*Owai la keia?*—Who is this?" "It is I," replied the youth; "it is I, Umi, your son." So saying, he displays his malo at the king's feet. At this token Liloa, while rubbing his eyes, recognized Umi, and had him proclaimed his son. Behold, then, Umi admitted to the rank of high chief, if not the equal of Hakau, his eldest son, at least his prime minister by birth—his lieutenant.

The two brothers lived at court on an equal footing. They took part in the same amusements, wrestling, drawing the bow, plunged with eagerness into all the noble exercises of the country and the time. The people of Umi's suite matched themselves with those of Hakau in the combat with the long lance (*pololu*), and the party of Umi was always victorious, compelling Hakau to retire in confusion.

Liloa, perceiving that his last hour was drawing near, called his two children to him, and said to them, "You, Hakau, will be chief, and you, Umi, will be his man." This last expression is equivalent to viceroy or prime minister. The two brothers bowed, in token of assent, and the old chief continued: "Do you, Hakau, respect your man; and do you, Umi, respect your sovereign. If you, Hakau, have no consideration for your man, if you quarrel with him, I am not disturbed at the results of your conduct. In the same way, Umi, unless you render your sovereign the homage you owe him, if you rebel against him, it will be for you two to decide your lot." Soon after, having made known his last wishes, Liloa gave up the ghost.

Umi, who was of a proud and independent character, foreseeing, no doubt, even then, the wicked conduct of his brother, would not submit to him, and refused to appear in his presence. Giving up his share of power, he departed from Waipio with his two *aikane*, and retired into the mountains, where he gave himself up to bird-catching.

Hakau then reigned alone, and ruled according to his fancy. Abusing his authority, he made himself feared, but, at the same time, detested by his people. He brought upon himself the censure of the chief attendants of his father, whom he provoked by all sorts of humiliations and insults. If he saw any one of either sex remarkable for good looks, he had them tattooed in a frightful manner for his good pleasure.

Meanwhile Umi, who had a taste for savage life, had taken leave of his favorites, and wandered alone in the midst of the forests and mountains. One day, when he descended to the shore at Laupahoehoe, in the district of Hilo, he fell in love with a woman of the people, and made her his companion without arousing a suspicion of his high birth. Devoting himself, then, to field labor, he was seen sometimes cultivating the ground, and sometimes going down to the sea to fish.

By generous offerings, he knew how to skillfully flatter an old man named Kaleihokuu, an influential priest, who at last adopted him as one of his children. Umi always kept at the head of the farmers and fishermen, and a considerable number, recognizing his physical superiority, voluntarily enrolled themselves under his orders and those of his foster-father; he was only known by the name of Hanai (foster-child) of Kaleihokuu. Meditating probably, even then, a way of acquiring supreme power, Umi exerted himself to gain the sympathies of the people, in whose labors he took an incredible part. There are seen to this day, above Laupahoehoe, the fields which Umi cultivated, and near the sea can be seen the heiau, or temple, in which Kaleihokuu offered sacrifices to the gods.

Hakau continued to reign, always without showing the least respect to the old officers of Liloa, his father. Two old men, high chiefs by birth, and highly honored under the preceding reign, had persisted in residing near the palace at Waipio, in spite of the insults to which the nearness of the court exposed them. One day when they were hungry, after a long scarcity of food, they said to one of their attendants: "Go to the palace of Hakau. Tell his Majesty that the two old chiefs are hungry, and demand of him, in our name, food, fish, and awa." [14] The attendant went at once to the king to fulfill his mission. Hakau replied with foul and insulting terms: "Go tell the two old men that they shall have neither food, fish, nor awa!" The two chiefs, on hearing this cruel reply, commenced to deplore their lot, and regret more bitterly than ever the time they lived under Liloa. Then rousing themselves, they said to their attendant, "We have heard of the foster-son of Kaleihokuu, of his activity, courage, and generosity. Lose no time; go directly to Laupahoehoe, and tell Kaleihokuu that two chiefs desire to see his adopted son." The servant went with all speed to Laupahoehoe, where he delivered his master's message. Kaleihokuu told him, "Return to your masters, tell them that they will be welcome, if they will come to-morrow to see my foster-son." The old men, at this news, hastened to depart. Arrived at the abode of Kaleihokuu, they found no one, except a man asleep on the mat. They entered, nevertheless, and sat down, leaning their backs against the walls of the pandanus house. "At last," said they, sighing, "our bones are going to revive, *akahi a ola na iwi.*" Then, addressing the slumbering man, "Are you, then, alone here?"—"Yes," replied the young man; "Kaleihokuu is in the fields."—"We are," added they, "the two old men of Waipio, come expressly to see the priest's foster-son."

The young man rises without saying a word, prepares an abundant repast—an entire hog, fish, and awa. The two old men admired the activity and skill of the youth, and said to themselves, "At all events, if the foster-son of Kaleihokuu were as vigorous a stripling as this, we should renew our life!" The young unknown served them food, and made them drunk with awa, and, according to the usage of those times,[15] gave up to them the women of Kaleihokuu, that his hospitality might be complete.

The next morning the old men saw Kaleihokuu, and said to him, "Here we have come to become acquainted with your foster-son. May it please the gods that he be like that fine young fellow who entertained us at your house! Our bones would revive."—"Ah, indeed," replied Kaleihokuu; "he who has so well received you is my *keiki hanai.* I left him at the house on purpose to perform for you the duties of hospitality." The two old men, rejoiced at what they learned, told the priest and his adopted son the ill treatment they had received at the court of Hakau. No more was needed to kindle a war at once.

At the head of a considerable troop of people attached to the service of Kaleihokuu, Umi went by forced marches to Waipio, and the next day Hakau had ceased to reign. He had been slain by the very hand of the vigorous foster-son of the priest.

THE REIGN OF UMI.

Umi ruled in place of Hakau. His two aikane, Koi and Omakamau, had joined him, and resided at his court. Piimaiwaa of Hilo was his most valiant warrior. *Ia ia ka mama kakaua*—to him belonged the bâton of war, a figurative expression denoting the general-in-chief. Pakaa was one of the favorites of Umi, and Lono was his kahuna.

While Umi reigned over the eastern shores of the island, one of his cousins, Keliiokaloa, ruled the western coast, and held his court at Kailua. It was under the reign of this prince, about two centuries before the voyage of Captain Cook, that a ship was wrecked near Keei, in the district of Kona, not far from the place where the celebrated English navigator met his death in 1779. It was about 1570* that men of the white race first landed in the archipelago. One man and one woman escaped from the wreck, and reached land near Kealakeakua. Coming to the shore, these unfortunates prostrated themselves on the lava, with their faces to the earth, whence comes the name

---

* The Hawaiian Islands were discovered in 1555, by Juan Gaetano, or Gaytan.—*Trans.*

Kulou, a *bowing down*, which the place which witnessed this scene still bears. The shipwrecked persons soon conformed to the customs of the natives, who pretend that there exists to our day a family of chiefs descended from these two whites. The Princess Lohea, daughter of Liliha,[16] still living, is considered of this origin. Keliiohaloa, who reigned over the coast where this memorable event took place, was a wicked prince, who delighted in wantonly felling cocoa-nut trees and laying waste cultivated lands. His ravages induced Umi to declare war against him.

He took the field at the head of his army, accompanied by his famous warrior, Piimaiwaa; his friends, Koi and Omakamau; his favorite, Pakaa; and Lono, his Kahuna. He turned the flanks of Mauna Kea, and advancing between this mountain and Hualalai, in the direction of Mauna Loa, arrived at the great central plateau of the island, intending to make a descent upon Kailua. Keliiokaloa did not wait for him. Placing himself at the head of his warriors, he marched to meet Umi. The two armies met on the high plain bounded by the colossi of Hawaii, at the place which is called *Ahua a Umi*.

Two men of the slave race, called Laepuni, famous warriors of Keliiokaloa, fought with a superhuman courage, and Umi was about to fall under their blows, when Piimaiwaa, coming to his rescue, caused the victory to incline to his side. Although history is silent, it is probable that the king of Kailua perished in the battle.

This victory completely rid Umi of his last rival; he reigned henceforth as sole ruler of Hawaii; and to transmit to posterity the remembrance of this remarkable battle, he caused to be erected on the battle-field, by the people of the six provinces, Hilo, Hamakua, Kohala, Kona, Ka'u, and Puna, a singular monument, composed of six polyhedral piles of ancient lava collected in the vicinity. A seventh pyramid was raised by his nobles and officers. In the centre of these enormous piles of stone he built a temple, whose remains are still sufficiently perfect to enable one to restore the entire plan. The whole of this vast monument is called, after the name of its builder, the Heaps of Umi—*Ahua Umi.*

Umi built another temple at the foot of Pohaku Hanalei, on the coast of Kona, called *Ahua Hanalei.* A third temple was also erected by him on the flank of Mauna Kea, in the direction of Hilo, at the place called Puukeekee. Traces of a temple built by the same king may also be recognized at Mauna Halepohaha, where are found the ruins of Umi's houses covered with a large block of lava.[17]

They give Umi the name of King of the Mountains. Tradition declares that he retired to the centre of the island, through love for his people, and these are the reasons which explain the seclusion to which he devoted himself. It was a received custom in Hawaiian antiquity that the numerous attendants of the chiefs, when traversing a plantation, should break down the cocoa-nuts, lay waste the fields, and commit all sorts of havoc prejudicial to the interests of proprietors or cultivators. To avoid a sort of scourge which followed the royal steps, Umi made his abode in the mountains, in order that the robberies of his attendants might no longer cause the tears of the people to flow. In his retreat Umi lived, with his retainers, upon the tribute in kind which his subjects brought him from all parts of the coast. In time of famine, his servants went through the forest and collected the *hapuu*, a nourishing fern which then took the place of poi.

Umi, however, did not spend all his time in the mountains. He came to live at various times on the sea-shore at Kailua. He employed everywhere workmen to cut stones, to serve, some say, in the construction of a sepulchral cave; according to others, to build a magnificent palace. Whatever may have been their destination, the stones were admirably hewn.[18] In our days the Calvinistic missionaries have used them in the erection of the great church of Kailua, without any need of cutting them anew. There are still seen, scattered in various places, the hewn stones of King Umi, *na pohaku kalai a Umi*. It is natural to suppose that they used to hew these hard and very large stones with other tools than those of Hawaiian origin. Iron must have been known in the time of Umi, and its presence is explained by the wrecks of ships which ocean currents may have drifted ashore. It is certain that they were acquainted with iron long before the arrival of Cook, as is proved by the already cited passage from an old romance: *O luna, o lalo, kai, o uka, a o ka hao pae, ko ke'lii.*

Umi, some time before his death, said to his old friend Koi: "There is no place, nor is there any possible way to conceal my bones. You must disappear from my presence. I am going to take back all the lands which I have given you around Hawaii, and they will think you in disgrace. You will then withdraw to another island, and as soon as you hear of my death, or only that I am dangerously sick, return secretly to take away my body."

Koi executed the wishes of the chief, his *aikane*. He repaired to Molokai, whence he hastened to set sail for Hawaii as soon as he heard of Umi's death. He landed at Honokohau. On setting foot on shore, he met a Kanaka, in all respects like his dearly-loved chief. He seized him, killed him, and carried his body by night to Kailua. Koi entered secretly the palace where the corpse of Umi was lying. The guards were asleep, and Koi carried away the royal remains, leaving in their place the body of the old man of Honokohau, and then disappeared with his canoe. Some say that he deposited the body of Umi in the great pali of Kahulaana, but no one knows the exact spot; others say that it was in a cave at Waipio, at Puaahuku, at the top of the great pali over which the cascade of Hiilawe falls.

From time immemorial it was the custom at Hawaii to eat the flesh of great chiefs after death, then the bones were collected in a bundle, and concealed far out of the way. Generally it was to a faithful attendant, a devoted *kahu*, that the honor of eating the flesh of his chief belonged by a sentiment of friendship, *no ke aloha*. If they did not always eat the flesh of high chiefs and distinguished personages, they always took away their dead bodies, to bury them in the most secret caves, or in most inaccessible places. But the same care was not taken with chiefs who had been regarded as wicked during their lives. The proverb says of this: *Aole e nalo ana na iwi o ke 'lii kolohe; e nalo loa na iwi o ke 'lii maikai*—The bones of a bad chief do not disappear; those of a good chief are veiled from the eyes of all the world.

The high chiefs, before death, made their most trusty attendants swear to conceal their bones so that no one could discover them. "I do not wish," said the dying chief, "that my bones should be made into arrows to shoot mice, or into fish-hooks." So it is very difficult to find the burial-place of such or such a chief. Mausoleums have been built in some places, and it is said that here are interred the nobles and kings; but it would seem that there are only empty coffins, or the bodies of common natives substituted for those of the personages in whose honor these monuments have been raised.

THE HISTORY OF KEAWE.

Whatever the historian, David Malo, may say, it is very doubtful whether there were several chiefs of the name of Keawe. It is probable that there was only one high chief of this name, that he was the son of Umi, and was called Keawe the Great—*Keawe nui a Umi.* David Malo was interested, as the natives know, in swelling the genealogy of the alii, and he wished to flatter both nobility and people by distinguishing Keawe nui, of the race of Umi, from another Keawe. There are two Keawe, as seven Maui, and nine Hina. It is not, indeed, so long a period from Umi to the present era, that we can not unveil the truth from the clouds which surround it.

The people, in general, only speak of one Keawe, who inherited the power of his father Umi. He was supreme ruler in the island of Hawaii, and is even said to have united, as Kamehameha has since done, all the group under his sceptre. Kamehameha conquered the islands by force of arms; Keawe had conquered them by his travels and alliances. While he passed through the islands of Maui, Molokai, and Oahu, he contracted marriages everywhere, as well with the women of the people as with the highest chiefesses. These unions gave him children who made him beloved of all the high chiefs of that time. He was regarded at Maui and Oahu as supreme king. The king of Kauai even went so far as to send messengers to declare to him that he recognized his sovereignty. Such is the origin of Keawe's power.

By his numerous marriages with chiefesses and common women without distinction, this king has made the Hawaiian nobility, the present alii say, bastard and dishonored. The chiefs descended from Keawe conceal their origin, and are by no means flattered when reminded of it. From Keawe down, the genealogies become a focus of disputes, and it would be really dangerous for the rash historian who did not spare the susceptibilities of chiefs on this subject.

The principle on which those who condemn the conduct of Keawe rests is the purity of the blood of the royal stock, required by ancient usages, whose aim was to preserve the true nobility without alloy. Disdaining this rule, Keawe contracted numerous marriages, which gave him as mothers of his children women of low birth. The posterity of this chief, noble without doubt, but of impure origin, likes not to have its lame genealogy recalled. It is with the sensitiveness of the Hawaiians on this subject, as with many other things in this world: they attack bitterly the amours of Keawe, and seem to forget that Umi, their great chief, whose memory they preserve with so much care, was of plebeian blood by his mother.

It seems certain that King Keawe usually resided at the bay of Hoonaunau, in Kona. The heiau of Hoonaunau, where may still be seen the stakes of ohia (*Metrosideros*) planted by Keawe, is called *Hale a Keawe*—The house built by Keawe. It served also as a City of Refuge.[19]

VARIOUS DOCUMENTS ON THE PROVINCE OF KA'U.

The people of Ka'u are designated in the group under the name of *Na Mamo a ke kipi*—The descendants of the rebellion. The province of Ka'u has always been regarded as a land fatal to chiefs. At the present day an inhabitant of Ka'u can be distinguished among other natives. He is energetic, haughty in speech, and always ready to strike a blow when occasion presents. He is proud, and worships his liberty. Several Hawaiian chiefs have been killed by the people of Ka'u, among others Kohaokalani, Koihala, etc.

THE HISTORY OF KOHAOKALANI.

He was, according to tradition, the most important chief on the island, and reigned in royal state at Hilea. He it was who built the heiau situated on the great plain of

Makanau. The sea-worn pebbles may still be seen, which Kohaokalani had his people carry up on to the height, about two leagues from the shore. These pebbles were intended for the interior pavement of the temple. The people, worn out by the great difficulty of transportation, tired of the yoke of royalty, and incited by disloyal priests, began to let their discontent and discouragement show itself. A conspiracy was soon formed by these two classes leagued against the chief, and a religious ceremony offered an occasion to rid themselves of the despot.

The temple was completed, and it only remained to carry a god up there. This divinity was nothing but an ohia-tree of enormous size, which had been cut down in the forest above Ninole. At the appointed day the chief priests and people set to work to draw the god to his residence. In order to reach the height of Makanau there was a very steep pali to be ascended. They had to carry up the god on the side toward Ninole, which was all the better for the execution of their premeditated plan. Arrived at the base of the precipice, all pulled at the rope; but the god, either by the contrivance of the priests, or owing to the obstacles which the roughness of the rock presented, ascended only with great difficulty. " The god will never come to the top of the pali," said the Kahuna, " if the chief continues to walk before him; the god should go first by right of power, and the chief below, following, to push the lower end; otherwise we shall never overcome his resistance." The high chief, Kohaokalani, complied with the advice of the priests, placed himself beneath the god, and pushed the end from below. Instantly priests and people let go the cord, and the enormous god, rolling upon the chief, crushed him at once. The death of Kohaokalani is attributed chiefly to the Kahuna.

THE HISTORY OF KOIHALA.

Koihala reigned at Ka'u. He was a very great chief—perhaps the entire island recognized his authority. An abuse of power hastened his death. He had commanded the people of Ka'u to bring him food upon the plain of Punaluu, at the place known under the name of Puuonuhe. A party of men set out with pounded kalo (*paiai*, differing from poi in not being diluted), bound up in leaves of ki, called *la'i* (a contraction for *lau-ki*). When they arrived at the top of the plateau, which is very elevated, they found that the chief had set out for Kaalikii, two leagues from Puuonuhe, and that he had left orders for them to bring him the provisions in this distant place. The bearers hastened toward Kaalikii. As soon as they came there, orders were given for them to proceed to Waioahukini, half a league's walk in the same direction, and beneath the great pali of Malilele, on the shore. They went on. Arrived at Waioahukini, they were ordered to go and join the chief at Kalae. There they had to climb again the great pali, and two leagues more to go. When they reached the cape of Kalae, the most southern point of the Hawaiian group, they were sent to seek the chief at the village of Mahana; but he had left for Paihaa, a village near Kaalualu, a little bay where the native vessels now anchor. There, at last, they must find the tyrant. Exasperated, dying of hunger, indignant at the cruel way in which the chief made sport of their pains, the bearers sat down on the grass and took counsel. First they decided to eat up the food, without leaving any thing for the chief who entertained himself so strangely in fatiguing his people (*hooluhi hewa*). They moreover determined to carry to him, instead of kalo, bundles of stones. The trial of Koihala is ended, his insupportable yoke is about to fall.

The determined conspirators, after satisfying their hunger, set off, and soon arrived, with humble mien, in the presence of the chief, between Paihau and Kaalualu. "Prince," said they, "here are your servants with provisions." They humbly laid at his feet their bundles wrapped in la'i. The wrappers were opened, and the scene changes. These people, apparently half dead, became in an instant like furious lions, ready to devour their prey. They armed themselves with stones, and showered them upon Koihala and his company, who perished together.

Two other high chiefs of the island were exterminated by the same people. One was killed at Kalae, beaten to death by the paddles of fishermen; the other was stoned at Aukukano.

These revolts against the chiefs have given birth to several proverbial expressions, applied to the district of Ka'u. Thus it is called *Aina makaha*—Land of torrents: a nation which removes and shatters every thing like a torrent; *Ka'u makaha*—Ka'u the torrent; *Ka lua kupapau o na'lii*—The sepulchre of the high chiefs; *Aina kipi*—The rebellious land.

LEGEND OF KALEIKINI.

He was a chief of the olden time.

On the sea-shore, between Kaalikii and Pohue, the waves were ingulfed beneath the land, and shot into the air by a natural aperture some fifty feet from the shore. The water leaped to a prodigious height, disappeared in the form of fine rain, and fell in vapor over a circuit of two leagues, spreading sterility over the land to such an extent that neither kalo nor sweet-potatoes could be grown there. The chief Kaleikini closed the mouth of the gulf by means of enormous stones, which he made the natives roll thither. It is plainly seen that this blow-hole has been closed by human hands. There still remains a little opening through which the water hisses to the height of thirty or forty feet.

Kaleikini closed at Kohala, on the shore of Nailima, a volcanic mouth like that of Ka'u.

On the heights of Honokane, he silenced the thunders of a water-fall by changing its course. At Maui Hikina, he secured the foundations of the hill of Puuiki, which the great-tides had rendered unstable. To do this, he put into the caverns of Puuiki a huge rock, which stopped the tumults of the sea, and put an end to the trembling of the hill.

For these feats of strength, and many others like them, Kaleikini was called *Kupua* —Wizard.*

DOCUMENTS ON THE PROVINCE OF PUNA.

According to common tradition, the district of Puna was, until two centuries ago, a magnificent country, possessing a sandy soil, it is true, but one very favorable to vegetation, and with smooth and even roads. The Hawaiians of our day hold a tradition from their ancestors, that their great-grandparents beheld the advent of the volcanic floods in Puna. Here, in brief, is the tradition as it is preserved by the natives:

LEGEND OF KELIIKUKU.

This high chief reigned in Puna. He journeyed to the island of Oahu. There he met a prophet of Kauai, named Kaneakalau, who asked him who he was. "I am," re-

---

* Kaleikini may be considered the Hawaiian Hercules.

plied the chief, " Keliikuku of Puna." The prophet then asked him what sort of a country he possessed. The chief said: "My country is charming; every thing is found
there in abundance; everywhere are sandy plains which produce marvelously."—"Alas!"
replied the prophet, " go, return to your beautiful country; you will find it overthrown,
abominable. Pele has made of it a heap of ruins; the trees of the mountains have descended toward the sea; the ohia and pandanus are on the shore. Your country is no
longer habitable." The chief made answer: " Prophet of evil, if what you now tell
me is true, you shall live; but if, when I return to my country, I prove the falsity of
your predictions, I will come back on purpose, and you shall die by my hand."

Unable, in spite of his incredulity, to forget this terrible prophecy, Keliikuku set sail
for Hawaii. He reached Hamakua, and, landing, traveled home by short stages. From
the heights of Hilo, at the village of Makahanaloa, he beheld in the distance all his
province overwhelmed in chaotic ruin, a prey to fire and smoke. In despair, the unfortunate chief hung himself on the very spot where he first discovered this sad spectacle.

This tradition of the meeting of Keliikuku and Kaneakalau is still sometimes chant-
ed by the Kanakas. It was reduced to metre, and sung by the ancients. It is passing
away in our day, and in a few years no trace of it will remain.

Whether the prediction was made or not, the fact is that Puna has been ravaged by
volcanic action.

LEGEND OF THE CHIEF HUA.

The high chief Hua, being in Maui, said to Uluhoomoe, his kahuna, that he wished
for some *uau* from the mountains (a large bird peculiar to the island of Hawaii). Uluhoomoe replied that there were no uau in the mountains—that all the birds had gone
to the sea. Hua, getting angry, said to his priest: "If I send my men to the mountains, and they find any uau there, I will put you to death."

After this menace, the chief ordered his servants to go to bird-hunting. They obey-
ed; but instead of going to the mountains (*mauka*), they set snares on the shores (*ma-
kai*), and captured many birds of different kinds, among others the uau and ulili. Returning to the palace, they assured the chief that they had hunted in the mountains.

Hua summoned his kahuna, and said to him: "There are the birds from the mountains; you are to die." Uluhoomoe smelled of the birds, and replied: "These birds do
not come from the mountains; they have an odor of the sea." Hua, supported by his
attendants, persisted in saying, as he believed truly, that they came from the mountains,
and repeated his sentence: "You are to die." Uluhoomoe responded: "I shall have a
witness in my favor if you let me open these birds in your presence." The chief consented, and small fish were found in the crops of the birds. "Behold my witness," said
the kahuna, with a triumphant air; "these birds came from the sea!"

Hua, in confusion, fell into a terrible rage, and massacred Uluhoomoe on the spot.
The gods avenged the death of the priest by sending a distressing famine, first on the
island of Maui, then on Hawaii. Hua, thinking to baffle the divine vengeance, went to
Hawaii to escape the scourge; but a famine more terrible yet pursued him there. The
chief vainly traversed every quarter of the islands; he starved to death in the temple
of Makeanehu (Kohala). His bones, after death, dried and shrunk in the rays of the
burning sun, to which his dead body remained exposed. This is the origin of the
Hawaiian epigram always quoted in recalling the famine which occurred in the reign

of Hua, an epigram which no one has understood, and which has never been written correctly:

Koele na iwi o Hua i ka la—The bones of Hua are dry in the sun.*

On the island of Hawaii are many places called by the name of this celebrated chief. At Kailua, in the hamlet of Puaaaekolu, a beautiful field, known by the name of Mooniohua, recalls one episode of Hua's misery. Here it was that, one day, running after food which he could never attain, he fell asleep, weary with fatigue and want. The word Mooniohua is probably a corruption of *Moe ana o Hua*—The couch of Hua.

THE STORY AND SONG OF KAWELO.

Kawelo, of the island of Kauai, was a sort of giant; handsome, well made, muscular, his prodigious strength defied animate and inanimate nature. In his early youth, he felt a violent passion kindle in his bowels for the Princess Kaakaukuhimalani, so that he sought in every way to touch her heart. But the princess, too proud, and too high a lady, did not deign to cast her eyes upon him.

Despairing of making her reciprocate his love, Kawelo poured into his mother's bosom his grief and his tears. "Mother," said he, "how shall I succeed in espousing this proud princess? What must I do? Give me your counsel."

"My son," replied his mother, "a youth who wishes to please ought to make himself ready at labor, and skillful in fishing; this is the only secret of making a good match."

Kawelo too eagerly followed his mother's advice, and soon there was not on the island a more indefatigable planter of kalo, nor a more expert fisherman. But what succeeds with common women is not always the thing to charm the daughters of kings. Kaakaukuhimalani could make nothing of a husband who was a skillful farmer or a lucky fisherman; other talents are required to touch the hearts of nobles, and hers remained indifferent, insensible to the sighs of Kawelo. Nobles then, as to-day, regarded pleasure above all things; and a good comedian was worth more to them than an honest workman.

In his great perplexity, Kawelo consulted an old dancing-master, who told him, "Dancing and poetry are the arts most esteemed and appreciated by those in power. Come with me into the mountains. I will instruct you, and if you turn out an accomplished dancer, you will have a sure means of pleasing the insensible Kaakaukuhimalani." Kawelo listened to the advice of the poet dancing-master, and withdrew into the mountains to pursue his duties.

He soon became a very skillful dancer, and an excellent reciter of the mele; so the fame of his skill was not slow in extending through all the valleys of the island.

One day when Kaakaukuhimalani desired to collect all the accomplished dancers of Kauai, her attendants spoke to her of Kawelo as a prodigy in the art, who had not his equal from one end to the other of the group, from Hawaii to Niihau. "Let some one bring me this marvel!" cried the princess, pricked with a lively curiosity. The old and cunning preceptor of the mountains directed his pupil not to present himself at the first invitation, in order to make his presence more ardently desired. Kawelo, understanding the value of this advice, did not obey until the third request; he danced before the

* The more common form is, *Koele na iwi o Hua ma i ka la*—Dry are the bones of Hua and his company in the sun.—*Trans.*

princess with a skill so extraordinary that she fell in love with him, and married him. So Kawelo found himself raised to princely rank.

The happy parvenu had three older brothers. They were: Kawelomakainoino, with fierce look and evil eye; Kawelomakahuhu, with unpleasant countenance and angry expression; Kawelomakaoluolu, with a lovable and gracious face. All three were endued with the same athletic strength as their younger brother.

Jealous of the good fortune which a princely marriage had brought their brother, they resolved to humble him for their pleasure. Taking advantage of the absence of Kaakaukuhimalani, they seized Kawelo and poured a calabash of poi over his head. Poor Kawelo! The paste ran down from his head over all his body, and covered him with a sticky plaster which almost suffocated him. Overwhelmed with shame at having to undergo so humiliating a punishment, Kawelo fancied that he could no longer live at Kauai; he determined to exile himself, and live in Oahu.

He had already embarked in his canoe and prepared to set sail with some faithful friends, when he saw his wife on the shore. Seated beneath the shade of a kou (*Cordia sebestena*), Kaakaukuhimalani waved her hand to Kawelo, crying:

Hoi mai	Return,
Hoi mai kaua!	Return with me!
Mai hele aku oe!	Go not away from me!

Kawelo, touched with love for his wife, but immovably determined to leave his island, chants his adieu, which forms the subject of the first canto.

PAHA AKAHI.	CANTO I.
Aloha kou e, aloha kou;	Thou lovest me still! Oh yes
Ke aloha mai kou ka hoahele	Thou lovest me; thou,
I ka makani, i ka apaapaa	The companion who hast followed me
Anuu o Ahulua.	In the tempest and in the icy
Moe iho nei au	Winds of Ahulua. I, alas!
I ka po uliuli,	Sleep in dark night, in dark
Po uliuli eleele.	And sombre night. My eyes
Anapanapa, alohi mai ana ia'u	Have seen the gleaming flashes
Ke aa o Akua Nunu.	Of the face of the god Nunu.
Ine ee au e kui e lei	If I resist, I am smitten as by
Ia kuana na aa kulikuli.	The thunder-bolts of the deepening storm.
Papa o hee ia nei lae.	Go, daughter of Papa, away from this
E u'alo, e u'alo	Headland; cease thy lamentations;
Ua alo mai nei ia'u	Cease to beckon to me
Ka launiu e o peahi e;	With thy fan of cocoa-nut leaves.
E hoi au e, e hoi aku.	I will come again. Depart thou!

On his arrival at Oahu, Kawelo was well received by the king of that island, Kakuihewa, who loaded him with favors, and even accorded him great privileges, to do honor to his wonderful strength. Kawelo did not forget himself in the midst of the pleasures his strength procured him. He had vengeful thoughts toward Kauai for the injury he had received from his brothers. Retiring to a secluded place, and concealing himself as much as possible from the notice of Kakuihewa, he secretly set about recruiting a small army of devoted men for an expedition against the island of Kauai. When he had collected enough warriors, he put to sea with a fleet of light canoes. Hardly had he left the shore of Oahu, when the marine monster, Apukohai, met him — an evil omen. He was but the precursor of another monster, Uhumakaikai, who could raise great waves and capsize canoes. The oldest sailors never fail to return to land at the first appearance of Apukohai; all the pilots then advised Kawelo to go back with all speed. But the chief, full of determination which nothing could shake, would not change his course; he persisted in sailing toward his destination. This is the subject of the second canto.

PAHA ELUA.	CANTO II.
O ka'u hoa no ia,	I had a friend with whom
E hoolulu ai maua i ka nahele,	I lived peacefully in the wilderness.
I anehu au me he kua ua la	I swung like a cloud full of rain,
I oee au me he wai la.	I murmured like a rivulet,
I haalulu au me he kikili la.	I shook like a thunder-bolt,
I anei wau me he olai la.	I overturned every thing like an earthquake,
I alapa au me he uila la.	I flashed as lightning,
I ahiki welawela au me he la la.	I consumed like the sun.
Melemele ka lau ohia,	Yellow was the ohia leaf;
Kupu a melemele,	Unfolding, it turned yellow
I ka ua o na' pua eha,	Under the rain of the four clouds,
Eha, o na ole eha eha,	In the month of the four *ole*,
O na kaula' ha i ke kua	When the fisherman, four ropes
No paihi, o ka paihi o malu.	Upon his back, enjoyed calm and fair weather.
A Haku, Haku ai i ka manawa,	Be Lord, be lord of the weather.
E Pueo e kania,	O Owl, whose cries give life!
Manawai ka ua i ka lehua,	Send down the rain upon the lehua;
E hoi ka ua a ka maka o ka lehua;	Let the rain come again upon
La noho mai;	The buds of the lehua. Rest, O Sun!
E hoi ka makani	Let the wind fly
A ka maka oka opua	Before the face of the clouds.
La noho mai	Rest, O Sun!
E hoi ko kai a manawai	Return, O Ocean of the mighty waters;
Nui ka oo, la noho mai.	Great is thy tumult! Sun rest here.
E kuu e au i kuu wahi upena	Rest, O Sun! I will cast my net
Ma kahi lae:	At the first headland;
E hei ka makani ia'u.	I shall catch the wind.
E kuu e au i kuu wahi upena	I will cast my net
Ma ka' lua lae,	At the second headland;
E hei ka ino ia 'u	I shall catch a tempest.
E kuu e au i kuu wahi upena	I will cast forth my net
Ma ke 'kolu lae,	At the third headland;
E hei ke kona ia 'u	I shall get the south wind.
E kuu e au e kuu wahi upena	I will cast forth my net
Ma ka' ha lae.	At the fourth headland;
E hei luna, e hei lalo,	I shall take above, below,
E hei uka, e hei kai,	Land and sea—
E hei Uhumakaikai.	I shall take Uhumakaikai.
I ke olo no Hina,	At a single word of Hina
E hina kohia i ka aa,	He shall fall; hard pressed
Uhumakaikai.	Shall be the neck of Ukumakaikai.

In the sixteenth verse of this second canto Kawelo invokes the owl, which the Hawaiians regarded as a god. In extreme perils, if the owl made its cries heard, it was a sign of safety, as the voice of this bird was sacred; and more than once has it happened that men, destined to be immolated on the altar of sacrifices as expiatory victims, have escaped death merely because the owl (*Pueo*) was heard before the immolation. It is easy to understand, after this, the invocation that Kawelo made to Pueo when he found himself in combat with the terrible Uhumakaikai.

In the third canto Kawelo endeavors to destroy the monster. He commences by saying that he, a chief (*ka lani*), does not disdain to work as a simple fisherman. Then he pays a tribute to those who have woven the net he is going to use to capture the monster of the sea. The olona (*Bœhmeria*), a shrub whose bark furnishes the Hawaiians with an excellent fibre, was regarded as a sort of deity. Before spinning its fibres, they made libations, and offered sacrifices of hogs, fowls, etc. Kawelo refers to all this in his song.

PAHA EKOLU.	CANTO III.
Huki kuu ka lani	I, a chief, willingly
Keaweawekaokai honua,	Cast my net of olona;
Kupu ola ua ulu ke opuu.	The olona springs up, it grows,
Ke kahi 'ke olona.	It branches and is cut down.
Kahoekukama kohi lani.	The paddles of the chief beat the sea.
O kia ka piko o ke olona,	Stripped off is the bark of the alona,
Ihi a ka ili no moki no lena,	Peeled is the bark of the yellow moki.
Ahi kuni ka aala,	The fire exhales a sweet odor;
Kunia, haina, paia,	The sacrifice is ready.
Holea, hoomoe ka Papa,	The bark is peeled, the board* is made ready,
Ke kahi ke olona,	The olona is carded,
Ke kau ko opua,	And laid on the board.
Ke kea ka maawe	White is the cord,
Kau hae ka ilo ka uha,	The cord is twisted on the thigh,
Ke kaakalawa ka upena:	Finished is the net!
O kuu aku i kai,	Cast it into the sea,
I kai a Papa; ua hina,	Into the sea of Papa; let him fall,
E hina, kohia i ka aa	Let him fall, that I may strangle the neck
O Uhumakaikai.	Of Uhumakaikai.

After having exterminated Uhumakaikai, the conqueror sailed unmolested toward Kauai, to defeat his other enemies. Kawelo had on this island two friends, who were at the same time his relations; they were the chiefs Akahakaloa and Aikanaka. When these chiefs learned that their cousin intended to return to Kauai, they enrolled themselves in the ranks of his enemies, and prepared to make a vigorous resistance to his landing. It was on perceiving their armies upon the shore that Kawelo commenced his fourth *paha*.

PAHA EHA.	CANTO IV.
O oe no ia, e ka lani Akahakaloa,	Ah! it is then you, chief Akahakaloa.
Kipeapea kau ko ohule ia	A roosting-place is thy bald head become
Kulamanu.	For the gathering birds.
Konia kakahakaloa:	Disobedient Akahakaloa;
I kea a kau io k'awa	Thou appearest as a warrior
Kiipueaua.	Offshoot of Kiipueaua.
Hahau kau kaua la.	Defeat has come upon you in the
E Aikanaka.	Day of battle, O Aikanaka!

---

* On which the bark is beaten to make kapa.

Kii ka pohuli	You require transplanting—
E hoopulapula	Yes, a nursery of warriors—
Na na na.	You do, indeed.
E naenaehele koa	Unfruitful of warriors
Kona aina.	Is his country.

In the following song Kawelo exhorts his two old friends, Kalaumaki and Kaamalama, who had followed him to Oahu, to fight bravely in the approaching battle. The return of Kawelo was expected, and, foreseeing it, the islanders had taken advantage of his absence to roll, or carry, to the bank of the Wailua River immense quantities of stones. The relatives and friends of Kawelo, who had remained at Kauai during his exile, had themselves assisted in these warlike preparations, ignorant of their object. It is on beholding the hostile reception prepared for him that Kawelo chants the fifth song—a proclamation to his army.

PAHA ELIMA.	CANTO V.
E Kaamalama,	O Kaamalama!
E Kalaumaki,	O Kalaumaki!
E hooholoia ka pohaku;	Behold how they heap stones.
E kaua ia iho na waa;	Let us draw our canoes ashore:
He la, kaikoonui nei;	This is a day when the surf rolls high;
Ke auau nei ka moana;	The ocean swells, the sea perchance
He kai paha nei kahina 'lii*	Portends another deluge.
Ua ku ka hau a ke aa;	Piles of pebbles are collected;
Ke ahu pohaku	A heap of stones
I Wailua.	Has the Wailua become.
O ua one maikai nai	This beautiful sandy country
Ua malua, ua kahawai,	Is now full of pits like the bed of a torrent;
Ua piha i ka pohaku	And all Kauai
A Kauai.	Has filled it with rocks.
He hula paha ko uka	A dance perchance brings hither
E lehulehu nei.	This great multitude;
He pahea la, he koi,	Games or a race—
He koi la, he kukini;	Games indeed.
I hee au i ka nalu, a i aia,	If I cast myself upon the surf,
Paa ia'u, a hele wale oukou:	I am caught: you will go free.
E Kaamalama,	O Kaamalama,
E Kalaumaki,	O Kalaumaki,
Ka aina o Kauai la	Fled is the land
Ua hee.	Of Kauai!

The combat has commenced. The people of Kauai rain showers of stones upon the landing troops. Kawelo, buried beneath a heap of stones, but still alive, compares himself to a fish inclosed on all sides by nets, and then to the victims offered in sacrifices. He then begins his invocations to the gods.

PAHA AONO.	CANTO VI.
Puni ke ekule o kai	The ekule of the sea is surrounded;
Ua kaa i ka papau	Stranded in a shallow,
Ua komo i ka ulu o ka lawaia.	It is within the grasp of the fisherman.
Naha ke aa o ka upena,	Broken are the meshes of the net
Ka hala i ka ulua.	Within the hala and ulua.

---

* The Hawaiians have a tradition of an ancient deluge, called Kaiakahinalii.

Mohaikea.	A sacrifice is to be offered.
Mau ia poai ia o ke kai uli.	Surrounded are the fish of the blue sea.
Halukuluku ka pohaku	The rocks fall in showers—
A Kauai me he ua la.	A storm of the stones of Kauai.
Kolokolo mai ana ka huihui	The coldness of death creeps over me.
Ka maeele io'u lima,	Numb are my limbs,
Na lima o Paikanaka.	The limbs of Paikanaka.
E Kane i ka pualena,	O Kane of the yellow flower;
E Ku lani ehu e,	O Ku, ruddy chief;
Kamakanaka!	Kamakanaka!
Na'u na Kawelo,	It is I, Kawelo,
Na ko lawaia.	Thy fisherman.

Left for dead beneath the heap of stones, Kawelo, perceiving his danger, continues his prayer.

PAHA EHIKU.	CANTO VII.
Ku ke Akua	O divine Ku,
I ka nana nuu.	Who beholdest the inner places.
O Lono ke akua	O Lono, divine one,
I kama Pele.	Husband of Pele.
O Hiaka ke akua	O holy Hiaka,
I ka puukii.	Dweller on the hills.
O Haulili ke akua	O Haulili, god
I ka lehelehe	Ruling the lips!
Aumeaume maua me Milu.	We two have wrestled, Milu and I.
I'au, ia ia;	I had the upper hand;
I'au, ia ia;	I had the upper hand;
I'au iho no:	Then was I beneath:
Pakele au, mai make ia ia.	I escaped, all but killed by him.

PAHA EWALU.	CANTO VIII.
He opua la, he opua,	Here is a cloud, there another.
He opua hao walo keia,	This cloud bears destruction;
Ke maalo nei e ko'u maka.	I have seen it pass before my eyes.
He mauli waa o Kaamalama.	The obscure cloud is the canoe of Kaamalama.
Eia ke kualau	This is the tempest,
Hoko o ka pouli makani,	Wind in the darkness;
Oe nei la, e Kaamalama	Thou art the sun, Kaamalama,
Ke hele ino loa i ke ao.	Rising clouded in the dawn.
Ua palala, ua poipu ka lani,	Dark and shaded are the heavens,
Ua wehe ke alaula o ke alawela,	A warm day begins to dawn.
He alanui ia o Kaamalama.	This is the path of Kaamalama.
Oe mai no ma kai,	Thou art from the sea,
Owau iho no ma uka;	I, indeed, beneath the land mountain.
E hee o Aikanaka	Fly, O Aikanaka,
I ke ahiahi.	In the evening!
E u ka ilo la i ko' waha;	Maggots shall fatten in thy mouth;
Ai na koa i ka ala mihi.	The soldiers eat the fragrant mihi.
Ai pohaku ko' akua.	Thy god is a devourer of rocks;
Ai Kanaka ko maua akua.	Our god eats human flesh.
Kuakea ke poo	Bleached shall be thy head
I ka pehumu.	In the earth-oven.
Nakeke ka aue i ka iliili.	Thy broken jaw shall rattle on the beach pebbles.
Hai Kaamalama ia oe,	Kaamalama shall sacrifice you,

Hae' ke akua ulu ka niho.	The god's tooth shall grow on the sacrifice.
Kanekapualena;	O Kane of the yellow flower;
E Ku lani ehu e;	O Ku, bright chief;
Kamakanaka,	Kamakanaka,
Na'u na Kawelo	I am Kawelo,
Na ko lawaia.	Thy fisherman.

In the following canto Kawelo reproaches and menaces the chief Kaheleha, who had deserted him for Aikanaka.

PAHA AIWA.	CANTO IX.
Kulolou ana ke poo o ka opua,	The head of the cloud bears down
Ohumuhumu olelo ana ia'u:	And whispers a word in my ear:
Owau ka! ka ai o ka la ua.	It is I! the food of a rainy day.
E Kaheleha o Puna	O Kahelaha, of Puna,
Kuu keiki hookama	My adopted son,
Aloha ole!	Heartless fellow!
O kaua hoi no hoa	We two were comrades
Mai ka wa iki	In times of poverty;
I hoouka'i kakou	In the day of battle
I Wailua;	We were together at Wailua.
Lawe ae hoi au, oleloia:	It might be said
Haina ko'u make	My death was proclaimed
Ia Kauai.	In Kauai.
E pono kaakaa laau	Good to look upon
Ka Kawelo.	Is the strength of Kawelo.
Aole i iki i ka alo i ka pohaku.	He knows not how to throw stones.
Aloha wale oe e Kaheleha	Farewell to you, Kaheleha
O Puna.	Of Puna.
A pa nei ko'poo i ka laau,	Thy head is split by my spear,
Ka laulaa o kuikaa.	A spliced container!
Nanaia ka a ouli keokeo.	The whitening form is to be seen.
Papapau hoa aloha wale!	O Aikanaka, loving only in name,
Aikanaka ma,	To you and yours,
Aloha,	Farewell!
Aloha i ka hei wale	Farewell to the ensnared,
O na pokii.	The youngest born.

History declares, and this ninth canto confirms it, that Kaheleha of Puna, Kawelo's friend from his youth, and one of his powerful companions in arms at the descent on Wailua, believed that Kawelo was mortally wounded beneath the shower of stones that had covered him, and this belief had induced him to go over to the camp of Aikanaka. Verses fourteen to sixteen are the words that Kawelo reproaches Kaheleha with saying before his enemies. Kaheleha was slain by the hand of Kawelo at the same time with Aikanaka.

PAHA UMI.	CANTO X.
Me he ulu wale la	Like a forest rising abruptly
I ka moana,	Out of the ocean,
O Kauai nui moku lehua;	Is Kauai, with flowery lehua;
Aina nui makekau,	Grand but ungrateful land,
Makamaka ole ia Kawelo.	Without friends or dear ones for Kawelo.
Ua make o Maihuna 'lii,	They have put to death Maihuna,
Maleia ka makuahine;	As also Malei, my mother.

Ua hooleiia i ka pali nui,	They have cast from a great pali
O laua ka! na manu	Both of them! Were they birds
Kikaha i lelepaumu.	To fly thus in the air?
Aloha mai o'u kupuna:	Love to you, oh my ancestors:
O Au a me Aalohe,	To you, Au and Aaloha,
O Aua, a Aaloa,	To you, Aua and Aaloa,
O Aapoko, o Aamahana.	Aapoko and Aamahana,
O Aapoku o Aauopelaea:	Aapoku and Aauopelaea,
Ua make ia Aikanaka.	Who died by the hand of Aikanaka.

Maihuna was the father of Kawelo, and Aikanaka was his first cousin. The latter put to death all the family of Kawelo, after having employed them, with the other inhabitants òf Kauai, in collecting the stones which were to repulse his cousin. It was before the great battle of Wailua that Kawelo's family was put to death.

In the last canto the hero reproaches his friends for abandoning him in the day of danger. At the sight of his old friends, whose bodies he had pierced with many wounds in punishment, he cries: "Where are those miserable favorites?" He had transfixed them with his lance—that lance made, he says, for the day of battle.

He compares Aikanaka to a long lance because of his power; he reproaches him with having betrayed himself, who was comparatively but a little lance—a little bit of wood (*laau iki*); then he ironically remarks that Kauai is too small an island for his conquered friends.

PAHA UMIKUMAMAKAHI.	CANTO XI.
Auhea iho nei la hoi	Where just now are those chiefs,
Ua mau wahi hulu alaala nei	Rebellious and weak,
Au i oo aku ai	Whom the point of the spear
I ka maka o ke keiki	Has transfixed—the spear of the
A Maihuna?	Son of Maihuna?
He ihe no ka la kaua.	The spear made for the day of battle.
Pau hewa ka'u ia	Stolen was my fish,
Me kau ai,	And the vegetable food—
Pau hewa ka hinihini ai	Stolen the food raised by
A ka moamahi.	The conqueror.
Komo hewa ko'u waa	Mischievously did you
Ia lakou.	Sink my canoes.
O lakou ka! ka haalulu	O wretches! ye trembled
I ka pohaku i kaa nei,	When the rocks rolled down,
Uina aku la i kahakaha ke one,	At the noise they made on the sand.
Kuu pilikia i Honuakaha.	When I was in danger at Honuakaha,
Makemake l ka laau nui,	Ye who desire long lances
Haalele i kahi laau iki.	And despise those that are small,
He iki kahi kihapai	Too small a place was Kauai,
Ka noho ka! i Kauai,	Your dwelling;
Iki i kalukalu a Puna.	Small was the kalukalu of Puna.
Lilo Puna ia Kaheleha	Puna shall belong to Kaheleeha,
Lilo Kona ia Kalaumaki,	Kona to Kalaumaki,
Lilo Koolau ia Makuakeke,	Koolau to Makuakeke,
Lilo Kohala ia Kaamalama,	Kohala to Kaamalama,
Lilo Hanalei ia Kanewahineikialoha.	Hanalei to Kanewahineikialoha.
Mimihi ka hune o Kauluiki ma.	The poverty of Kauluiki and his friends grieves me.
Alona na pokii i ka hei wale.	Farewell, little ones caught in the net!

Here ends all that we were able to collect of this original and very ancient poetry. Tradition relates that Kawelo became king of Kauai, and reigned over that island to an advanced age.

When old age had lessened his force, and weakened his power, his subjects seized him and cast him from the top of a tremendous precipice.

THE TARO PLANT.

NOTES.

(1.) The name of Alapai is not found in the genealogy published by David Malo. Neverthe-less, we have positive information from our old man and other distinguished natives that Alapai was supreme chief of Hawaii immediately before Kalaniopuu.

(2.) Poi is a paste made of the tuberous root of the kalo (*Colocasia antiquorum*, var. *esculenta*, Schott.). More than thirty varieties of kalo are cultivated on the Hawaiian Islands, most of them requiring a marshy soil, but a few will grow in the dry earth of the mountains. The tubers of all the kinds are acrid, except one, which is so mild that it may be eaten raw. After it is freed from acridity by baking, the kalo is pounded until reduced to a kind of paste which is eaten cold, under the name of poi. It is the principal food of the natives, with whom it takes the place of bread. The kalo leaves are eaten like spinach (*luau*), and the flowers (spathe and spadix), cooked in the leaves of the cordyline (*C. terminalis*, H. B. K.), form a most delicious dish. It is not only as poi that the tubers are eaten; they are sliced and fried like potatoes, or baked whole upon hot stones. It is in this last form that I have eaten them in my expeditions. A tuber which I car-ried in my pocket has often been my only provision for the day.

In Algeria, a kind of kalo is cultivated under the name of *chou caraibe*, whose tubers are larger, but less feculent. [In China, smaller and much less delicately flavored tubers are common in the markets.]

(3.) The Hawaiians have always been epicures in the article of dog-meat. The kind they raise for their feasts is small and easily fatted, like pig. They are fed only on vegetables, espe-cially kalo, to make their flesh more tender and delicately flavored. Sometimes these dogs are suck-led by the women at the expense of their infants. The ones that have been thus fed at a woman's breast are called *ilio poli*, and are most esteemed.

(4.) The Kahualii are still genuine parasites in the Hawaiian nation. They are, to use the lan-guage of a Catholic missionary, the Cretans of whom Paul speaks: "Evil beasts, slow bellies;" a race wholly in subjection to their appetite, living from day to day, always reclining on the mat, or else riding horses furiously; having no more serious occupation than to drink, eat, sleep, dance, tell stories; giving themselves up, in a word, to all pleasures, lawful and unlawful, without scruple or distinction of persons. The Kahualii are very lazy. They are ashamed of honest labor, think-ing they would thus detract from their rank as chiefs. Islanders of this caste are almost never seen in the service of Europeans. When their patron, the high chief of the family, has made them feel the weight of his displeasure, these inferior chiefs become notoriously miserable, worse than the lowest of the Kanakas (generic name of the natives).

(5). [Kamehameha IV. and V. were only noble through their mother, Kinau, the wife of Ke-kuanaoa. They were adopted by Kamehameha III. (Kauikeaouli).]

(6.) The old historian Namiki, an intelligent man, and well versed in the secrets of Hawaiian antiquity, has left precious unedited documents, which have fallen into our hands. His son, Kui-kauai, a school-master at Kailua, one of the true historico-sacerdotal race, has given us a genealo-gy of his ancestors which ascends without break to Paao.

(7.) A tradition exists, mentioned by Jarves, that Paao landed at Kohoukapu before the reign of Umi. According to the same author, Paao was not a Kanaka, but a man of the Caucasian race. However this may be, every one agrees that Paao was a foreigner, and a *naauao* (scholar; literally, a man with enlightened entrails, the Hawaiians placing the mind and affections in the bowels).

(8). Hina, according to tradition, brought into the world several sons, who dug the palis of Hulaana. It may be asked whether *Hina*, which means *a fall*, does not indicate a deluge (Kaia-kahinalii of the Hawaiians), or some sort of cataclysm, and whether the islanders have not person-ified events.

(9.) It is, however, improbable that there were ever genuine sorcerers among the Hawaiians, in the sense that word has among Christians. It may have happened, and indeed it happens ev-ery day, that people die after the machinations of the kahuna-anaana; but it is more reasonable to refer these tragical deaths to the use of poison, than to attribute them to the incantations of the sorcerers. It is moreover known that there are on the group many poisons furnished by trees, by shrubs and sea-weeds; and the kahuna-anaana understood perfectly these vegetable poisons. The many known examples of their criminal use inclines us to believe that these kahuna were rather poisoners than magicians. [Kalaipahoa, the poison-god, was believed to have been carved out of a very poisonous wood, a few chips of which would cause death when mixed with the food.]

(10.) During the summer of the year 1852, while I was exploring the island of Kauai, I was near being the victim, under remarkable circumstances, of an old kahuna named Lilihae. I was then residing under the humble roof of the Mission at Moloaa. Lilihae had been baptized, and professed Christianity, although it was well known that he clung to the worship of his gods. He was introduced to me by the missionaries as a man who, by his memory and profession, could add to my historical notes. I indeed obtained from him most precious material, and in a moment of good nature the old man even confided to me the secret of certain prayers that the priests alone should know. I wrote down several formulæ at his dictation, only promising to divulge nothing before his death. The old man evidently considered himself perjured, for after his revelations he came no more to see me.

Some days had passed after our last interview, and I thought no more of him. All at once I lost my appetite and fell sick. I could eat nothing without experiencing a nausea, followed imme-diately by continual vomiting. Two missionaries and my French servant, who partook of my food, exhibited almost the same symptoms. Not suspecting the true cause of these ailments, I attrib-uted them to climate and the locality, and especially to the pestilent winds which had brought an epidemic ophthalmia among the natives. Things remained in this condition a fortnight without improvement, when one morning at breakfast a marmalade of bananas was served. I had hardly touched it to my lips when the nausea returned with greater violence; I could eat nothing, and soon a salivation came on which lasted several hours. In the mean while a poor Breton who had established himself on the island some years ago, and had conformed to savage life, came to see me. Bananas were scarce in the neighborhood, and he found that I had a large supply of them, and I offered him a bunch. Fortin, it was his name, on his way back to his cabin with my pres-ent, broke a banana off the bunch and commenced to eat it. He felt under his tooth a hard sub-stance, which he caught in his hand. To his great surprise, it was a sort of blue and white stone. He soon felt ill, and fortunately was able to vomit what he had swallowed. Furious, and accusing me of a criminal intention, he returned to my quarters to demand an explanation. I examined the substance taken from the banana, and found that it was blue vitriol and corrosive sublimate. The presence of such substances in a banana was far from natural. I took other bunches of my supply, and found in several bananas the same poisons, which had been skillfully introduced under the skin. After some inquiries I found, from Fortin's own wife, that similar drugs had been sometimes seen in the hands of Lilihae, who had bought them of a druggist in Honolulu for the treatment of syph-ilis. The riddle was at once completely solved. A few days passed, and Lilihae killed himself by poison, convinced that all his attempts could not kill me. In his native superstition, he was satis-fied that the gods would not forgive his indiscretion, since they withheld from him the power of taking my life; and he could devise no simpler way to escape their anger, and the vengeance of my own God, than to take himself the poison against which I had rebelled. It was discovered that

Lilihae had, in the first place, tried native poisons on me, and finding them ineffective, he thought that my foreign nature might require exotic poisons, which he had accordingly served in the bananas destined for my table. He went, without my knowledge, into the cook-house where my native servants kept my provisions, and, under pretext of chatting with them, found means to poison my food. The unfortunate kahuna died fully persuaded that I was a more powerful sorcerer than he. It was to be feared that, when he discovered his impotency, he would intrust the execution of his designs to his fellows, as is common among sorcerers; but his suicide fortunately removed this sword of Damocles which hung over my head.

(11.) At the present day, useless old men are no longer destroyed, nor are the children, whom venereal diseases have rendered very rare, suffocated; but they do eat lice, fleas, and grasshoppers. Flies inspire the same disgust, and the women still give their breasts to dogs, pigs, and young kids.

(12.) [This operation is certainly still practiced extensively, if not universally; and the ancient form of *kahiomaka*, or slitting the prepuce, has given way, generally, to the *okipoepoe*, or the complete removal of the foreskin. The operation in a case that came under my notice on the island of Oahu was performed with a bamboo, and attended with a feast and rejoicings; the subject was about nine years old.]

(13.) The islanders, who admire and honor great eaters, have generally stomachs of a prodigious capacity. Here is an example: To compensate my servants, some seven in number, for the hardships I had made them endure on Mauna Kea, I presented them with an ox that weighed five hundred pounds uncooked. They killed him in the morning, and the next evening there was not a morsel left. One will be less astonished at this when I say that these ogres, when completely stuffed, promote vomitings by introducing their fingers into their throats, and return again to the charge. [It is equally true that the Kanakas will go for a long time without much food, and it can not be said they are a race of gluttons.]

(14.) Awa (*Piper methysticum*) grows spontaneously in the mountains of the Hawaiian group. The natives formerly cultivated it largely [and since the removal of the strict prohibition on its culture fields are not uncommon]. From the roots the natives prepare a very warm and slightly narcotic intoxicating drink. It is made thus: women chew the roots, and having well masticated them, spit them, well charged with saliva, into a calabash used for the purpose. They add a small portion of water, and press the juice from the chewed roots by squeezing them in their hands. This done, the liquid is strained through cocoa-nut fibres to separate all the woody particles it may contain, and the awa is in a drinkable state. The quantity drunk by each person varies from a quarter to half a litre (two to four gills). This liquor is taken just before supper, or immediately after. The taste is very nauseous, disagreeable to the last degree. One would suppose he was drinking thick dish-water of a greenish-yellow color. But its effects are particularly pleasant. An irresistible sleep seizes you, and lasts twelve, twenty-four hours, or even more, according to the dose, and the temperament of the individual. Delicious dreams charm this long torpor. Often when the dose is too great or too small, sleep does not follow; but in its place an intoxication, accompanied by fantastic ideas, and a strong desire to skip about, although one can not for a moment balance himself on his legs. I felt these last symptoms for sixty hours the first time I tasted this Polynesian liquor. The effects of awa on the constitution of habitual drinkers are disastrous. The body becomes emaciated, and the skin is covered, as in leprosy, with large scales, which fall off, and leave lasting white spots, which often become ulcers.

(15.) This usage still exists in certain families toward great personages or people they wish especially to honor; but it is disappearing every day. Formerly when a Kanaka received a visit from a friend of a remote district, women were always comprised in the exchange of presents on that occasion. To fail in this was regarded as an unpardonable insult. The thing was so inwrought in their customs, that the wife of the visitor did not wait the order of her husband to surrender her person to her host.

(16.) [Liliha was the wife of Boki, governor of Oahu under Kamehameha II.]

(17.) The most curious thing which attracts the traveler's eye in the ruins of the temples built by Umi is the existence of a mosaic pavement, in the form of a regular cross, which extends throughout the whole length and breadth of the inclosure. This symbol is not found in monuments anterior to this king, nor in those of later times. One can not help seeing in this an evidence of the influence of the two shipwrecked white men whose advent we have referred to. Can we not conclude, from the existence of these Christian emblems, that about the time when the great Umi filled the group with his name, the Spanish or Portuguese shipwrecked persons endeavored to introduce the worship of Christ to these islands? Kama of Waihopua (Ka'u) has given us, through Napi, an explanation of the four compartments observed in the temple of Umi, represented by the following figure; but if we accept this explanation of Kama, it is as difficult to understand

Place of the god Kaili.	Place of the god Ku.
Place of the priest Lono.	Place of the chief Umi.

why this peculiarity is observed in the monuments of Umi, and not in any other heiau; as, for example, Kupalaha, situated in the territory of Makapala; Mokini, at Puuepa; Aiaikamahina, toward the sea at Kukuipahu; Kuupapaulau, inland at Kukuipahu-mauka. The remains of these four remarkable temples are found in the district of Kohala. Not the least vestige of the crucial division is to be seen. The god Kaili [see the first page of the Appendix], a word which means a theft, was not known before the time of Umi. [The temple of Iliiliopae, at the mouth of Mapulehu Valley, on Molokai, is divided as in the diagram, and the same is true of many other heiau; and as it seems to have been the usual form, it is not probable that the form of the cross had any thing to do with it.]

(18.) It does not seem improbable that a premature death removed the foreigner who could have given Umi the idea of an art until then unknown; and had the foreigner lived longer, these curious stones would have served to build an edifice of which the native architects knew not the proportions.

(19.) [The cities of Refuge were a remarkable feature of Hawaiian antiquity. There were two of these *Pahonua* on Hawaii. The one at Honaunau, as measured by Rev. W. Ellis, was seven hundred and fifteen feet in length and four hundred and four feet wide. Its walls were twelve feet high and fifteen feet thick, formerly surmounted by huge images, which stood four rods apart, on their whole circuit. Within this inclosure were three large heiau, one of which was a solid truncated pyramid of stone one hundred and twenty-six feet by sixty, and ten feet high. Several masses of rock weighing several tons are found in the walls some six feet from the ground. During war they were the refuge of all non-combatants. A white flag was displayed at such times a short distance from the walls, and here all refugees were safe from the pursuing conquerors. After a short period they might return unmolested to their homes, the divine protection of Keawe, the tutelary deity, still continuing with them.]

THE END.